AN ENGRAVER'S PILGRIMAGE

JAMES SMILLIE IN QUEBEC, 1821–1830

AN ENGRAVER'S PILGRIMAGE

JAMES SMILLIE IN QUEBEC, 1821–1830

MARY MACAULAY ALLODI ◆ ROSEMARIE L. TOVELL

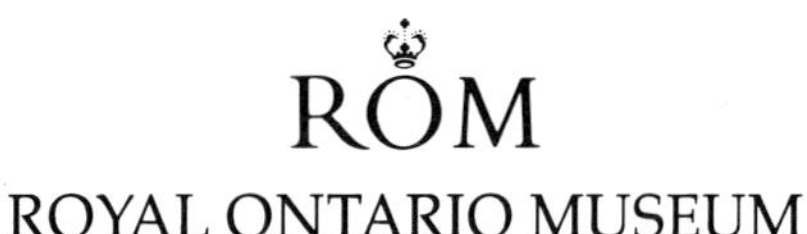

ROYAL ONTARIO MUSEUM

Mary Macaulay Allodi is curator, Canadian Decorative Arts Department, Royal Ontario Museum.

Rosemarie L. Tovell is associate curator, Canadian Prints and Drawings, National Gallery of Canada, Ottawa.

Cover: Edward Heaton, *James Smillie, Quebec 1825*, watercolour over graphite, touches of gum arabic, 14.0 × 11.5.

Photographs
We are grateful to the following for permission to reprint their photographs. All photographs not listed are by the Royal Ontario Museum photography department.

(Musée et) Archives du Séminaire de Québec, Guy Rainville, photographer, pp. 35, 39; Bibliothèque de la Ville de Montréal, p. 40, *top left*; Cartographic and Architectural Archives, National Archives of Canada, Ottawa, p. 83; McCord Museum of Canadian History, Montreal, p. 8; National Archives of Canada, Ottawa, pp. 7, 34, 38, 82, 94; National Gallery of Canada, Ottawa, pp. 6, 70–74; Private collection, p. 49.

Canadian Cataloguing in Publication Data
Allodi, Mary, date
An engraver's pilgrimage : James Smillie in Quebec, 1821–1830

Bibliography: p.
Includes index.
ISBN 0-88854-335-2

1. Smillie, James, 1807–1885. 2. Quebec (Province) - Description and travel - 1764–1850 - Views.* 3. Smillie family. 4. Engravers - Quebec (Province) - Biography. I. Tovell, Rosemarie L. II. Smillie, James, 1807–1885. III. Royal Ontario Museum. IV. Title.

NE543.S52A85 1989 769.92'4 C89-093550-5

---

100 Queen's Park, Toronto, Canada, M5S 2C6
ISBN 0-88854-335-2
PRINTED AND BOUND IN CANADA AT UNIVERSITY OF TORONTO PRESS

Contents

Works in the Catalogue

Supplementary Illustrations

In memory of Kathleen M. Fenwick (1901–1973),
curator of prints and drawings at
the National Gallery of Canada,
who inspired us with her love of prints

Acknowledgements

Although there were two of us working on this study, its many-faceted aspects required us to draw upon the knowledge and assistance of numerous friends and colleagues. To them we express our gratitude.

Foremost among the individuals who assisted with our study on James Smillie are his great-grandchildren Barbara Curtis, James Smillie, and David Smillie. Without the interest, support, and patience of the engraver's descendants, this book could not have been undertaken.

A friend and colleague who deserves special mention is Honor de Pencier. Honor constituted our major cheering section throughout every phase of this study. She also gave us advice and assistance on early Canadian silversmiths.

Information and assistance on prints, history, maps, artists, and a variety of other subjects were generously given by the following individuals: Marie Babayant and Daniel Olivier, Bibliothèque de la Ville de Montréal; Eileen Marcil, Charlesbourg, Quebec; Laurier Lacroix, Condordia University, Montreal; Allan Hally, King City, Ontario; Luc Noppen and John R. Porter, Université Laval, Quebec; John Crosthwaite, Metropolitan Toronto Library; Conrad E. W. Graham and Peter Winkworth, McCord Museum, Montreal; Robert Derome, Université de Québec à Montréal; John L. Russell, Montreal; Thierry Ruddel, Museum of Civilization, Ottawa; Jacqueline Hunter, National Gallery of Canada, Ottawa; Helen E. Smailes, Scottish National Portrait Gallery, Edinburgh; Robert Rainwater, New York Public Library; Marie Elwood, Nova Scotia Museum, Halifax; Office of the Surveyor of the Queen's Works of Art, London; René Chartrand, Parks Canada, Ottawa; Jim Burant, Anita Burdett, Edward H. Dahl, Gilbert Gignac, and Douglas Schoenherr, National Archives of Canada, Ottawa; Walter Tovell, Royal Ontario Museum, Toronto; the late A. Murray Vaughan and David M. Vaughan, Toronto; Peter N. Moogk, University of British Columbia, Vancouver; Joan Winearls, John P. Robarts Research Library, University of Toronto; and Jane Pomeroy, Washington, D.C.

Colleagues at the Royal Ontario Museum helped in many ways during the preparation of the manuscript for publication. Thanks go especially to our editor, Barbara Ibronyi; to Brian Boyle and Allan McColl for the photography of the Smillie Family Collection; and to Louise Mackie and John Hayes of the Royal Ontario Museum Art and Archaeology Editorial Board. For support and help throughout the production and design of the book, we thank Hugh Porter, Lorna Hawrysh, and Virginia Morin of Publication Services. In the Canadian Decorative Arts Department, Janet Holmes provided constant support, and Barbara Chisholm and Bette Shepherd researched specific problems. A very special acknowledgement is extended to Pat Heimbecker for her good-natured patience and skilful handling of many drafts and rewrites of the manuscript.

This book has been published with the help of a grant from the Canadian Federation for the Humanities, using funds provided by the Social Sciences and Humanities Research Council of Canada. The colour cover was made possible by a donation from John Laurel Russell, C.M.

Explanatory Notes

All works have been measured in centimetres, with height given before width. Every effort has been made to cite the most constant physical size of the object.

Drawings and Watercolours: All measurements are sheet dimensions.

Prints: Whenever possible, plate (or block) dimensions are recorded.

If dimensions are recorded as sheet size, it is implied that the impressions located have been trimmed within the plate. If more than one impression has been located, measurements are given for the impression with the largest dimensions. Where dimensions are recorded as image size, it is implied that the impressions located have been measured to the maximum dimensions of the image or its outer ruled margins.

All illustrated works not otherwise credited belong to the Smillie Family Collection.

Abbreviations

AEAC	Agnes Etherington Art Centre, Kingston
AGGV	Art Gallery of Greater Victoria
AGH	Art Gallery of Hamilton
ANQ	Archives nationales du Québec
arch. mat.	Archival Material section of the Bibliography
ASQ	(Musée et) Archives du Séminaire de Québec
BSQ	Bibliothèque, Séminaire de Québec
BVMG	Bibliothèque de la Ville de Montréal (Collection Gagnon)
CAA	Cartographic and Architectural Archives, National Archives of Canada, Ottawa
McC	McCord Museum of Canadian History, Montreal
McG.RBD.LR	The Lawrence Lande Collection of Canadiana in the Department of Rare Books and Special Collections, McGill University Libraries, Montreal
MQ	Musée de Québec
MTL	Metropolitan Toronto Library
NA	National Archives of Canada, Ottawa
NGC	National Gallery of Canada, Ottawa
NLC	National Library of Canada, Ottawa
NPGL	National Portrait Gallery, London, England
NSM	Nova Scotia Museum, Halifax
NYPL	New York Public Library, New York City
Pilgrimage	Smillie manuscript autobiography, Smillie Family Collection
ROM	Royal Ontario Museum, Toronto
Scrapbook	"In Memoriam," Smillie Family Collection
Supplementary Scrapbook/ss.	Supplementary scrapbook of James Smillie's work assembled by James David Smillie, Smillie Family Collection

James Smillie Chronology

1807	Born in Edinburgh, Scotland, on 23 November.
1819	Apprenticed to silver engraver James Johnston, Edinburgh, Scotland, from 22 October 1819 to 29 August 1820.
1820	Apprenticed to pictorial engraver Edward Mitchell, Edinburgh, Scotland.
1821	Immigrates to Canada with his family. Leaves Scotland on 20 April; arrives in Quebec on 6 June. Living at 16/24 Mountain Street, his uncle's house.
1822	Living at 8 Garden Street.
1823	Business entitled David Smillie & Son.
1826	Living at 10 Ste. Anne Street; business entitled D. Smillie & Sons.
1827	Sails for England on 16 October 1827; in late November leaves London for Edinburgh, Scotland. Apprenticed to Andrew Wilson, Edinburgh.
1828	Leaves Scotland; arrives in Quebec on 10 August.
1829	Working on St. Stanislas Street with his brother David; business entitled D. & J. Smillie.
	First visit to New York City, for printing of *Picture of Quebec*. Arrives on 14 May; leaves on 11 June.
	Second visit to New York City, working on commission for Robert W. Weir and others. Returns to Quebec about December 1829.
1830	Moves to New York City between late May and late July. Six-month partnership with George Hatch in New York during production of views of the city for George Melksham Bourne. In the autumn his mother, brother William, and three sisters leave Quebec and settle in New York.
1831	Publication of the Bourne views of New York City in the spring. Working vacation in the summer at Tappan, New York, with engravers Robert W. Weir and William Main. In the autumn brothers David and George arrive from Quebec.
1832	Marries Katherine Van Valkenburgh on 29 March; elected associate member, National Academy of Design.
1833	Eldest son James David born, followed in subsequent years by seven more children. Sends for engraver Robert Hinshelwood, paying his passage from Scotland.
1834	Sister Margaret marries Robert Hinshelwood, who begins work on his own.
c. 1836	Moves to Kingston, New York; returns to New York City after eighteen months.
c. 1837–1838	Takes up banknote engraving, specializing in vignettes.
c. 1840	Visits Montreal to see his brother David. On return, works for banknote printers Rawdon, Wright & Hatch; after six months becomes a partner.

1842	Moves to Poughkeepsie, New York, commuting to New York City for business. Rawdon, Wright, Hatch & Smillie faces bankruptcy; Smillie returns to New York City.
1845	Starts again in full partnership with Robert Hinshelwood.
1847–1850	Partnership dissolved. Smillie works on his own; starts making prints for American Art Union after Thomas Cole and Asher B. Durand.
1851	Contracts to engrave entire series of Thomas Cole's *Voyage of Life*.
1852	Elected full member of National Academy of Design.
1861	Works for National Bank Note Company.
1862	Visits Europe for four months with his son James David.
1864	Contracts to engrave print after Albert Bierstadt's *The Rocky Mountains* (completed 1866).
1868	Leaves National Bank Note Company; works for American Bank Note Company with his son William Main.
1871	His nephew George Frederick Cumming Smillie (son of his brother David) joins the company.
1873	Travels to Montreal and Quebec with his son James David in July. In Quebec is called upon by Dr. William Marsden and his cousin's sons Walter and Thomas Drysdale.
1874	Moves to Poughkeepsie, New York; continues contract work for American Bank Note Company.
1882	Concludes his autobiography, "A Pilgrimage."
1885	Dies on 4 December at Poughkeepsie.

Introduction

Studies of pictorial printmaking in Canada have produced little information about the earliest craftsmen who plied that trade. Printmakers before 1830 worked in relative obscurity, and they are known mostly by their few printed works that happen to have survived the passage of time. For this reason, the information provided by James Smillie about his youth as an engraver in Quebec brings to life a forgotten portion of the Canadian heritage.

James Smillie (1807–1885) completed his autobiography, "A Pilgrimage," in 1882 and illustrated it with an accompanying scrapbook of his prints and drawings, entitled "In Memoriam." The memoir was the concluding work in a long and notable career that began in Lower Canada and continued in the United States. The present publication covers the early part of Smillie's career, from his childhood in Scotland until the year 1830, when he left Canada. It contains his autobiography to 1830 (proportionately the largest and most detailed part of that manuscript) and a catalogue of his known work to that date, compiled from various collections. The manuscript autobiography, the scrapbook, and numerous other documents, which together constitute the Smillie Family Collection, were made available to the authors by the engraver's direct descendants.

Smillie's memory was excellent, and in his autobiography he gives a detailed account of life in Quebec and of the insecure climate in which engravers tried to make a living. He tells of the Scottish artisans who settled in Quebec following the Napoleonic Wars, especially the Smillie clan of jewellers and silver workers. He also introduces the reader to a group of military artists in the circle of the governor in chief, the Earl of Dalhousie.

The Early Engravers

James Smillie was the first pictorial engraver to practise his trade in 19th-century Quebec, then the administrative centre of British North America. There had been a flurry of activity during the 1790s, when the proprietors of the *Quebec Magazine* engaged John George Hochstetter (act. 1791–1796), about whom little is known, to etch pictorial plates for their periodical.[1] The name of no other professional printmaker of pictorial material in that city has come down to us before the publication of Smillie's first Quebec prints in 1823.

In the period between Smillie's arrival in Quebec in 1821 at age thirteen and his departure in 1830, fewer than a dozen pictorial single-sheet engravings (that is, prints for framing) are known to have been printed in the whole of what is now Canada—excluding Smillie's work. In comparison, Smillie etched or engraved at least sixteen single-sheet subjects, twenty-two book illustrations, and six maps before leaving Quebec. These numbers do not include his commercial work (pictorial trade cards, bookplates, and billheads) or work done in Scotland for the Canadian market.

Smillie's contemporaries were engravers of varying abilities. His only rival in Quebec was Edward Bennet (act. Quebec 1821–1828), who produced city plans and trade cards. Surviving examples of Bennet's work show him to have been a less accomplished engraver than Smillie, whom he refused to apprentice (Appendix C). At the same time in Montreal a few pictorial engravers produced interesting and attractive views. The most notable was William Satchwell Leney (1769–1831), who emigrated from New York in 1820, towards the end of a long career as a reproductive engraver. Despite his abilities, he was commissioned only rarely. In Lower Canada he etched six single-sheet city views and two plates for periodicals.

Professional engravers in Nova Scotia were equally underemployed. The most successful seems to have been Charles W. Torbett (act. 1812–1834), who worked in Halifax. Apart from two single-sheet etchings, his commissions were mostly for commercial work and magazine illustrations.

Without a firsthand account one could only guess at what life was like for these professional printmakers, economically and socially. Smillie's autobiography is relevant here, for his experiences and commissions were probably similar to those of his confrères. That Smillie eventually gave up on Canada is significant, particularly when one notes that among his peers he seems to have been the most productive of Canada's early engravers.

The Smillies

Although the subject of this study is James Smillie, a review of the lives of other artisan members of the family provides the context within which he developed his career and which remained an important framework throughout his life.

Biographies published to date on the Smillie family members have tended to be fragmented. Historians have not been helped by the Smillie propensity for using the same given names and practising essentially the same craft over several generations. The variations "Smillie," "Smellie," and "Smilie" in the spelling of the family name have added to the confusion. The Smillies themselves, however, cannot be faulted for this. In every autographic or legal document located to date, they have consistently spelled their name "Smillie" (pronounced smile-ee). Only when the spelling of the name fell into other hands, such as those of newspaper typesetters or clerks, did the variations appear.

A brief explanation should be made about the designation of family members as senior and junior. James Smillie, the engraver, and his uncle James Smillie, the jeweller, used the designations junior and senior only while the younger man was working in Quebec. The David Smillies, father and son, never tried to differentiate between themselves in that manner, probably because the father died before his son David was in business on his own and achieved success. The addition of these suffixes to their names is used in this book only when confusion about the generations might occur.

The first member of the Smillie clan to emigrate to Canada was James Smillie, Sr. (?–1841). He was born in Edinburgh, Scotland, where he worked as a manufacturing jeweller in partnership with his brother David. About 1812 their partnership was dissolved and in time James, Sr., removed his business to London.[2] In 1819 he emigrated to Quebec and opened a business as a goldsmith, seal engraver, and lapidary, announcing that he had "just arrived from Britain (whence he has brought several of his best workmen)."[3] Established in his own house and shop,[4] James, Sr., appears to have prospered in business, and he was a frequent contributor to charitable organizations.[5] Although he had a family of his own,[6] he also helped his brother David to settle in Quebec in 1821 and assumed a parental role towards his nieces and nephews when his brother died in 1827.[7]

James, Sr., was a working jeweller, with business contacts extending at least as far as Montreal.[8] He does not seem to have been a practising silversmith, and it has not been conclusively proved that the punch marks given to "J. Smellie, Quebec," are his marks.[9] He probably imported or purchased silver objects, which he modified to suit his clients. His trade card illustrated the variety of items sold in his shop (Cat. No. 23). The pinnacle of his career was reached in 1824, when he was awarded a royal warrant as "Jeweller in Ordinary and Lapidary to King George IV."[10] In late 1829 James, Sr., planned to retire to the country and held a sale of his stock and attached houses at 16 and 24 Mountain Street.[11] The building evidently did not sell, and the following May his nephew David, Jr., announced that he would take over the premises and business.[12] When David, Jr., left Quebec in the autumn of 1831, James, Sr., resumed his business.[13] He was still working from the Mountain Street address when he, his wife, and an apprentice died in the fire that consumed the house on 4 February 1841.[14]

David Smillie, Sr. (1781–1827),[15] started in business as a manufacturing jeweller in Edinburgh with his brother James, Sr. In 1801 he married Elizabeth Cumming (1782–1852), and they eventually had eight children.[16] Although he was a loving husband and father, the responsibility of this ever-growing family did not prevent David, Sr., from embarking on new ventures. In 1812 he left his business in the care of his partner and joined a geological-mineralogical expedition to the Faeroe Islands. Upon his return he found his business in ruins. A few years later he joined a similar expedition to Norway and returned home to face the same consequences. Probably economic circumstances, as well as

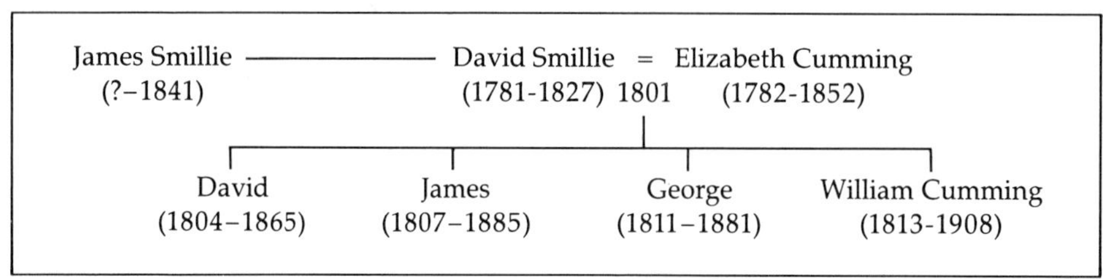

The Artisan Members of the Smillie Clan

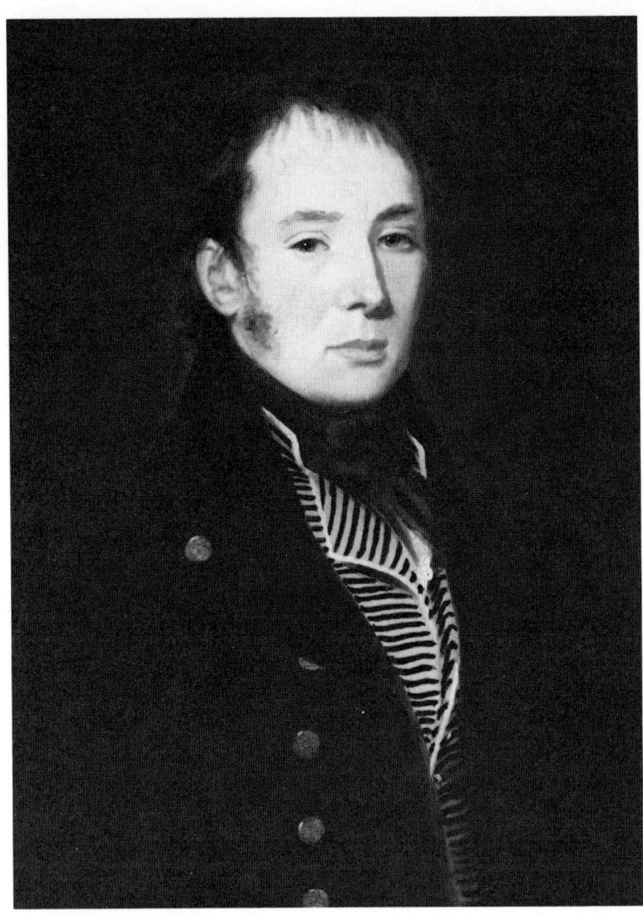

Unidentified artist, Scottish school, *David Smillie, Sr., before 1821*, oil on canvas.

family ties, decided him to emigrate to Quebec with his wife and children in June 1821.

David, Sr., suffered a debilatating spinal injury during the passage to Quebec and had neither the financial resources nor the strength to establish himself as a jeweller on his arrival.[17] For the first year the family lived in his brother's house and ran a bakery. By 1822 David, Sr., returned to his trade, now described as silver-plating and engraving, at 8 Garden Street. His son James, Jr., probably attended to the engraving side of the business, which was called David Smillie & Son. When the eldest son, David, Jr., had finished his apprenticeship with his uncle James, probably late in 1823, he joined his father's business, and by 1826 the name of the firm was changed to D. Smillie & Sons. From the description of this business given by James, Jr., the firm depended largely on contract and private work given out by the military. David, Sr., also collected minerals and zoological specimens for the Quebec Literary and Historical Society.[18] Having encouraged his sons to make a start in their professions, and after many years of ill health, David, Sr., died on 26 October 1827.

David Smillie, Jr. (1804–1865), completed his apprenticeship as a jeweller with his uncle James, Sr., about 1823. He then joined his father and brother James, Jr., at the shop, first on Garden Street and later at 10 Ste. Anne Street.[19] Following the death of David, Sr., and upon the return of James, Jr., from Scotland in August 1828, the name of the firm was changed to D. & J. Smillie. The brothers advertised their business as "Jewellers & Engravers," adding that "Silver and Brass Crests would be made to any pattern."[20] David, Jr., also appears to have been an agent for, or maker of, gold medals.[21]

In 1829 D. & J. Smillie moved to St. Stanislas Street.[22] The following year it was advertised that "David Smillie, Jeweller and Lapidary" had taken over his uncle's business at 24 Mountain Street as of 1 May 1830.[23] This business lasted for little more than a year, and in October 1831 P. & W. Ruthven announced that it had power of attorney to collect debts owed to "Mr. David Smillie, Jeweller, now of New York lately of this city."[24]

New York was apparently not as attractive to David, Jr., as it was to his brothers and sisters. He returned to Canada, this time to Montreal, in the spring of 1837 (Appendix L.16). He first appeared in the Montreal directory in 1842, listed as a "working jeweller." He continued to work in Montreal, winning a prize for goldsmith's work at the 1850 Provincial Industrial Exhibition.[25] He died there on 2 December 1865.

James Smillie, Jr. (1807–1885), the subject of this study, was the second of the four sons of David, Sr. His autobiography, which follows, describes his life, so that it is only necessary at this stage to sketch its principal turning points. At the age of twelve he was apprenticed to a silver engraver in Edinburgh for a period of ten months and to a picture engraver for another few months. When the family emigrated to Quebec, he continued to practise engraving by himself until he was experienced enough to cut letters and ciphers on silver and brass items sold by his uncle and father.

By 1823 he was etching pictorial subjects, and it was to this branch of art that he dedicated all his efforts. His talents brought him to the attention of the governor in chief, and in October 1827 he was given free passage to England, so that he could study engraving further. With few contacts and virtually no money, he eventually made his way to Edinburgh, where he apprenticed for six months with a pictorial engraver. On his return to Quebec in August 1828, he worked in partnership with his brother David, Jr.

Two brief visits to New York in 1829 convinced him that he had found a more suitable centre in which to make a living. He moved there permanently during the late spring or early summer of 1830 and within a few

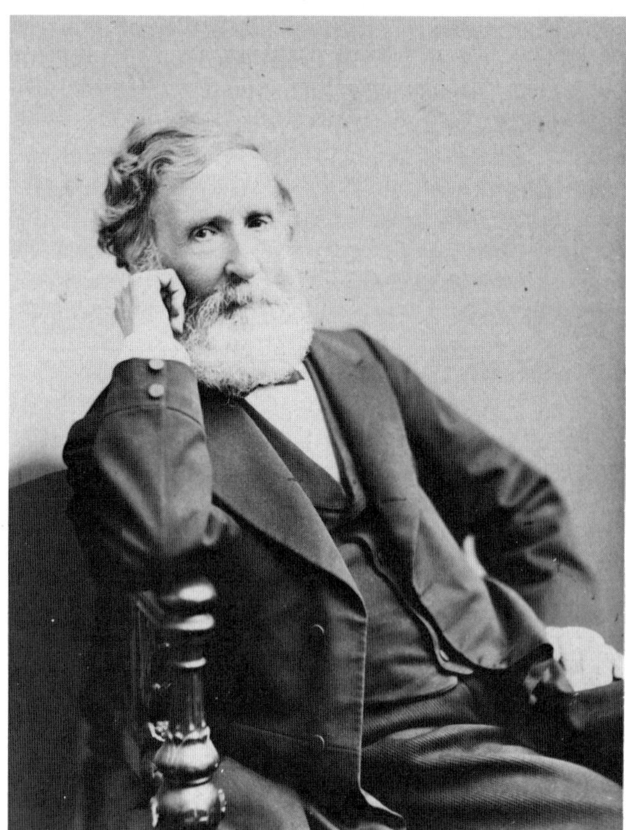

James Smillie, Jr., in later life.

months was able to send for his mother, sisters, and brother William. His talents were not only honoured (as they had been in Quebec), but also sought after and remunerated. He became one of the most prolific and respected reproductive engravers in the United States, where he lived until his death in 1885.

The third brother, George Smillie (1811–1881), was trained in the jewellery side of the family business. He worked as a jeweller with his brother David, Jr., in Quebec in 1830 and left that city for New York in 1831. In 1837 he took up residence in Montreal (Appendix L.17), where he advertised in 1839 as a "Mechanical Dentist."[26] These were years of recession, and he soon returned to the United States, where he continued to practise dentistry. He died at Plainfield, New Jersey, on 29 December 1881.

The youngest brother, William Cumming Smillie (1813–1908), learned to engrave under the supervision of James, Jr. While James, Jr., was in Scotland, "Willie" helped David, Jr., with the engraving side of the jewellery business, but he is not known to have etched pictorial views at this early period.[27] By October 1830 he had joined James, Jr., in New York (Appendix L.11), and he eventually became a banknote engraver, working for the American Bank Note Company and other firms.

About 1859 William returned to Canada and in that year was listed in the Montreal directory as a banknote engraver. With Confederation close at hand, he could sense that there would be need for a Canadian currency. He obtained support from politicians and in 1864 set up the British American Bank Note Company in Ottawa, which is still making Canada's banknotes. In 1866 this company merged with a rival company formed under George Burland (1829–fl. 1903); the two interests continued under the name of William's company, with William as president. In 1881 William resigned and the following year formed his own Canada Bank Note Company, which he sold in 1891. He died in Poughkeepsie, New York, on 2 July 1908.[28]

Quebec: 1819–1830

The city to which the Smillies emigrated in the early 19th century was the home of a society in transition. From the time of its establishment by the French and following its conquest by the British, Quebec had been the administrative, religious, commercial, and cultural centre of British North America. For nearly fifty years after the conquest of 1759, the social structures of the colony were remarkably similar to those of the French regime. There were changes, naturally, such as the rapid growth of an English-speaking merchant class. In the late 18th and early 19th centuries, however, the British worked comfortably within the existing mercantile community. It was only during and after the Napoleonic Wars that the situation changed, when acute economic and social unrest in Great Britain caused the emigration of an ever-growing number to the most established British colony.

Quebec was usually the port of entry for immigrants destined for settlement in Upper and Lower Canada, and many of the new arrivals remained in that city. In 1795 about one-third of the seven thousand inhabitants of Quebec were English speaking; by 1831 approximately half of the twenty-seven thousand inhabitants claimed English as their mother tongue.[29] Many of these new arrivals came from the urban artisan class of Great Britain.[30] The Smillies, therefore, would most likely have felt at ease and been able to blend into a society relatively similar to the one that they had left in Edinburgh.

The rapid change in the social make-up of Quebec was accompanied by a boom of activity that required the work of both skilled craftsmen and manual labourers. The lumbering industry, dominated by an English-speaking merchant class, was quickly supplanting the less labour-intensive fur trade as the colony's chief industry. A direct offshoot of the lumber business was a shipbuilding industry, also controlled by English-speaking merchants.

The military were occupied building new defensive works following the War of 1812. These projects included the construction of the Rideau Canal and the new fortifications of Fort Henry at Kingston, all administered from Quebec. Most important for the city itself was the large undertaking of the expansion of the Citadel, the impact of which was felt at all levels of the community.[31] Although the military tried as much as possible to use their own men for much of the construction, in order to keep expenses down, they had to turn to the civilian population for the craftsmen. The craftsmen of British descent were the ones who benefited most from the military contracts.[32] The use of British artisans did not only involve those skilled in various aspects of the construction industry; it also meant contracts to cobblers for shoes and to silversmiths for bayonet scabbard mounts.

The effect of the influx of British settlers and their takeover of the local economy is evident to a certain extent in James Smillie's autobiography. The Smillie jewellers, as purveyors of luxury goods, would naturally have had clients who were wealthy and socially active. According to the memoir and the few documents recording their jewellery business, their clients were primarily, but not exclusively, from the British sector of Quebec society and the officer class of the military. As an engraver, Smillie had talents that were useful to a wider segment of the community, regardless of social status and mother tongue. His clients included both Catholics and outspoken anti-Catholics, tradesmen and governors, and artists, both French and British.

If Smillie was favoured by any particular social group, it was by his own race, the Scots. Being a Scottish artisan in Quebec during this decade had its benefits. Not only was the English-speaking merchant class dominated by men of Scottish descent, but a distinguished Scottish lord, the Earl of Dalhousie, was governor in chief. He seemed to have a preference for taking care of his own people; the officers closest to Dalhousie were, for the most part, Scottish.

Lord Dalhousie and His Artists

The period of Lord Dalhousie's governorship in Quebec (1819–1828) coincided with James Smillie's years in the city. Dalhousie's presence in Quebec had a direct effect on the young engraver's career and was the impetus that turned him from an engraver of silver to an engraver of pictorial prints.

George Ramsay, ninth Earl of Dalhousie (1770–1838), was descended from one of Scotland's oldest families. After a career in the army, which included service with Wellington in the Peninsular Wars and at Waterloo, Dalhousie continued in public service, accepting the lieutenant governorship of Nova Scotia in 1816. Upon the death of the Duke of Richmond in 1819, Dalhousie was appointed to replace him at Quebec as the governor in chief of British North America.

Dalhousie was a man true to his age, class, and heritage. Very much the product of the Age of Enlightenment in Scotland, he fully believed in developing non-sectarian institutions that encouraged learning in the sciences and the arts. He founded Dalhousie College in Halifax and the Literary and Historical Society in Quebec. His own interests centred around the new science of agriculture and the visual arts.

In his wife, Christian Broun (1786–1839), he found a partner whose interests complemented his own. Lady Dalhousie was a patron of the arts and literature, as well as a keen botanist and mineralogist. In 1827 she delivered a paper to the Quebec Literary and Historical Society, which catalogued the Canadian plants she had found and classified. Smillie tells of her personal encouragement, when she gave him instructions in drawing.

Dalhousie had a remarkable propensity for surrounding himself with men of artistic talent. John Elliott Woolford (1778–1866), Captain John Crawford Young (1788–c. 1859), Lieutenant Colonel Charles Ramus Forrest (c. 1787–1827), and Lieutenant Henry Pooley (act. 1812–1843) were all at one time or another on Dalhousie's staff. Officers stationed at Quebec during Dalhousie's governorship included Colonel Andrew Brown (act. Quebec 1825–1828), Lieutenant Andrew Brown (act. Quebec 1827–1828), and Lieutenant Colonel James Pattison Cockburn (1779–1847). When Dalhousie's patronage extended beyond this tight circle, it was screened through these officer-artists. Dalhousie assisted fellowship among talented garrison officers by

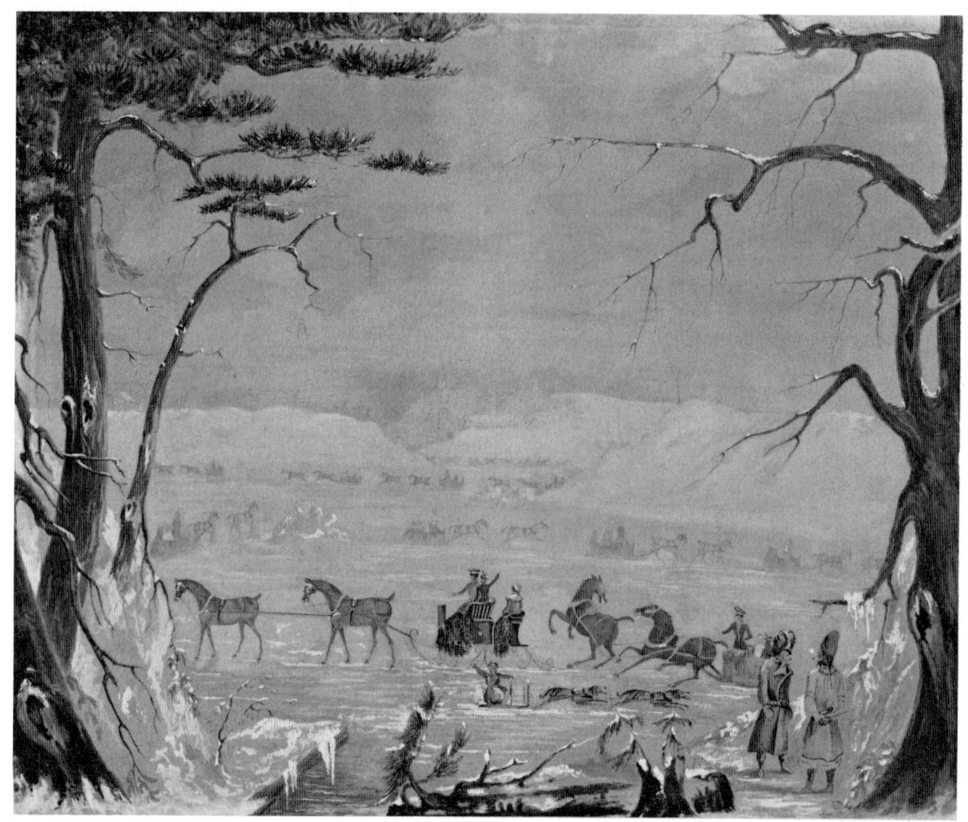

Andrew Brown, *Tandem Club*, watercolour and gouache over graphite (NGC 16659).

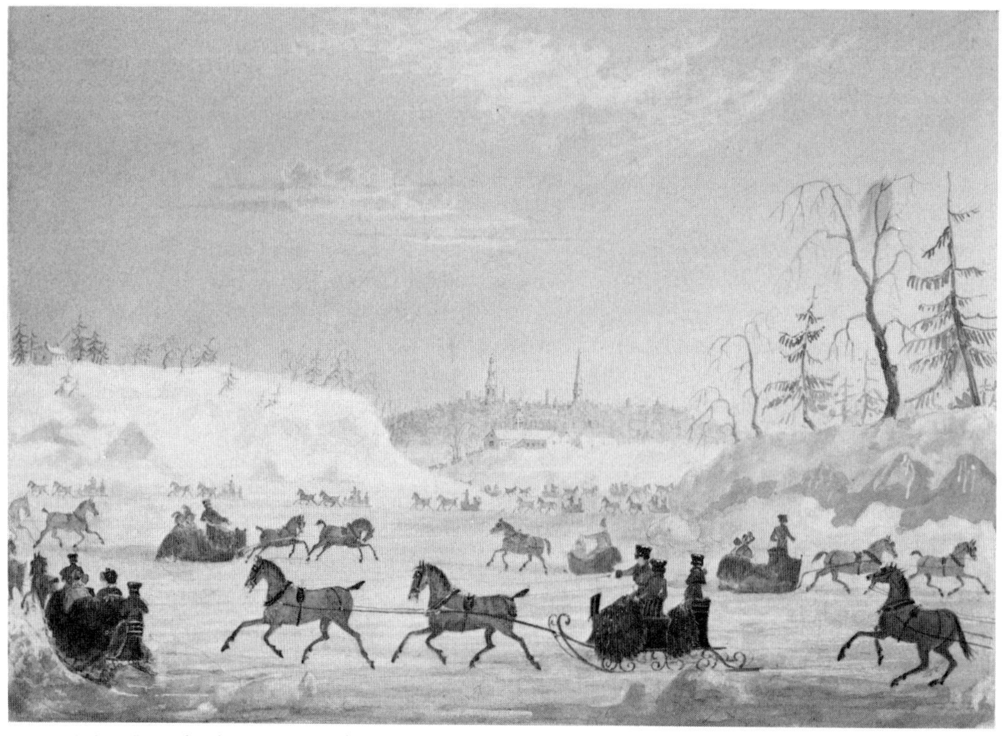

John Crawford Young, *Tandem Sleigh Club on the Saint Charles River*, watercolour over graphite (NGC 29214.23).

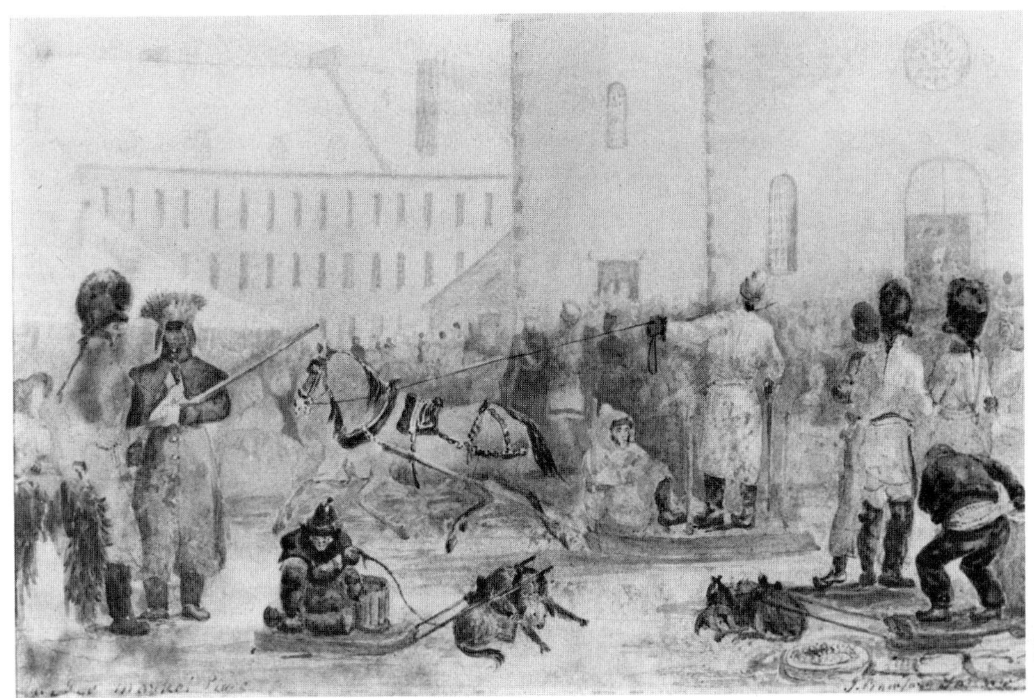
John Crawford Young, *Quebec Market Place*, watercolour over graphite (NA C40088).

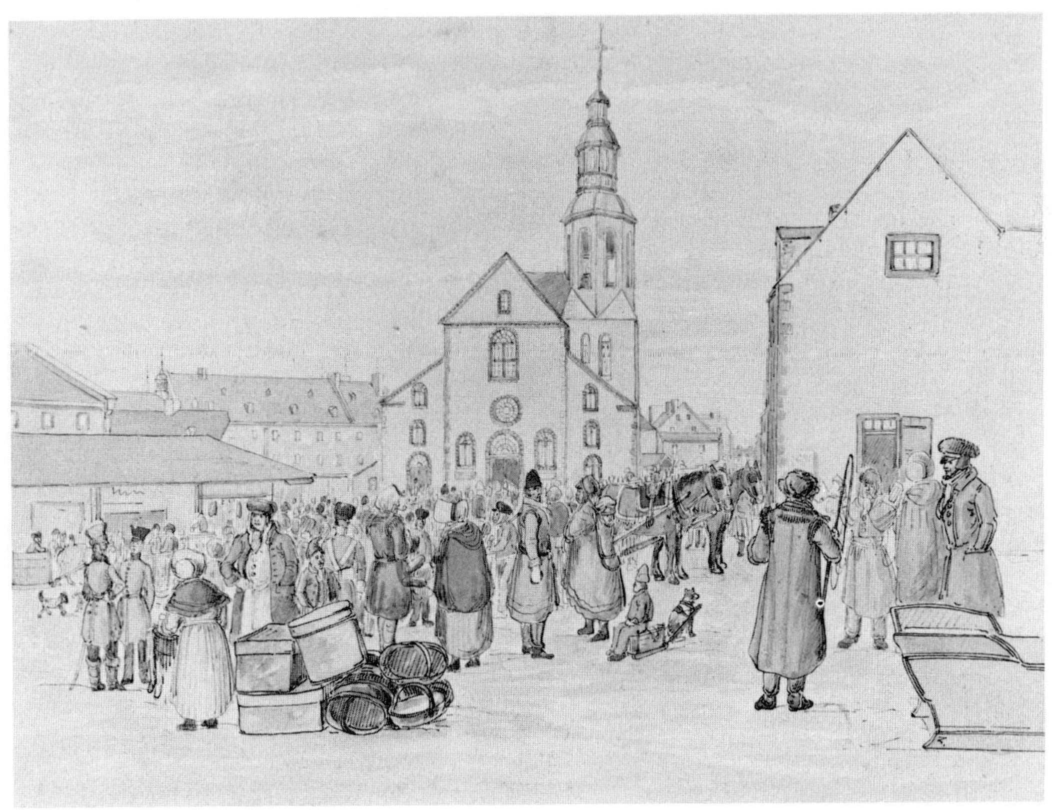
James Pattison Cockburn, *Upper Town Market*, watercolour, pen and ink (NA C38728).

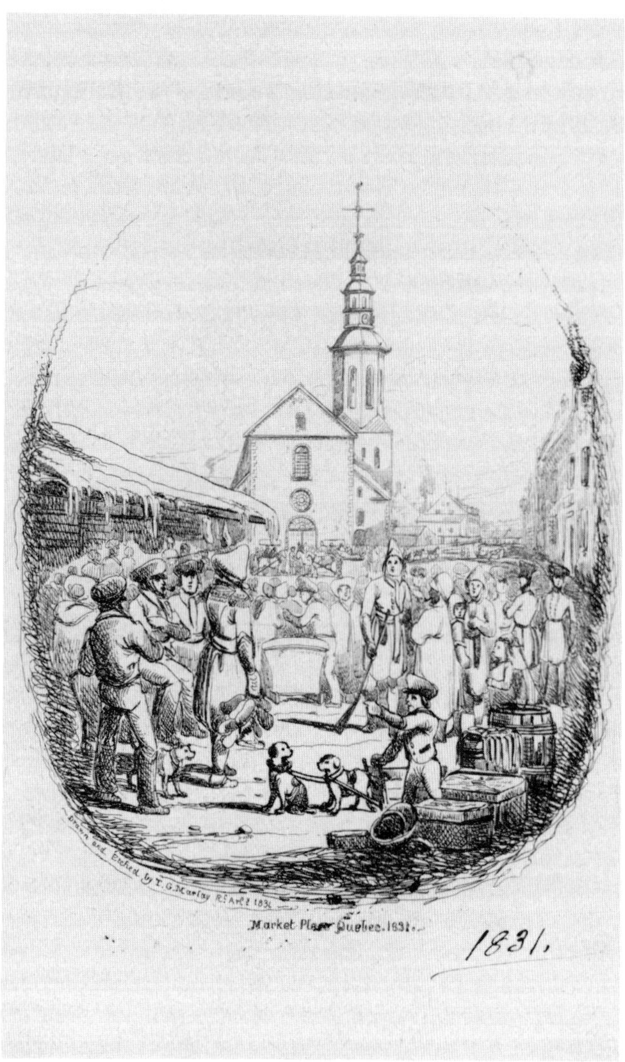

Thomas George Marlay, *Market Place, Quebec 1831*, etching (McC M919).

asking them along on his various official tours and allowing them leave to travel and sketch on their own or with each other.[33]

An informal association of watercolourists and landscape artists developed, evidently directly fostered by Dalhousie and centred to a great extent around the work of Woolford. Woolford came to Canada with Dalhousie as his personal draftsman and the visual recorder of his tours throughout the country. Dalhousie amassed a collection of Woolford's watercolours, as well as copies of these by William Roebuck (c. 1797–1847) and Forrest.[34]

A second group of artists centred around Captain Young of the Seventy-ninth Regiment, and Lieutenant Colonel Cockburn of the Royal Artillery. The close association of this group is demonstrated in the artists' works by a similarity of style and of subject matter. The watercolours of the Tandem Sleigh Club by Brown[35] (p. 6) and one attributed to Young[36] are remarkably alike in style and composition. Both are variants of the watercolour by Young in the album that he presented to the Earl of Dalhousie in 1827 (p. 6). The rendering of the figures, horses and sleighs, and dog carts in these watercolours also resembles the treatment of the same elements in Smillie's print (Cat. No. 32) after Ensign William Wallace (fl. 1824-1841). Similar comparisons can be made with Young's watercolour of the Upper Town Market and the same subject by Cockburn, Lieutenant Thomas George Marlay,[37] and young Smillie (p. 7, 8; Cat. No. 69h). Numerous documentary sources demonstrate that Cockburn sketched with Young, Forrest, and Marlay. This association explains some of the similarities in painting style, but the resemblances of the Brown and Young watercolours also suggest an exchange or copying of each other's works.

A further illustration of the collaboration between these artists is recounted in Smillie's memoir. He tells of a planned co-publication by Young and Cockburn of a set of engraved or etched views (Cat. Nos. 64–66). The Young and Cockburn project was never fully realized, although some plates were produced. Nevertheless, Cockburn completed a similar project with Marlay by publishing some of the Smillie-etched prints as illustrations to his 1831 book *Quebec and Its Environs* (Cat. No. 55).

It was first through Woolford, and then through Wallace, Young, and Cockburn that Smillie was repeatedly brought to the attention of Lord and Lady Dalhousie.[38] It was Young, and possibly also Cockburn, who persuaded Dalhousie to arrange for the young engraver's passage to England and to provide a letter of introduction that would help Smillie find an engraver for his apprenticeship.[39]

The Patronage of an Engraver

Because James Smillie had virtually no competition in Quebec during the 1820s, one would expect to see a wide variety of engraved works attributed to him, and this is indeed the case. Furthermore, it is not surprising that the commissions Smillie received reflect the interests within certain Quebec communities at the time; after all, printing was the best means of broadcasting one's economic, social, intellectual, and political concerns.

The business community's need for an engraver was clearly practical. Personalized receipts, insurance certificates, brochures, and business cards as advertisements were the major requirements. As merchants developed more and more economic control within the colonies, they made increasing demands on the government and found new uses for engraved material. For example, James George, an import-export agent in Quebec, wrote pamphlets—one illustrated with a Smillie etching (Cat. No. 76)—arguing for improved internal transportation facilities.

Educationalists were also commissioners of prints. William Gale, a schoolmaster from Scotland, ordered a print, an essay on the Crucifixion, either as a prize to his students or as a model for penmanship (Cat. No. 6). The Ursuline Convent commissioned a print of the Virgin and Child, also probably for distribution to students (Cat. No. 18). In both cases the religious subjects of the commissions emphasize the close connection that existed between education and the church, whether the schools were Protestant or Catholic, private or parochial. In contrast is the print of the non-denominational École Élémentaire Française, probably commissioned by the school's founder, Joseph-François Perrault (Cat. No. 71).

Despite the slim amount of book publishing in Canada at this time, Smillie was involved with four publications between 1829 and 1831: Lieutenant F. H. Baddeley's article on rocks and fossils in the Saguenay River area (Cat. No. 67), the Reverend George Bourne's guide book *Picture of Quebec* (Cat. No. 69), Adam Kidd's volume of poems *The Huron Chief* (Cat. No. 73), and James Pattison Cockburn's guide *Quebec and Its Environs* (Cat. No. 55). In all cases the authors were responsible for the contract with Smillie as their engraver.

As an institution the British military establishment did not require the services of an engraver. The Royal Engineers had their own lithographic press to be used for official purposes. Views by travelling artists, however, were sought after by London publishers who catered to the British public's interest in illustrated travel books. As a result, some of the more talented garrison artists were familiar with the commissioning of prints after their watercolours, and it became a natural extension of their production as artists. In this context, Smillie's employment by the military was strictly through the private patronage of the amateur artists of the garrison.

Cockburn was one of the military artists who, from 1807 to 1842, had many of his watercolour views issued as aquatints, etchings, and lithographs by the best printers and publishers in London. In Quebec he consistently supported Smillie in his attempts to learn the craft of engraving. Cockburn must have envisioned the satisfaction of having a competent engraver nearby during a long and isolated tour of duty. Cockburn's stature seems to have influenced his fellow officer-artists: for example, John Crawford Young, who had never previously had prints made after his watercolours, started to supply Smillie with his sketches and took the greatest interest in the production of the etchings. Considering the potential prints that could have resulted from Smillie's close association with these military artists, it is a pity that so little was actually produced. As amateurs and gentlemen, the officers did not have to rely on publication in order to earn their livelihood, and the projects were often left unfinished. Nevertheless, it was as a consequence of his contact with the garrison artists that Smillie began a career as an engraver of topographical views.

Another source of employment for Smillie came from the civilian administration of the government. The Legislative Assembly of Lower Canada, through its committees and the Surveyor General's Office, commissioned maps to be printed to illustrate reports. Five maps were etched by Smillie for two separate but not unrelated government projects: the settlement of the boundary dispute between the state of Maine and British North America (Cat. Nos. 52, 54), and Surveyor General Joseph Bouchette's long-term project of surveying and mapping the Canadas (Cat. Nos. 12, 53, 68). In 1828 Smillie received first prize from the Society for the Encouragement of Arts and Sciences in Canada for the etching of one of these maps (Cat. No. 54). Nevertheless, when Bouchette completed work on his *Topographical Dictionary of the Province of Lower Canada* and advertised for subscribers in July 1829, he announced that it would be printed and published in London.[40] This must have been a bitter blow to Smillie, then seeking commissions. It is not surprising to find he left for New York only months after having lost any chance of participating in the major publication project to come out of Quebec at that time.

The Engraver in Quebec

James Smillie's story shows that he had the initiative and ability to succeed as an engraver. He persisted in learning his craft, overcame many difficulties in a new country, and gained official patronage early in life. His prints were praised, and he eventually collaborated to publish the first illustrated guide to the city of Quebec. Why, then, did he not succeed in making a living in Canada?

His ability as an engraver-etcher was not the limiting factor, except during his earliest years. By 1826, and especially after 1828, when he had returned from an apprenticeship in Edinburgh, he was an accomplished reproductive engraver whose work could be "looked [upon] . . . as the works of a London Engraver."[41] His abilities were confirmed by the success he achieved as soon as he arrived in New York in 1829, where he was engaged by two of that city's most eminent artists, Asher B. Durand (1796–1886) and Robert W. Weir (1830–1889), to reproduce their paintings.

One major difficulty that Smillie could not overcome in Quebec was, according to his own statement, the lack of a press and printer to pull quality impressions of his work. The press that he owned and used was small, in poor condition, and unable to match the quality of his plates or print them in quantity. When he had control over a publication, as with *Picture of Quebec*, he took his etched plates abroad for quality printing, instead of engaging commercial printers in Quebec, such as William Augustus Leggo or Neilson & Cowan.

Smillie was a reproductive printmaker rather than an original artist, and he needed good models for his etchings. The precision and assurance that he exhibits when working on copper contrast with his tentative style when drawing. His sketches are usually copies of works by other artists, and the few watercolours or drawings in his scrapbook that are specified as "from life" are his weakest productions. By the same token, most of his print subjects are based on the work of others, although he claimed that the illustrations for *Picture of Quebec* were an exception. But even in this case he had examples of similar subjects to draw upon, such as the many views of the Upper Town Market by garrison artists.[42]

During the 1820s there were professional painters in Quebec, notably François Baillairgé (1759–1830), Joseph Légaré (1795–1855), and Jean-Baptiste Roy-Audy (1778–c. 1848). These artists never had their paintings reproduced as prints, nor is there evidence that they were interested in such an idea. The situation was quite the reverse, for they were often given European prints as models to follow when painting religious subjects on commission. The only local professional painter with whom Smillie worked was the relatively minor artist Louis-Hubert Triaud (1794–1836). Smillie, therefore, had to rely for the most part on the military watercolourists—who could be and were posted out of the city at any time—and on the occasional itinerant painter to supply him with subject matter. The uneven quality and sporadic availability of these sources were not conducive to compiling a varied stock of subjects or building a continuing partnership.

In competition with Smillie's etchings were imported prints depicting prominent persons, battles, marines, landscapes, sporting scenes, political cartoons, flowers, and historical, religious, and genre subjects. As early as 1790 the office of *La Gazette de Québec* was importing from England an "assortment of Landscape and other Prints most superbly executed."[43] Other booksellers, such as Thomas Cary, were importing prints from abroad in the 1820s. In 1829 John Clark, a bookseller located next door to the shop of James Smillie, Sr., was also selling imported prints.[44] In 1831 George Melksham Bourne, the New York art dealer, brought a large group of European prints to Quebec for a highly successful exhibition and auction.[45] The large number of reproductive prints found in the collections of the painter Joseph Légaré, the Ursuline Convent, and the Séminaire de Québec indicates how popular such images were.[46] Smillie himself collected prints, which he copied.

Smillie's lack of success in finding buyers for his works was certainly related to the small population of Quebec, which represented a mere fraction of the market reached by European and American print publishers. Quebec did not have enough inhabitants or a sufficiently developed economy to support an art-printing business. Instead of publishing his set of London views in Quebec, Smillie would probably have had more success by selling a set of Canadian views in London or Edinburgh.

An analysis of Smillie's known production from 1823 to 1830 reveals that only a small proportion of his work consisted of prints to be framed or kept in the connoisseur's portfolio. Most of his etchings were made on commission for a flat fee, and many of these were trade cards or business forms. Only two of his single-sheet prints were published in any quantity, if one is to judge from the number of those surviving today. Smillie issued *The Quebec Driving Club* (Cat. No. 32) sporadically and did not advertise in the press, and he etched *New Roman Catholic Church, Montreal* (Cat. No. 74) on commission. The three fine landscape prints after watercolours by James Pattison Cockburn and John Crawford Young might have met with success, had they ever been officially published. These prints were intended as part of a portfolio of Canadian views, a project which was discontinued when both Young and Smillie left Quebec. Other single-sheet subjects that Smillie published himself consisted of one religious print (Cat. No. 18), three portraits of persons not connected with Canadian history (Cat. Nos. 24, 58, 60), and two Scottish views (Cat. Nos. 4-5)—none of which sold well. His set of five London views (Cat. No. 56), which he advertised at seven shillings and sixpence, met with critical success, but the same review that praised his work advised him to concentrate on Canadian scenes. This comment may have affected his sales, which amounted to 20 sets out of 150 printed.

Although energetic in seeking work, Smillie lacked business experience. In the early years he allowed the client to set the price and he tended to underestimate the time required to engrave a plate. It is also possible that on occasion he was not paid at all: money is never mentioned in connection with prints for Dalhousie, Cockburn, and Young. Furthermore, Smillie demonstrated a reluctance to pursue outstanding payments, such as the money Bourne owed him for the plates for *Picture of Quebec.* (Appendix L.11). Nevertheless, the publication of that book was his principal Canadian success and the only instance in which he had the help of a business partner, particularly one with publishing contacts.

Even after moving to New York, Smillie was reluctant to enter the business side of printmaking and generally preferred to work independently on a commission basis for publishers. He was steadily employed and became one of the most sought-after engravers in New York. Looking back on his decision to leave Quebec, he reflected in his autobiography, "I was satisfied that whatever might be in store for Canada in the future in Fine Arts, it was too far off to suit my purpose."

The Manuscript and the Scrapbook

James Smillie wrote his autobiography, "A Pilgrimage," on ninety-eight pages of unbound, ruled foolscap, of which fifty-five describe his career before 1830 and are published in this book, without changes to spelling, punctuation, and paragraphing. As an *aide-mémoire* he compiled a scrapbook of his work, which he entitled "In Memoriam."[47] In it he mounted approximately two hundred of his prints, drawings, and watercolours, as well as some documents and souvenirs, arranged and numbered in chronological order to the best of his memory. Also attached to the Scrapbook are his own manuscript comments about its contents, which often cite information not contained in the autobiography. In the autobiography he refers to the Scrapbook entries by number, and with only two exceptions, these items are still in the Scrapbook.[48] A supplementary scrapbook containing duplicate impressions was assembled by his son James David Smillie (1833–1909).

Smillie's autobiography has been used as the basis for several articles on his later career, but with little reference to his nine years in Canada.[49] In 1901 James David Smillie planned to have the autobiography printed as a private publication and etched a portrait of his father as he appeared in 1825 (p. 12). Publication did not take place, and this is the first time that Smillie's story of his youth in Scotland and early life in Quebec has appeared in print.

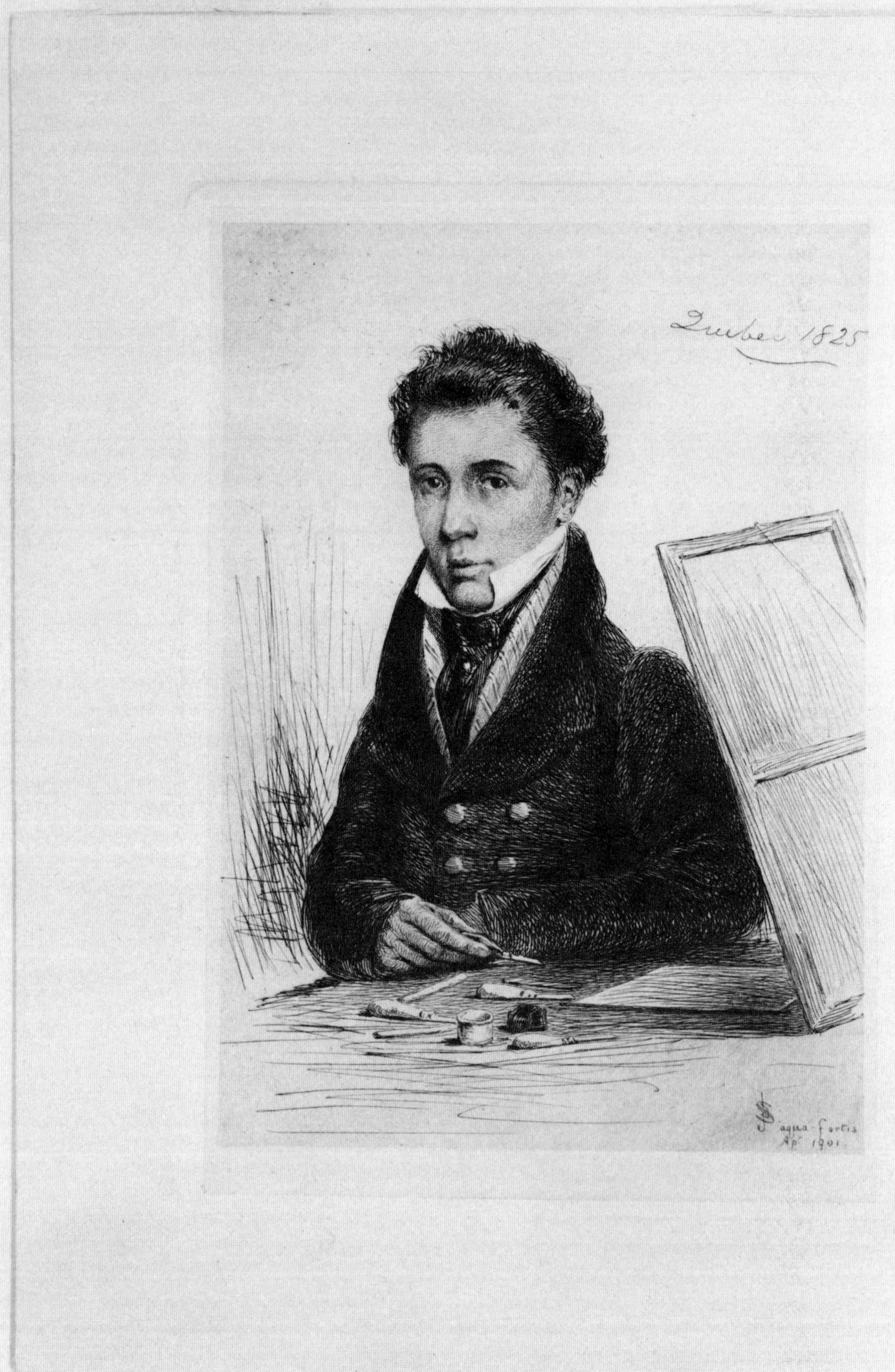

James David Smillie, *James Smillie*, 1901, etching after Edward Heaton (ROM 985.90.1).

A Pilgrimage

By James Smillie 1807-1885

On the 23rd of Nov. 1807. I was born in the city of Edinburgh, Scotland.

There are but three events only, which I can remember with any degree of distinctness previous to the year 1815. The first, when I was in petticoats, one day seeing father bring into the house a large paper bag full of old worn out english shillings, and emptying them on the table. I thought he was so rich! He had bought them to melt.

The second event was the death of my grandmother. (on father's side) I can well remember how proud I was in a new suit of black cloths, and black silk stockings, and we all went to the graveyard of the old "Chapel of Ease".

The third, was a great event, the return of a small remnant of the 42nd 1815.
regiment of Highlanders, from the Battle of Waterloo! As Rev. Thos, Guthrie, in his autobiography gives it, "The town was wild with joy, and as the small but gallant remnant of that noble regiment entered with tattered colors, some with their arms in slings, patches still on the naked limbs that trode, and on the brave browned faces that looked upon that bloody field, the roll of drums and shrill sound of their bagpipes were drowned in shouts that rent the air."[1] That scene is very vividly stamped on my mind, as I stood by the old Tron Church and witnessed the throng marching up to the castle.

At this period, of things in general, I have but a vague recollection, further than being a good deal in father's shop. He was a manufacturing Jeweler. About this time I went to a school for small children. I continued there but a very brief period however, as circumstances in the family had greatly changed.

Father and his brother (Uncle James) were then in partnership, and doing very well. Everything was comfortable and promising.

Father had a great passion for mineralogy, and was a good deal of a naturalist. He was approached by Sir George McKenzie and Mr. Allen (a banker) both of Edinburgh. A proposition was made that he should accompany them in an exploring expedition to the Faro Islands.[2] Nothing could have pleased father more than this. He made arrangements at once for a start, leaving the business entirely in the hands of his brother, which in time proved to be a fatal step.

During a protracted absence of the party, father's partner had given himself up very much to gay company, and completely neglected business. The result was that mother and children had to suffer. I can well remember some of our hardships at that time. My opportunity to attend school was cut off, and many other privations ensued.

In due time father returned home, and found things very much deranged. He strove hard for some time to make matters right, but became very much discouraged. He began to look round for something else to do, outside of his legitimate business. A chance presented itself in the way of taking the oversight of an extensive chemical work in Porto-bello, three miles from Edinburgh. He applied, and secured the situation.

This was a pleasant little village on the shore of the Frith of Forth. We very 1817.
soon made a move here, and remained for three years. Here I first became enamoured of nature. To this day, my experience of those three years rise up before me with a freshness and delight I cannot express. I can still hear the lark

and the blackbird which especially enchanted me at that time. I can see my linnets, and tame sparrows so familiar that, always at meal time they would be on hand, hopping about on the table, getting on the shoulder of one and another and eating from our mouths. —Here, in a ditch running near by our house, I used to make dams, and build mills and houses.

There was a very extensive brick yard joining the chemical works, where I used to spend a good deal of my time, laying brick (to dry in the sun) I became quite expert in that line. From this yard I used to procure a quantity of spoiled brick, for building purposes. On one occasion I erected a a house large enough so that two or three of us boys could creep in and enjoy ourselves. Many a long rumination I have had alone there, young as I was, looking forward to America!

I remember being once rambling over some of the fields in an adjoining farm. I happened to meet a stray goose. I did not think for a moment that it belonged to any one, so I caught the creature and carried it to my little house and kept it there for several days, until my parents got wind of my possession and they showed me my error and folly in keeping it. I had to let the prisoner go free. In the act I was taught a lesson.

We had a little garden, which I undertook to manage myself. I raised a large quantity of vegetables of all kinds, watching their growth with the keenest interest.

The workmen in the establishment had each of them a patch of ground along side of our garden, and I had a good opportunity of observing them in their management of the ground.

Another thing here that afforded me great pleasure was, after harvest, came gleaning time. I used to go out with sister Margaret,[3] and a number of the children of the neighborhood, and pick up the odd ears of wheat left on the field after all the grain had been taken in. When we gathered as much as could be held (clasping) with one hand, it was tied with a few straws; this we called a "dibble".

One season sister and self were very successful, and had piled up in the house so large a quantity that we were advised by the neighbors to have it ground, and thus profit by our labor. I knew there was a mill at Northfield about two miles distant but how was it to be conveyed there? A thought struck me at once. There was an old Irishman living close by, whom I knew very well. He owned an ass, with which he used to go about the country peddling salt. I gave him a call and asked him if he would have any objections to lend me the animal for the purpose of carrying our grain to the mill. He kindly consented, so that, on a certain day it was arranged that Margaret and myself should set out for the mill. At the time appointed, the old man came along not only with the animal, but it was fully equiped with his salt creels (two large baskets) hung across the asses back. This was just charming. I had made a nice whip for the occasion, and I am sure that no jockey with four in hand could have felt more pleasure than did I on our way to Northfield. We arrived there all right, gave orders, and left our grain. This however, was not the end of our trip to the mill.

Both Margaret and myself thought as our creels were now empty we might as well enjoy a ride home! We each got into a creel, and felt just happy. The day before our excursion it had rained very hard, so that the roads, in some places were very bad, and now and then we had to wade through puddles. When we were about half way home, we came to one of these puddles which extended the entire width of the road, and pretty deep too. In about the middle of this water our donkey took a notion of coming to a dead halt. I used my whip freely, but to no purpose. I tried coaxing and every thing possible to make a start without avail. At last, when we were well nigh tired out, the gentleman very quietly lay right down in the water without asking our leave!

It was a very ludicrous plight for us, and I think we must have given a good deal of sport to passers by. Through the aid of some one standing near we managed to raise his lordship, and about dusk we reached home. Many times poor Margaret and I have laughed over that adventure.

These are some of the reminiscences of our sojourn at Porto-bello.

Father became dissatisfied with his position here and resolved to return to
the city and try once more to make a business. This was in 1818. After another 1818.
struggle father had succeeded in recovering some of his old customers, and had several hands at work, when another expedition was gotten up (I do not remember by whom) to go to Norway. He was absent a long time and things were again badly managed. The business had been left in hands of one in whom father had confidence. During this period mother and children suffered more than on the former trip to the Faro Islands. I could not go to school. The only chance I ever had in that way was while we lived in Porto-bello, which did not amount in all, to probably, two years.

I was now about eleven years old, and had a great desire to be engaged in some way. I remember getting hold of a piece of sheet lead, and I procured a graver and amused myself in cutting figures of various kinds. In this way I filled up a good part of my time. This gave rise to my first thought of becoming an engraver.

I proposed to mother that she should try to find a place for me to learn the business. She only laughed at me, saying I was too young, and I must wait until father's return. I was put off in this way for a considerable time. My patience at last became exhausted, so I determined to set out myself in quest of a master.

I had not tried long when I found a silver engraver, by name James Johnston, who was willing to receive me.[4] When I told mother she tried to disuade me, but it was of no use. I was bound to go. I knew no difference between one branch of engraving and another. It was enough for me that it was engraving.

When father returned home, I was an indentured apprentice! I felt myself 1819
quite a man.

Father was once more greatly disappointed in finding his affairs in such a low condition, but determined to do what he could to retrieve his loss by close attention to business.

In 1820. A young man by the name of James Salker Miller became 1820
aquainted in our family. He gave himself out as a Lieut. in the Royal Marines. He paid his addresses to sister Margaret. He was quite intelligent, and of winning manners. In a short time they were married. Sister was then about seventeen years old. Suffice it to say, after a short period, he started with his wife to Greenoch with the intention of sailing from there to Quebec.

Our family was thrown into great and serious trouble by certain developments which were now made, proving that this same Miller was a villanous imposter. He had abandoned a wife and several children.

Father had frequently expressed the desire to go to Quebec, having been pressed by his brother who had been settled there for some time, and doing well. The circumstance of his daughters misfortune, tended to quicken fathers desire to emigrate to America.

In the mean time my master died, after I had been at the business about ten months.

A short time after this father procured a place for me in the establishment of Edward Mitchel, a very good picture engraver.[5] During the time I was here (which was only a few months) I never tried anything at engraving. I simply made four or five drawings from heads. Two of that number, in scrapbook, marked No. 2. were done there [Cat. No. 1].

Father and mother had become so anxious about poor Margaret that they could not remain any longer at home. Soon a sale was made of their little
1821. effects, and on the 20th April 1821. we sailed from Leith, on board the Brig "Neptune", Capn. Bell, and arrived in Quebec on the 6th June.[6]

We were kindly welcomed by Uncle James, (fathers brother,) who had been settled in business there for several years and had been quite successful.

Here we found sister Margaret, and the man Miller, who had established himself as a teacher of penmanship.[7] In this line he was quite an expert. In many instances he had proved himself to be a very base man.

In the course of a little while, sister gave birth to a little girl who, in God's mercy, in a few month's was taken from the evil to come.

From all the testimony father had brought with him from Scotland, proving beyond all doubt that Miller was a married man, it was determined to take the case into Court, and a trial of considerable length was carried out. When he saw how things were going to terminate he absconded, and never has been heard of up to this day. The case made a great stir in the city. The sympathy expressed for sister, by the community was very marked.———

On our passage out, one stormy day, on deck father was thrown from his feet by a lurch of the vessel, and injured his spine, which in time proved fatal.[8]———

1822 In Uncles house there was a vacant store. The thought struck him that inasmuch as father was not able to do much at his own business it might be well to try some other way of making a living. To this end, he started a bakery in this store. An old Scotchman, a practical baker was secured to carry on the business under fathers superintendence.

The new project succeeded very well for a time. This made (for the present) an opening for me. I could not tell as yet what I should pursue, but as to engraving, I had abandoned that idea, thinking it impossible to learn without instruction.

During the ten months I had been an apprentice with Mr. Johnston I had had very little chance of doing much in the way of engraving, from the fact that I had to run messages, and do many little matters about the establishment being the youngest boy.

I was now put to a new line of the fine arts. Part of my time was occupied in the bake-house making mutton pies. In the mornings I had to go out with the bread wagon to supply our customers. The rest of my time, (when father was not able to be on hand) I had to attend to the shop.

Even now, under all these adverse circumstances father insisted that I must not give up the idea of engraving. Back of the shop there was a small room where all our flour barrels were kept. In this apartment, with a bit of copper and a graver I set to work, using one of the barrels for my table, and did the best I could.[9] My only aim then was, to make letters. In time, I became quite interested in my pursuit. Uncle encouraged me not a little by saying that his customers were constantly enquiring about having things engraved. I continued practicing until I was able to make a tolerable cypher on a spoon, cut a name on a ring &cc.

In a short time my aspirations began to rise above a bakers wagon, or a mutton pie. From spoons, rings &c. I was soon able to undertake a visiting card, next in turn, all the other branches of commercial engraving.

The baking business had now fallen sadly behind, so that it had to be wound up with considerable loss. This change of affairs unfortunately resulted in alienation between father and his brother, and for a considerable time we had a very hard struggle. Father was scarcely able to do anything.

Brother David having finished his apprenticeship at the Jewelery business 1823.
with Uncle, we rented a shop.[10] Thus unitedly we did what we could. There were always two full regiments, besides artillery and sappers and miners in Quebec, so that, if there was little or nothing to do in Jewelery, there was always something in the way of military ornaments.

We also struck out in another new branch viz. making crests for gentlemens harness. There was a good deal of pride in this way especially among the members of the Tandum Club.[11] This line of business opened up something new for me also. For many of the crests new models had to be made, so father put this department into my hands.

I modeled the subject in wax, from which a brass stamp was cast, then with very thin silver or brass plate the crests were "struck up." Father was originally a silver-plater, a knowledge of which business he found very valuable in those days.

I frequently helped along myself in the making of military ornaments, crests &c &c.

All these things interfered with the proper application to my legitimate branch, but we were glad to do anything that was honest for a living.

My window in the shop was right behind the forge, so that, with bellows blowing, and frequent use of the anvil, with many other distracting sounds I had difficult work sometimes to get along.

My only time for quiet was in the evening. I would frequently return after tea and keep at work until ten, and eleven oclock.

The chief part of my work was engraving spoons, door-plates, dog collars &c now and then a card plate. I was now however, becoming very anxious to aquire a knowledge of etching, making pictures. All my spare chances were used in that direction.

By slow degrees I worked into that line which was more congenial to my feelings. Among my first efforts in etching were two views of Dalhousie Castle, Scotland. The originals were loaned me by an officer in the army.

When finished, I had the pair colored by a young officer (like those in Scrapbook Nos 3. & 4. [Cat. Nos. 4–5]) and submitted them to Lord Dalhousie, then Governor of Canada. This made for me an introduction in high places. The effect of this on the whole, was good inasmuch as it brought me in contact with some of the officers of the respective regiments. I tried to publish these views, but never sold any.

At this date I engraved a map of Upper Canada for a Mr. Smith. It measured six feet long, and three feet wide. (in three separate plates.) I was engaged on many months. For this work I received One hundred and twenty dollars [Cat. No. 9].

The only copy I had was destroyed when Uncles house was consumed.[12]

I was constantly told to get up some views in Canada, which would be sure to pay me. The chief difficulty lay in the fact that I knew of no one who could furnish me with drawings.

At this time I used to do a good deal in drawing with the pencil. (copying from engravings) I made two drawings of this kind, quite large, and much elaborated. The subjects were "The Holy family [Cat. No. 8]." and "Gaston de Foi [Cat. No. 7]." I had them framed and presented them to Lady Dalhousie, who was quite an artist.[13] She sent for me, and thanked me for my pictures. She gave me some good instructions about drawing in sepia, and presented me with a cake of that color.

Everything seems to conspire against me in my attempts to keep at picture engraving. There was no demand for anything of that kind, so that I had to do my part in trying to keep the pot boiling.

Things began to wear a more doleful aspect, as father evidently was becoming more and more unfit to do anything himself.

1824. At this period my second sister Eliza took sick, and gradually sank into consumption. This proved another serious blight in my path. With all that brother David and self could do, it was simply from hand to mouth.

We removed to a more eligable part of the city, with the hope of improving business.[14] Here I had a very large sign board made, and painted it myself, in leafed letters gilt. It read Davd Smillie and Sons, Jewelers, Silver platers and engravers. In this new start, I again frequently took part in the way of tinkering, mending jewelery &cc. In this place I remember painting a sign representing a mangle, for a poor woman, as part payment on a old rickety wooden printing press, which had come into her possession through a man who had boarded with her for some time and could not pay her.[15]

I here saddled myself with a debt of $60. thinking that, as now I could engrave visiting cards I might add to our income by printing them. This same mangle woman, her husband and children, proved to be perfect ghosts who haunted me for years, almost every day for whatever trifle I might be able to give toward the payment of the press.

This press was so bulky, and warped, and everything but an article that was fit for use that it required almost horse power to turn it. It was no small matter when I had fifty cards to print. It seemed however, in good keeping with everything else about us at that time.

1824. I engraved a large copper plate, a piece of lettering, for a Mr William Gale.[16] The original was published in London about one hundred years ago.

I undertook the work for the sum of ten dollars. I was engaged on it constantly, for six weeks. During the progress of the work, Mr G. had the conscience to see that I had made a great mistake in estimating my labor, and encouraged me with the assurance that, when I finished my task he would make it all right. Good hope!

When pay day came Mr Gale the magnanimous gave me one dollar to heal my mistake!

The subject was the "Crucifixion of Our Savior and the two thieves [Cat. No. 6]", an impression of which is among my old work, and from which brother Willie made a copy and attempted to publish in New York, but failed.

Father kept moving about, and did a little occasionally, but at the same time giving evidence of his gradual unfitness for any kind of labor. His spine was increasing in pain all the time. One of the vertibrae protruded very much, and frequently caused him to cry out with all his might from perfect agony. He began now to totter, his limbs becoming paralized. For a long time he was not able to lie in bed, but had to sit in an arm chair day and night.

Sister Eliza was constantly sinking. Her case was sealed. This was perhaps the most trying time in our troubles. No relief! I remember on one occasion father began talking with me very seriously about his case, and said that his hope was firmly fixed in his Savior! At that time I knew but little myself of the value of such an assurance, but many times since, have I taken much comfort from the sounding of these words from my father's lips.

In all our distress in sickness, it would have been much more tolerable if it had not gone hand in hand with extreme poverty.

One morning we arose not knowing where we were to get a loaf of bread for breakfast! God had never left us absolutely to want, but this was the sharpest point we had ever met. That morning He opened for us a narrow way, by which we escaped actual hunger.

A little boy came in from one of the jewelers shops in town, with a thimble to engrave. I immediately sat down and did the work as quickly as possible, carried to the shop myself, for which I received sixpence. Thank God! I was able to return home with a loaf of bread!

Brother David and myself were now the only props upon which the family could lean for support. Brothers George and Willie had attended school and had never yet done anything in the way of business.

Sister continued sinking until, after six months close confinement she died, 1824.
at the age of sixteen years.[17]

In those early days of Sunday school effort, Eliza was a staunch adherent, and was well enlightened on the subject of religion. She died in the triumphs of faith.

The funeral occasion was a very sad one, to see poor father in his chair, in great suffering, to witness the carrying out the corpse of his child, knowing too, that there was nothing for him but a continuance of bodily suffering, and to see his family struggling in poverty. It is comforting to know however, that he was leaning on the arm of his Beloved!

"E'en the hour that darkest seemeth
Will his changeless goodness prove;
From the gloom his brightness streameth:
God is wisdom, God is love."

Shortly after this event, we removed, to occupy a half house.[18] Father had now entirely lost the use of his lower extremities, but was so far relieved from pain that he could lie in bed, where he continued for nearly two years. This change was a great tax on poor mother, father being utterly helpless she had, very frequently to shift him from side to side as he soon became weary.

Here our expences were somewhat lighter, and business became somewhat better. We received a contract to make new mountings for the bayonet scabbards of a whole regiment which proved quite a lift. Brother David and myself kept hard at work on this order for a considerable time.[19]

At this time I had orders from the House of Assembly to engrave a map of the Valley of S.t John, showing a boundry line in dispute between the United States and Canada [Cat. No. 54].——— For this effort I was presented with a silver medal by the "Society for the encouragement of Arts and Sciences" and was elected a member of the Society.[20]

Brother Willie had now started in the practice of the graver with me, and brother George turned his attention to brother Davids line of business. We were encouraged to hope that, in time we would be able to overcome our poverty.

I attempted to publish a large plate at this time representing the "Tandum 1825.
Club [Cat. No. 32]," from a sketch by a young officer. (from this plate was taken the small view, afterwards published in "Picture of Quebec" [Cat. No. 69f].) From this I made very little.

I engraved also a large plate, to order, of the new Roman Catholic Parish Church, Montreal [Cat. No. 74].

My most daring undertaking was a plate for the Ursuline Convent. The size of engraving was about 12 × 18 inches, after an excellent print by some old Italian master. Subject, The Virgin and infant Savior [Cat. No. 18]. I engaged to do the work for forty dollars! It took me six months hard labor, and working too under the most unfavorable circumstances, behind the forge and in all the racket in the shop. I would keep at it (for the sake of quiet) till ten oclock some nights.

When finished with my great undertaking, I presented a proof, (or poor impression rather) to Mère Superior and other nuns.[21] I soon discovered that I had not made a very favorable hit with my patrons. They were evidently a good deal embarrassed, which state I began to experience myself. It was a trying moment. After a lengthened pause Mere Superior asked me if I would have any objections to publish the plate myself, and they would pay me twenty dollars toward my expences.

All things duly considered, I felt that this was rather magnanimous than otherwise. I settled the bargain on the spot and was only too glad to get out.

I had a number of impressions taken, and colored (in an attractive style of course!) to please the habitants, hoping to sell them in the country.—I could not push this enterprise very far however for want of means and understanding of the business. All I made out of it amounted to very little.

I possess no impression of this wonderful work. I had a number of them in a working desk, left in Uncles house, which was afterward occupied by us, and was destroyed by fire, when Uncle and Aunt lost their lives. See page 174. Scrap book.[22]

We had left the house previous to this catastrophy.

1826. Captn. Young of the Royal Artillery, and Aid-de-camp of Lord Dalhousie, was in the habit of coming a good deal about our shop, and found out what I was trying to do in the way of making pictures, took quite an interest in my case. He was a very good draughtsman, and had taken a great many views in Quebec and vicinity.[23]

At this same period Col. Cockburn, of the Royal Artillery also.[24] He too, had taken a large number of views in different parts of Canada, and was very anxious that I should devote as much of my time as possible to the engraving such views. He kindly offered to furnish me with subjects. He etched several plates himself, which I bit in, and put in shape for him. No's. 50. 51. are examples. No's 48. 49. I got up myself with the intention of starting a publication [Cat. No. 55]. It went no further.

I shall always remember with gratitude, the kind interest Col. Cockburn manifested in my welfare.

1827. Captn. Young called at our shop one day to say that if I felt disposed to go to London, to further my knowledge in engraving, the Governor, Lord Dalhousie, would be pleased to furnish me a free passage, on board of a Transport then lying in the river. He gave me to understand also, that certain plans would be carried out for me on my arrival in London that would accrue greatly to my advantage. Altogether, I was led to infer that a high way was opening up for me.

I was elated, and at the same time greatly depressed, on account of father's condition.

No 45. is a note I received from Lord Dalhousie in reference to the matter.[25]

On reflection, I have often thought whether Captn. Young did actually so state the case to me as to give me reason to expect something tangible at the hand of the Governor on my arrival in London, or whether my own sanguine temperament did not magnify and misconstrue what he said, in such a way as to be the means of leading me into serious disappointment and suffering as the sequel will show.

In the mean time, how was it possible for me to go at all. I could not bear to leave father in his suffering condition.

My case was fully canvassed at home, and poor father, although he well knew that his days were very near the end, insisted that I should go by all means. He believed that, however keenly he might feel the separation, it would prove an ultimate benefit to the family, and pressed me to avail myself of the offer.

This aspect of the subject went far to convince me that it was after all, a reasonable step although a very painful one for me. Mother, and the family all, fully acquiesced in the measure. Brother David determined to do all in his power to meet the requirements of the family, and by this time, brothers George and Willie were making advances in their respective brances, so that I felt satisfied everything would be done that could be done, by them all.

With a struggle, my mind was made up. I had no reason to suppose that father could possibly recover, but I was brought to a trying juncture, and God gave me courage to face it.

Leaving for London.

On the 11th October 1827, I received a communication stating that I must be on the vessel, Ship "Heydon", that day, as she was going to sail immediately. It was Sunday, but it did not take long to pack up all I had to carry.

My patience was very much tried when, after having passed through a fiery ordeal in the way of parting at home, I found we would not sail that day. I had made everything right on board the vessel, with the expectation of an immediate start, and I would not go ashore. I did not desire a repetion of the scene I had already passed through.

The vessel remained in port until Tuesday 13th inst. In the interim many of family and friends came on board to see me. Poor Aunt Smillie was very kind, knowing that my means must necessarily be very limited. She put three sovereigns into my pocket. Of how much I was under obligation I never could express, and how much they were greatly needed not longer than five weeks later, the Lord knows.

Up to this time I had not heard a word of instruction from any one. I was going, not knowing wither. After the vessel had got under weigh, a small boat came off to us, and a letter was handed to me, addressed to Mr. Aiken, Secretary to the Society of Fine Arts London.[26] I now felt greatly relieved. I thought that my way was now clear as far as that matter was concerned.

We left in the midst of a very severe snow storm which added greatly to the gloom of my departure.[27]

We had no sooner started than we found our vessel almost fast in the rocks about Point Levi. We had just taken our pilot on board! We strove all day to get loose, but could not succeed until about dark. After leaving two anchors behind, we made a fair start. The wind blew very strong all night. In the morning, the country was covered with snow, and our vessel rushing along with only two storm sails set.

The storm continued all the way across the ocean, and yet the vessel went steadily. I did a good deal of engraving. There was quite a number of officers on board. When they found that I was engaged in business, they brought along quite a lot of little matters to be marked. Perhaps a good deal from curiosity in having the work done on the sea.

When we reached the English Chanel we met a perfect calm. In due time we came in sight of the Isle of Wight. The weather was delightfully mild, and on the Island everything was green and beautiful. I could not but make a contrast between what I now saw and what I had left four weeks previously.

Arrived at Portsmouth.

We arrived in Portsmouth on the 13th Novr where I remained until next day.

I must here mention an unpleasant occurrance which took place after coming to anchor. The Captain gave me permission to go ashore in the first boat (appoint. for the officers only) which I felt to be a great kindness. After all the officers had taken their places I attempted to decend with a small portable writing desk in which I had a few trinkets from persons in Quebec to their friends in London, and being anxious to avoid the Custom House officers coming on board, I took the precaution to take this desk with me. One of the officers in the boat (a very spruce young man the very pink of neatness who was going to meet his young wife who resided in Portsmouth) immediately reached up his hand for my desk. At that unlucky moment when I took hold of one of the end handles to lower it, my ink bottle inside had lost its cork and its contents streamed right into the bosom of my kind benefactor! Our mutual plight can better be imagined than described. Ever after that I had a sharp look out for the cork of my ink bottle.

After making arrangements at a public house for a stay over night, I went out for a stroll through the city. I had not gone far before I was attracted by seeing in a booksellers window a copy of the "Amulet" for 1828 just published. This is one of the English "Annuals", all the rage in those days. Of course, this was too much for me to look over the engravings and not make a purchase, and notwithstanding the fact that three sovereigns was the whole amount of money I had, and did now know where I was going or what was before me I committed myself in the act.

I took out my passage for London, securing a seat on top of the stage coach. I was greatly charmed with my ride. Never did anything strike me more gratefully than the English scenery. The farms so beautifully cultivated. Here was another contrast with what I had left, in the way of agriculture. In Canada, everything so primitive. Here, everything so polished.

During my ride, notwithstanding my mind was so occupied with the landscape, it was continually disturbed with the fear of entering London.

I was alone, and we would not arrive in that city before dark. Where should I go? Fits of fear would overtake me at times as greatly to mar my enjoyment.

Arrive in London.

We at last arrived. 8 o'clock. Of such a place I had formed no conception.

I began to look round and make inquiry as to where I should go. Some one recommended me to the "White Horse Inn". There I took lodging for the night. It gives me even now, the horrors to think of my experience of nightmare.

Letter to Captn Bowie's friends

In the morning, I went out to deliver some letters which I had brought from friends in Quebec. I had a letter of introduction from a Captn Bowie, a retired officer from the British Army to one of his relatives in London. The family gave me a hearty invitation to make their house my home while in the city. I gratefully accepted it, and for two or three days I enjoyed their hospitality.

Called on Mr. Aiken.

During my stay here, I went to the Adelphi, where I saw Mr. Aiken, to whom, my letter from Lord Dalhousie was addressed. I was on tip-toe notwithstanding the gentleman received me with an air of dignity.

I was greatly disappointed when, instead of hearing words of cheer, after he had read the letter, he coolly told me he could only give me the names of the most eminent engravers, on whom I could call myself. This put things in a very different shape from what I had anticipated.

Called on Mr. Landseer.

I had with me a letter of introduction from Col. Cockburn to Mr. J. Landseer.[28] Father of Sir Edwin.[29] He held a high rank as a landscape engraver somewhat in the old school. The old gentleman received me very cordially. I found him seated in his arm chair, with an ear trumpet in his hand, perfectly deaf. He sent for his son Thomas,[30] the one who has immortalized his name by his large engravings of Deer subjects, after his brother Sir Edwin.

Thomas, I found nearly as deaf as his father. He was exceedingly pleasant, showed a plate he had just finished for one of the "Annuals", "The Falkoner". He called in a sister, also an engraver she seemed quite interested in the art of engraving.[31]

On that same occasion, I was introduced to another son, Charles,[32] who was at the time engaged in painting a large picture. I do not recollect the subject. Edwin was at that time on a sketching tour in the Highlands of Scotland.

I had a letter also to Mr Warrener an eminent engraver. (historical).[33] He received me very kindly, but could do nothing for me.

Called on Mr Warrener.

I had still another letter to George Cruikshank the caricaturist.[34] He was remarkably friendly, and very interesting, but of course quite out of my line, and could render me no assistance.

Called on Mr Crukshank.

I found that without paying a very high premium I could do nothing in London.

After making a good deal of effort to find a suitable place, without success, I became quite discouraged. I had no means to fall back on. But for the three sovereigns which Aunt put into my pocket on leaving Quebec, I would have been almost penniless.

Having spent some days at the house of Captn Bowies kind friends, I began to feel that it was imposing on their generosity to remain any longer.

Sauntering along the streets in the evening, ruminating on my situation, I looked in at the window of a music store. There I saw some theatre tickets for sale, "For the benefit of George B. Gale", at the Surrey Theatre that night. At this my heart leaped for joy, having known Mr. Gale in Quebec while he was connected with a company there.[35] He had always been very friendly, and I thought my next step had better be towards the Surrey Theatre.

Gale's Benefit Tickets.

I bought a ticket, and immediately I went back to the house of my kind friends and told them I would not return that night.

I set off for the Theatre. I witnessed the performance, recognizing my old friend all through the play. When the drop curtain fell, I made rapid strides to the stage, and enquired for Mr. C. A man went to him with my name, and in a very short time I stood with him face to face. He appeared very glad to see me, and insisted at once that I should accompany him home. He was a widower (having lost his wife in Quebec.) He, and a little daughter lived with his widowed mother in Chelsea.

Went to Surrey Theatre.

I accepted the kind invitation of my friend, went home and slept with him. In the morning, at the breakfast table I was introduced to his mother, who proved to be a mother to me. No one could have shown more genuine kindness, than she did to me, though an utter stranger.

Nothing would satisfy my friends but that I should make their house my home as long as I remained in London.

My mind, for the present at least, was greatly relieved. I went to the house of my friends where I had been living, and had my trunk removed to Mrs. Gale's. I found myself very pleasantly situated indeed. Everything that could be done was done for my comfort.

I had nearly three miles to walk every morning into the city, where I wandered about in quest of something to do, and every evening returning more and more depressed.

Seeing at last that there was no chance for me in London, I determined to direct my course to Edinburgh, believing that, among my relatives, I could accomplish something.

Left Mrs. Gales.

On the 26th Novr I told my friend Gale and his mother, that I was going into town to secure my passage by Smack, for Scotland, which was to sail next day, and that I would call on my friends in the city to bid them good-bye. I told Mrs. Gale that she need not look for me that night, as I expected to stay with my friends, but that next day I would come for my trunk.

Could not find Captn Bowie's friends.

After getting into the city and doing my best for hours, I could not, for the life of me, find the place. I had forgotten the name of the street, and obliged at last, I had to give up the chase. It was night, and I had walked the streets all day. I felt very tired. What was to be done? I was two or three miles from Chelsea. I had paid my passage to Berwick, which took all but my last shilling, so that I could not afford to take lodging any where or even pay for a ride. I walked back to my old quarters.

Returned to Chelsey

When I reached Chelsea, it was about midnight. I had my fears as to gaining admittance at Mrs. Gales at so late an hour, but I must try. I rang the bell several times without answer. Then looked round in every direction to see what I should do next. I walked about for some time before I could discover any place with a light. It seemed as if every body had retired. At last I saw a glimmering light in a closed store, which appeared to me like a tavern. I knocked at the door, but no answer. I kept repeating my raps, but not a sound within.

Met a man at the tavern door.

I was about leaving, when a man with a jug in his hand made his appearance. He had come for his *hale.* I told him it was no use trying to get entrance there, as I had been knocking for a considerable time. He replied, I'll get in you'll see. In the mean time I related to him my situation. He at once said, if you have no objections to sleep with me—come, and I will give you a bed.—He had given his rap and now the door opens! After getting *"'is hale"* we walked off together, and I resumed my story to him. He says I live in a very poor house, but will make you welcome if you choose to go with me. What else could I do? Was not that man a messenger of mercy to me at that moment? I at once accepted his kind offer and followed him to his house, which I found to be a wretched hovel indeed. He was a common porter—When we entered the abode, he told his wife my situation, and arrangements were immediately made for my accommodation. It was necessary to make a "shake-down" for me in the garret. A doleful looking hole it was to be sure, but I was thankful for any place to lay my head.

In a short time he and I were bed-fellows!—Tired as I was I could not find a chance to go to sleep. He kept up his gab for nearly half the night.

In the morning, the good-wife prepared a very comfortable breakfast. I of course sat down with the family. (there were several children to add to their poverty)

When through with my meal, I made arrangements with my host to convey my trunk to the vessel, in his hand-cart.

I called at Mrs. Gales to bid them all good-bye there, and to get my trunk. The good old lady seemed to feel very badly when I related to her my troubles.

Left for Smack.

I made a final start, following my coachman to the smack. . a distance of about three miles. This man did certainly appear to be a very honest good fellow. I had nothing to complain of in the way of his charges. For my lodging and breakfast and carrying my trunk such a distance I paid him five shillings! His own price. I was sorry that my pecuniary condition was such that I could not afford to be generous. I felt thankful that I had met with such a benefactor.

Sailed for Berwick.

My Sail to Berwick was coasting all the way. We were five days in reaching our journey's end. I kept my bed the whole time. The vessel was very small, and in a very short, cross sea, made such motion that I suffered tenfold more from sea-sickness than I did all the passage over from Quebec to Portsmouth.—Slept the night in Berwick, suffering another terrible fit of nightmare.

Left Berwick for Edinburgh.

Next day I engaged my passage, (on top of the stage coach) for Edinburgh. My funds were now reduced to merely twenty five cents. I knew of course, that I would require something to eat before the day was done, and when the coach halted at an Inn for dinner, I felt very much embarrassed as to whether I should venture down from my seat, or try to hold out. I determined at all risks to order something to eat. When pay time came, I found the demand only two pence more that I had. I compromised with the host very pleasantly however, and we made a fresh start on our journey with renewed zest.

Arrival in Edinburgh.

About six o'clk. in the evening, (Dec 3d?) we arrived in "Auld Reeky". I left my trunk in the stage office, (head of Leith walk) and made my way to Aunt Haxton's. Found all well there, and met a hearty welcome. I had my trunk brought from the office, and I felt that now, I could almost say I had got home. Aunt had ever proved to be a true friend to our family, and she never could do enough for any of us from the love she bore her brother. (my father)[36]

Father's death.

Two or three days after my arrival I received a letter from brother David in Quebec, informing me that father died three days after I left home![37] This was a severe blow for me. Notwithstanding I knew that it was hoping against hope to suppose that father could ever recover, I was not prepared for the sad event then.

I now felt more anxious than ever, to have a knowledge of my business, that I might be an assistance at home.

I began at once looking out for an instructor. For about six weeks I was baffled in my search.

Andrew Wilson.

I at last found one in Mr. Andrew Wilson, a man of very moderate talents as an engraver, but he was good and kind.[38]

He agreed to receive me into his establishment for six months, by paying a premium of ten pounds sterling. Here I was again put to my wits end. My Uncle had just met with some heavy pecuniary losses so that I could not borrow the amount from him.

There was a good friend of our family, Captn McDougal, a sea-faring man, who had always shown a great deal in interest in my welfare. I know that he had just then arrived in London, from Quebec. I wrote to him, and told him my situation, and ventured to ask him the loan of the needed amount. To my great delight I received from him immediately, a very kind letter containing a ten pound note! Now I saw my way clear for a little while ahead [see Appendix L.6, 7].

I at once, commenced under Mr. Wilson's instruction.

At that time, a series of views of "London and its vicinity", were published. The work was just commenced. The engravings were all by George Cooke of London. It was considered that I could not lay a better foundation in the way of etching, than to copy some of these plates [Cat. No. 56].

Hornsey Church.

My first effort was a view of "Hornsey Church [Cat. No. 56b]. At this time I was quite undecided as to which branch of engraving I should really pursue, and as Mr. Wilson was ready for either (in his way) I undertook for my next subject, a portrait of "Sir William Temple" [Cat. No. 58]. I determined to alternate between portraits and landscapes.

My next subject was a view of "Ship-breaking, opposite Wapping" [Cat. No. 56c]. Then followed a portrait of Ochlenshlager, (a Danish poet) [Cat. No. 60].

My next, and last plate was "Woolsey's Well" [Cat. No. 56f]. Just at this time there was a vessel announced to sail from Leith to Quebec. I had still a month of my time to fill with Mr. Wilson, but as it was a rare thing for a vessel to sail to Quebec from Leith, I made up my mind, that I would wind up and make my way home. My home now, was in America.

Wilson's pupil.

There was a young man, (Colin Campbell) a pupil with Mr Wilson while I was there. He had been practicing on Cookes views also. The thought struck me that I might make something out of my plates in the way of a republication in Quebec. To this end I bargained with my companion for two of his plates, "Session's House, Clerkenwell Green", and "Tooting Church" [Cat. Nos. 56d–e]. His price was certainly very moderate, five dollars each! I had no money, but he trusted to my honesty in remitting him the amount when I was able. I had one hundred and fifty copies of each of the landscape plates printed, and as many covers, to make up No. 1 of a republication of Cookes "London and its vicinity" (No. 61, 63, 64, 65, 66, 67 in scrap book) hoping that I might find it to my advantage to continue the work [Cat. No. 56, Appendix E].

Took out my passage to Quebec.

I went down to Leith, and saw the Captain of the vessel about to sail. I told him frankly my situation, and asked him if he would for trust my honor for the payment of my passage till we arrived at Quebec. He was very kind indeed, and gave me a steerage passage, for which I was to pay three pounds.

During the time I was engaged with Mr. Wilson, I used to do little jobs in the way of lettering jewelery &c for a friend, Mr. Thomas Drysdale [Cat. No. 62]. With what I made in this way I laid in a stock of provisions for the passage.

My cousin Richard Haxton, now made up his mind to accompany me to America.

1828

About the 1st May 1828 we set sail, on board the bark "Margaret", Capn. Black.[39]

Escape from fire.

We had a very long tedious passage of sixty three days. We had a very narrow escape from burning at sea. One day, with the wind right aft, and our sails beautifully rounded, a live coal was carried from the steerage passenger's fire on deck, right into the lap of one of them. In an instant the sail was in a blaze. If it had not been that some one happened to see it at once, and had the sail (which fortunately was a studden sail) hawled in quickly, the whole ship would have been on fire. Surely this was a providential escape.

Short provisions.

My cousin and self began to find out that we had made short reckoning in laying in our provisions. In fact, before we got near the end of our journey, the passengers generally, were crying out in the same way, and the Captn. had nothing to spare, so that we were all on short allowance.

Cod-fishing.

We had had a good deal of very rough stormy weather, but when we reached the banks of Newfoundland we were very mercifully favored with a dead calm. This was just the right condition of things for cod fishing. All on board who could, set to work in rigging out fishing lines. We were most fortunate in catching a large quantity.

Mackerel fishing.

In the afternoon, a light breeze came up, enabling us to move along at the rate of about three knots per hour which was just suitable for mackerel fishing. We prepared ourselves for the change, adapting our lines for other game. In this, we were as fruitful in our efforts as in the former, so that during the rest of our way we were amply supplied with food, and the change was very grateful.

Arrived at home.

On my arrival home I found all my people well, and I was greeted with a very hearty welcome. During my absence the family had bridged matters tolerably well. Brothers George and Willie had made themselves useful, and helped considerably.

I now felt that I had arrived at a new era in my life, quite sanguine that I was going to make a field for the Fine Arts!

Published London views.

I immediately set about publishing my London views. Alas. Alas. I do not believe that I sold twenty copies altogether.

Col. Cockburn's call.

Col. Cockburn, who had interested himself on my behalf previous to my leaving for Europe, called to see me. He expressed a great desire (as he had formerly done) that I should turn my attention to the publishing of views in Canada. He and Captn Young together were ready to furnish me with drawings.

As other business would allow, I got out three plates (Nos. 74, 75, 77 [Cat. Nos. 64–66]) but fell through with my project. I found that, in order to accomplish anything, I must have means, and the demands of the family were such that I could not possibly carry out my wishes in this matter.

working on silver &c.

I was now engaged almost exclusively on silver engraving, or anything else that might offer. There was no choice left me. I consequently became very despondent. I fought against the grain for many months.

A new enterprise presented itself for my consideration. Rev. George Bourne,[40] a congregational minister then settled in Quebec, proposed that he and I should undertake the publication of a small book to be called "The Picture of Quebec", a guide for travellers [Cat. No. 69]. I thought there was reasonable hope for final success in this project.

Picture of Quebec

We made our contracts [Appendix G]. Mr. Bourne was to furnish the literary matter, and the illustrations were put into my hands.

We started a subscription list, and in a short time we numbered fifteen hundred subscribers at one dollar each. I thought this very encouraging, and began to work with some heart.

I commenced making drawings of all the public buildings in the city, with a general view of Quebec, making fifteen subjects in all.

When my plates were finished I found that it was quite impossible to have them printed in Quebec. There was but one person who made any pretentions to the business, and he printed only cards.[41]

I go to New York.

It was resolved that I should go to New York to have my plates printed there. With this arrangement I was much pleased, as I expected to meet with something that would stimulate me in the way of picture making.

1829.

In 1829, I set out for New York full of hope. I thought a brighter day was dawning. When I arrived, I called on Mr. Geo. M. Bourne, son of the gentleman who was compiling our forthcoming book.[42]

Plates printed for Picture of Quebec

By Mr. B's direction I put my plates into the hands of a Mr Miller a plate printer, who, in due time finished my order.[43]

After a stay of two or three weeks in New York, I returned to Quebec greatly pleased and much encouraged from all I had seen and heard, and with a feeling that, if I could not succeed in Canada, I might at some future day return.

As soon as possible after my return our book was published. The subscribers seemed well pleased with the effort. See Scrap book, No. 81. to 92 inclusive [Cat. No. 69].

After all the debts connected with the publication were paid, the amount in our pockets were very trifling [Appendix K].

Once more I was back into the old rut with no prospect of anything better ahead. I struggled along, doing everything, and anything.

1830. Returned to New York. I resolved at last to return to New York and try my fortune there.

I took with me an order to engrave a frontispiece for a book of poems by Adam Kidd of Quebec, then about to be published. Title, "Huron Chief". No. 94 [Cat. No. 73].

Mr Gimber. On my arrival, I became acquainted with an Enlish Engraver Mr. Stephen H. Gimber, who showed me a great deal of friendship.[44] He invited me to a seat in his establishment. Here I engraved the "Huron Chief" after a sketch by this gentleman.

When I finished this plate I had to look about for some employment. I scarcely knew what sort of work I was fit for, but must do something.

Mr G. had very little to do himself, and what he had was of the poorest kind: He had an order on hand for a lot of labels for cigar boxes. He said if I felt like doing that kind of work, I was welcome to a part of it. For this I felt thankful, as it gave me a chance of being on the ground where I could be looking round.

Introduced to Mr Weir. While engaged here, Mr Weir (now Prof. Weir of West Point)[45] called to see Mr. Gimber, who gave me an introduction. Mr Weir invited me to his studio to see a picture he had just finished, "The Convent Gate". No. 95–99. Mr. Weir had quite recently returned from Italy, where he had been studying for some time. The picture was quite a favorite both with himself and the public.

I called at the studio and saw the picture. It impressed me very favorably. Mr W. asked me if I would like to engrave it. I replied that nothing could please me more, but I had no confidence that I had the ability to satisfy him in such an undertaking. He then proposed that, if I felt inclined to accept, the hospitalities of his house, he would be glad to have me come there and engrave the plate in his studio.

At Mr Weirs Studio. With fear and trembling I accepted his offer, and in a few days I was under way on my very first attempt to engrave from a painting, which I often felt during its progress to be a very daring act on my part.

On this work I continued Mr Weir's guest for two months, at No. 47 Canal Street. During that period he and his young wife (he had just married) did everything in their power to make me feel comfortable.

I commenced this plate with the understanding that it was to be a joint affair.

When I had finished my work quite to Mr Weirs satisfaction, we had a number of proofs taken, but we employed no publisher, so that there was no chance given to the enterprize. I never sold one copy here. The impressions were equally divided, but I did not know how to dispose of my half.

From this affair I made nothing. It was now cold winter weather (December) I had become very homesick, and was greatly in want of many little things for my comfort but had not one cent.

Mr. A. B. Durand had just commenced a work in connection with Elim Bliss publisher of New York, entitled "The American Landscape".[46] He called at Mr Weirs to see me before I left his house, and asked me if I would undertake part of his work. I was of course very anxious to find some thing to do that I might realize enough to buy a pair of boots, (my naked feet were on the ground) and my hankering for home had become intolerable.

My first Steel plate. When I found that the work was to be done on steel, I shrank from it at once. I had never touched a steel plate.

Etched Fort Putnam. After expressing my fears on that account to Mr. Durand, he proposed that I simply etch the subject and he would "bite it in" and assume all the responsibility. I thought this was very encouraging, and I engaged to etch one plate, "The Ruins of Old Fort Putnam", from a painting by Mr Weir.

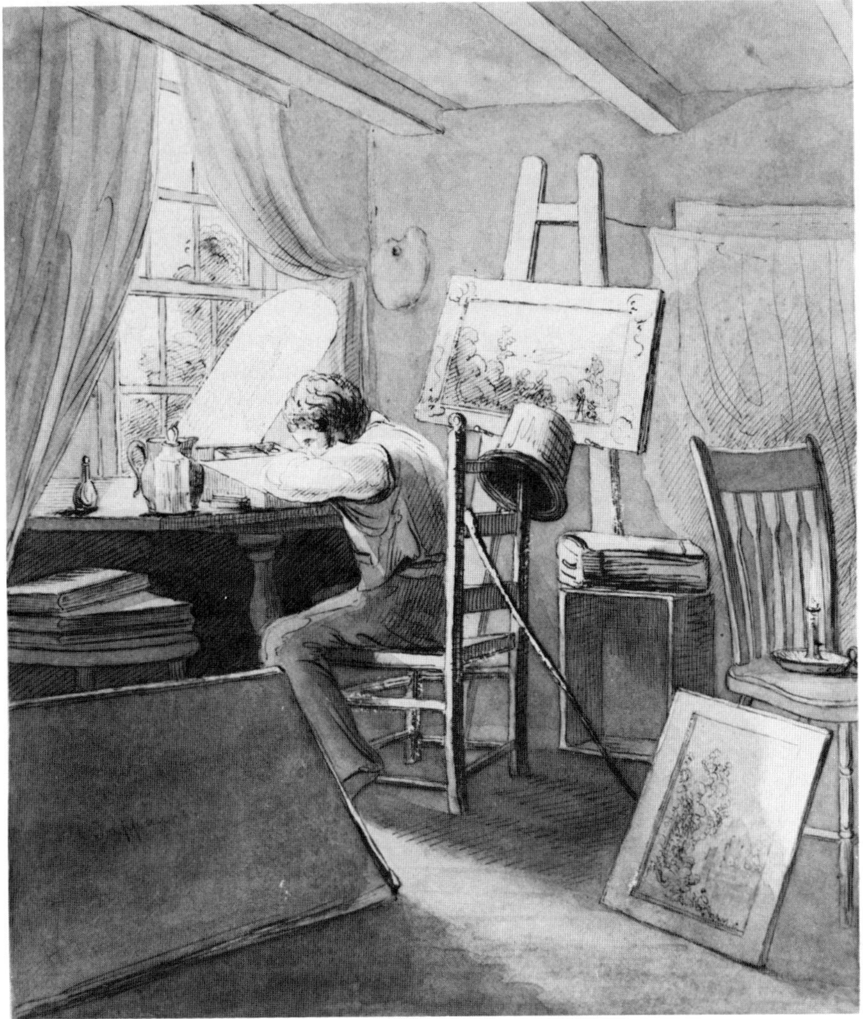

Attributed to Robert Walter Weir, *James Smillie at Tappan, N.Y., 1831*, brown wash, pen and ink.

My next difficulty was where was I to settle myself. I could not expect to remain at Mr. Weir's, and I had no money to take board. At this junction Mr. Rowland Bourne, son of Rev[d] Geo Bourne (with whom I had been connected in my "Picture of Quebec" speculation) had just started a small store in Canal St[t] branch of his brother George's business in Broadway. He very kindly offered me quarters there.

Lodged with Rowland Bourne.

In a small dark room back of the store we slept; friend Bourne also cheerfully divided his meals with me. So far so good, but where was I to etch my plate?

Happy thought! I had met with the family of an old friend of my father, an Edinburgh man. He himself had returned to Scotland to receive some money which had been left his wife by the death of a relative. He found it necessary to remain there a long time on account of legal difficulties. In the interim his family had become very much reduced. This good mother could not see her children cry for bread and was not ashamed to do anything for a living. She lived in an old delapidated house in Spring St. In the basement of which she had a mangle erected, and commenced business in that line of the Fine Arts.

Called on Mrs. McLeod.

In my extremity I called there and stated my situation to Mrs. McLeod, asking her if she could in any way accommodate me with a place to work in. She replied, "If you could do anything in one of our sleeping rooms in the garret you will be most welcome." Again I thought, very good! But it was cold, and what was I to do for want of fire? There was no alternative, I must do without fire. I accepted the kind offer and commenced my etching at once.

In two weeks I completed my work, and lost no time in making my way to Mr. Durand. He looked at it carefully then asked my price. I felt great delicacy in naming a sum as I did not even know whether it would answer. I secretly wished however, with all my heart, that I might receive enough to carry me back to Quebec as I could not stay from home any longer. With fear I asked Mr. D. if he thought thirty dollars would be too much. He immediately took out his pocket book and handed me forty dollars! and expressed himself perfectly satisfied, and wanted me to undertake another plate.

Under all the circumstances I did not feel that it was possible for me to remain any longer in New York. I felt conscious at the same time that, in all probability I was missing a good chance for the future. Mr. Durand had shown himself to be very well disposed to help me. I explained my situation and departed.

I bought a pair of boots, some socks and other little matters greatly needed, and made arrangements to start for the north.

Return to Canada.

I took passage by boat to Albany, and from there all the rest of my way to Quebec by Sleigh. I suffered much from cold and fatigue being three days on my journey.

at Three Rivers.

By the time I reached Three Rivers my funds were completely exhausted. I here took the liberty of calling on Mr. David Chisholm Postmaster of that place. He was a Scotchman. We had had some little transactions with him and found him a fine fellow. I made my case known to him. He was exceedingly cordial and helped me out of my trouble at once. After that interview he was always very friendly [see Appendix L.9, 15].

Home again!

In Quebec again.

Home is home even though it be near the north pole. I found mother and family well but struggling hard for a subsistance.

I again fell into my old line of business. It took a very short time to convince me that there was no improvement in my new line of engraving, (a taste of which I had just had in New York) I was satisfied that, whatever might be in store for Canada in the future in Fine Arts, it was too far off to suit my purpose.

Letter from Mr Bourne.

A few months rolled on and I received a letter from Mr Geo M. Bourne of New York, containing a proof of an engraving, No. 102.[47] He wished to know if I would be willing to return to New York and undertake for him the engraving of a series of small views of the city similar to the inclosed specimen sent. He promised a continuance of employment, and expressed the belief that I could make on the work at least ten dollars per week, and no doubt more as I improved. All this seemed to me like a providential opening to try once more, my fortune in the United States [Appendix L.10].

The getting up this work was suggested to Mr. Bourne's mind by the small engravings I had done for the "Picture of Quebec". I accepted Mr. B's terms and made arrangements for another move from home, with the determination never again to return to Canada as a place for final settlement.[48]

Catalogue

1. Two Heads, after Raphael 1820
Pen and black ink on wove paper; 15.9 × 17.5
Inscribed in pencil l.r. *Edinburgh 1820*; in ink l.r. *JS*

The artist's manuscript note attached to the Scrapbook page identifies this drawing as "No. 2. Two Heads, pen sketches from engravings under the direction of Mr. Ed[d] Mitchell, Engraver, Edinburgh, 1820."

James Smillie was apprenticed to Edward Mitchell (act. 1805–1821) for a few months in 1820. The heads are copied from one of the numerous prints after the Raphael cartoons in the Royal collections, now on loan to the Victoria and Albert Museum, London. The head on the left is after the head of the physician from *The Sacrifice at Lystra*. The head on the right is a disciple from *Feed My Lambs*.

REFERENCES: Scrapbook, no. 2; Pilgrimage, p. 16.

2. Facsimile Legal Document c. 1822–1823
Etching on seven sheets of onionskin; 36.0 × 23.4 (each plate)

James Smillie comments on this etching in a manuscript note attached to the Scrapbook.

> No. 18. A true facsimile from the original writing of a law case. The defeated man employed me to engrave it for publication, being convinced that it was his duty to expose a great fraud. I engraved the whole in twelve days, for which I received forty eight dollars. The best paying work I ever did in Canada.

The document, dated 17 November 1819, is a notarial act between John Boyle & Brothers and its creditors. The fascimile print reproduces the original manuscript, including marginal notes and cross-outs, on sheets that are watermarked "G PIKE / 1819" and "J. WHATMAN / TURKEY MILL." From references in two lawsuits involving George Arnold (one of the creditors), it appears that the facsimile was engraved between May 1822 and January 1823. The facsimile is referred to in an appeal heard in the January term of 1823 and again in the spring of 1823, when David Smillie, Sr., testified that he was employed by George Arnold to engrave a facsimile of an original document, and that he had some help with the plate. The actual engraving was evidently carried out by James Smillie, who was a minor at that date and did not testify.

REFERENCES: Scrapbook, no. 18; Arnold 1822; Arnold 1823a, pp. 1–3; Arnold 1823b, pp. 24–27.

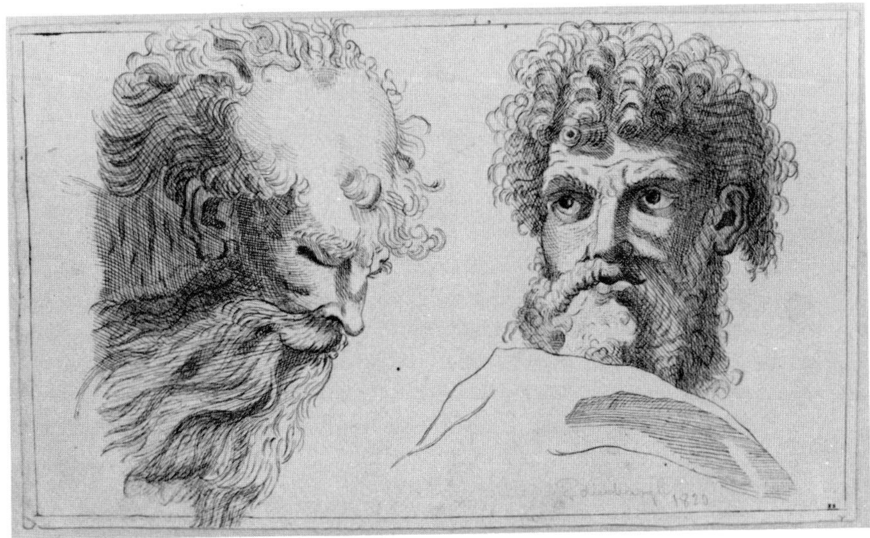

1

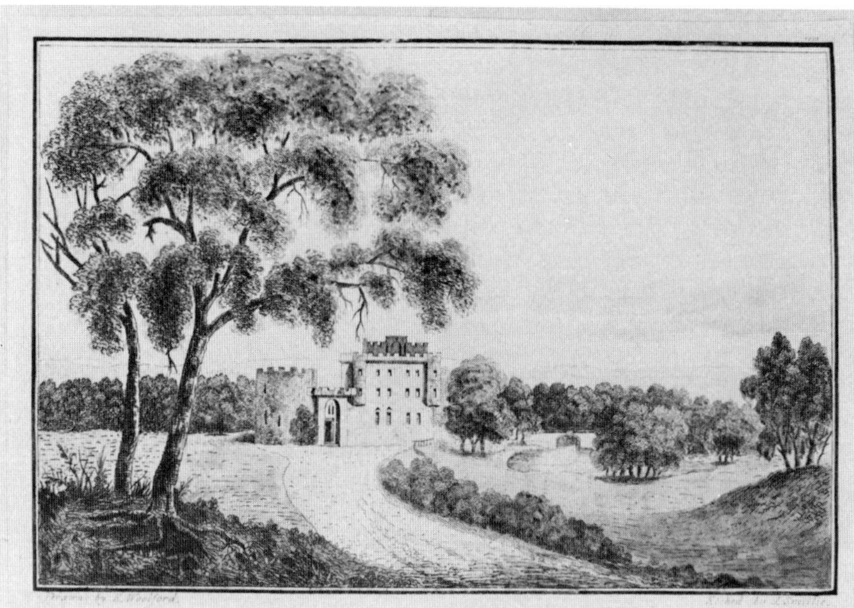

4

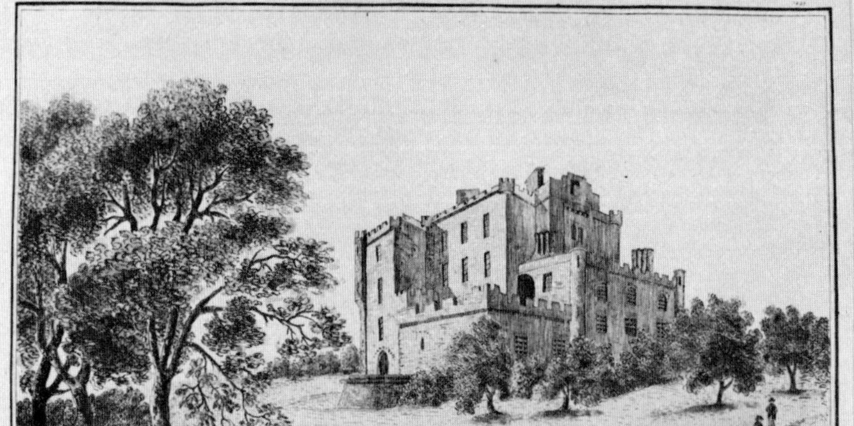

5

3. Chaudière Falls near Quebec c. 1822–1823
Etching or engraving, and drypoint; approximately 7.9 × 11.1
No impressions located

James Smillie's manuscript note attached to the Scrapbook reads as follows:

No. 17. The first plate I ever carried through as a finished picture! The sky and falling water are dry point, and about the very first of my attempts in that method. The view (from my own drawing) is the Falls of Chaudier near Quebec.

A later note in the Scrapbook by the artist's son James David Smillie records that he removed this etching from the album in April 1901 and presented it to the NYPL. The print was never recorded, however, as entering that collection. The approximate size of the etching represents the space cut out of the album page.

REFERENCES: Scrapbook, no. 16.

4. Dalhousie Castle from the N.W. 1823
Etching and watercolour on card; 14.0 × 21.0 (image), 16.6 × 22.2 (sheet)
Inscribed in plate l.c. *DALHOUSIE CASTLE / from the N.W.*; l.l. *Drawn by E. Woolford.*; l.r. *Etched by J. Smillie.*; u.r. *1823.*

In a manuscript note attached to the Scrapbook, James Smillie describes his two views of Dalhousie Castle.

No. 3–4. The original from which these etchings were taken, were furnished me by an officer in the garrison. I published them but utterly failed. The proprietor of this castle, the Earl of Dalhousie was at this time (1823) Governor of Canada. The views being in Scotland were without interest to the Canadians. They were colored by a young officer in the army.

John Elliott Woolford (1778–1866) was a professional artist on the personal staff of George Ramsay, ninth Earl of Dalhousie. He had served under Dalhousie in the army and had worked for a period at Dalhousie Castle in Scotland before accompanying the earl to Halifax and Quebec. Woolford was in Quebec in 1820 and remained there through part of 1823. Smillie, therefore, had the opportunity to meet him and see his works.

An early drawing of Dalhousie Castle by Woolford was engraved by Edward Mitchell (see Cat. No. 1) and published by Verner & Hood, London, in 1805. It shows the building from the northwest, but with a different roofline from the one in Smillie's etching. While in Halifax, Woolford advertised two views of the castle as being ready for sale on 3 July 1819; these etchings have not been located. A watercolour view of the castle by Woolford (MTL 902-1-34) does not correspond with Smillie's composition.

REFERENCES: Scrapbook, no. 3; Pilgrimage, p. 17; *Acadian Recorder*, 3 July 1819.

5. Dalhousie Castle from the S.W. 1823
Etching and watercolour on card; 13.8 × 21.1 (image), 16.3 × 22.0 (sheet)
Inscribed in plate l.c. *DALHOUSIE CASTLE / from the S.W.*; l.l. *Drawn by E. Woolford.*; l.r. *Etched by J. Smillie.*; u.r. *1823*

This composition, without the figures, was included in a specimen of penmanship that David Henderson of Halifax (c. 1795–fl. 1828) dedicated to the Earl of Dalhousie in May 1820 (NSM #N13, 826). Henderson was a teacher of plain and ornamental writing, who must also have copied the unlocated drawings or etchings by John Elliott Woolford (see Cat. No. 4).

REFERENCES: Scrapbook, no. 4; Pilgrimage, p. 17; MacDonald 1986; *Acadian Recorder*, 4 November 1820.

6. Crucifixion of Our Saviour and the Two Thieves 1823
Engraving on wove paper; 42.2 × 29.5 (sheet)
Inscribed in plate u.c. *On the / Crucifixion of our Savior and the two Thieves.*; l.l. *Eng*[d] *by J. Smillie Jun*[r]; l.r. *Quebec, March, 1823.*; l.c. *Published by W. Gale: School-master, Hope Street, Quebec.*

James Smillie's own impression of this print (NYPL) bears his pencil note, "I was six weeks engraving this plate for which I received ten dollars." In his memoir he describes the print as "a piece of lettering" taken after an original published in London "about one hundred years ago." Such lettered prints were not uncommon; for example, a similar print was advertised for sale in 1775, entitled *The Crucifixion of Christ, with Texts of Scripture thereto*. William Cumming Smillie made a copy of his brother's engraving (steel engraving, 1840, NYPL), which he failed to have published in New York.

Penmanship was always a part of the curriculum at William Gale's school, and the Crucifixion print may have been intended as a prize in this course or as an example to copy.

REFERENCES: Pilgrimage, p. 18; *Sayer and Bennett*, p. 142, no. 34; Pilgrimage, n. 16.

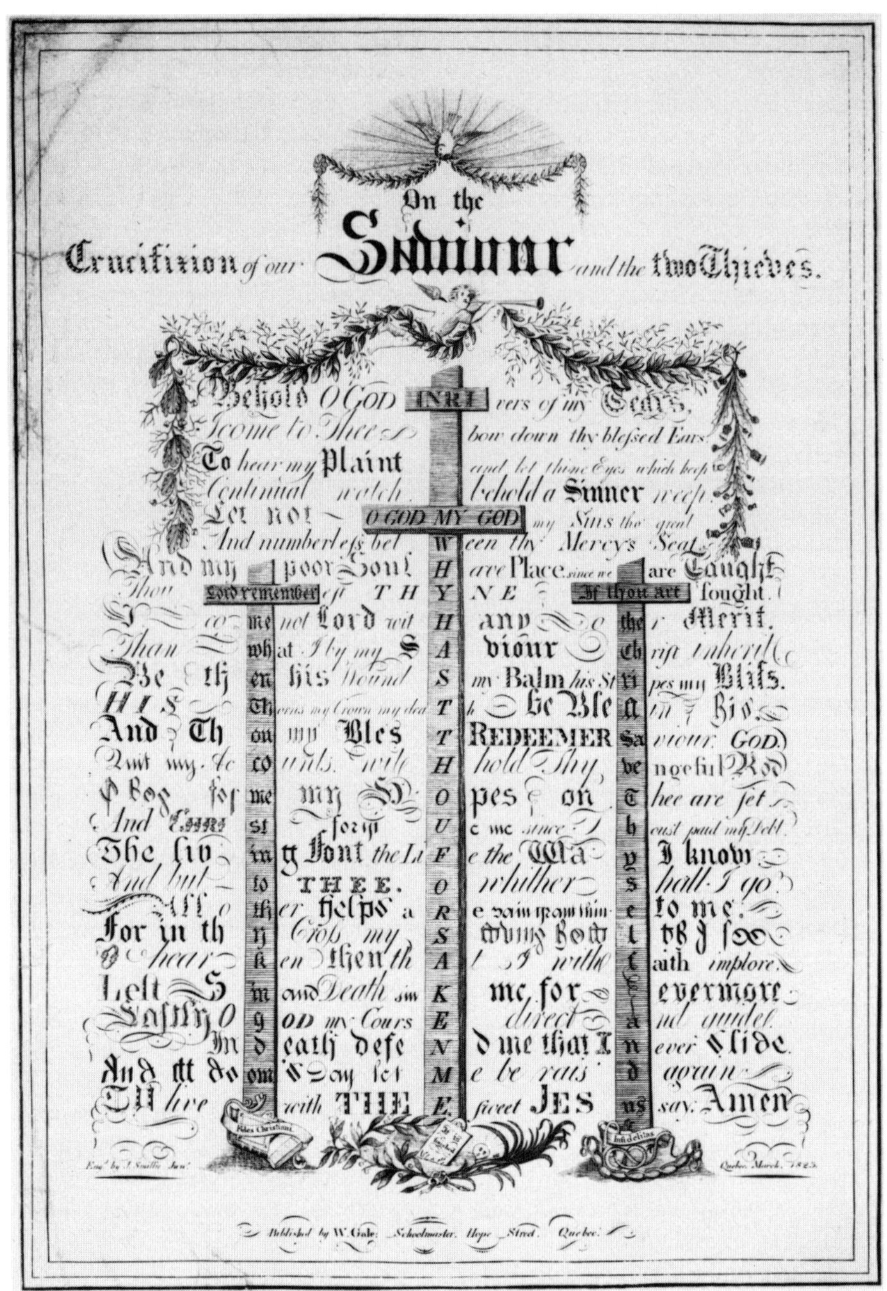
On the
Crucifixion of our Saviour and the two Thieves.
Behold O GOD
INRI
vers of my Sighs,
I come to Thee
bow down thy blessed Ears
To hear my Plaint
and let thine Eyes which keep
Continual watch
behold a Sinner weep
O GOD MY GOD
Lord remember
If thou art
WHY HAST THOU FORSAKEN ME
REDEEMER
Published by W. Gale. Schoolmaster. Hope Street. Quebec.

NA C121073

7. Gaston de Foix c. 1823
Graphite
Unlocated

Gaston de Foix (1489–1512) was a celebrated French general. James Smillie describes his drawing as "quite large, and much elaborated" and copied after an engraving. A possible source is an engraving by Michel Lasne (c. 1595–1667).

References: Pilgrimage, p. 18; Firmin-Didot 1977, no. 1081.

8. The Holy Family c. 1823
Graphite
Unlocated

This drawing was copied after an unidentified engraving. James Smillie framed this drawing and Cat. No. 7 and presented them to Lady Dalhousie.

References: Pilgrimage, p. 18.

9. Part of the Province of Upper Canada 1823
Etching and engraving on three plates; 78.6 × 136.7 (image)
Surveyor: James G. Chewett
Scale: 10 miles to 1 inch
Inscribed in plate l.r. *PART / OF PART OF THE / PROVINCE / of / UPPER CANADA / Organized, / TAKEN FROM THE MOST RECENT COMPILATIONS &c. / PUBLISHED & / ENGRAVED BY / David Smillie & Son, / QUEBEC.*

In his autobiography James Smillie notes the following:

> At this date (1823) I engraved a map of Upper Canada for a Mr. Smith. It measured six feet long, and three feet wide, in three separate plates. I was engaged on [it] many months. For this work, I received one hundred and twenty dollars. The only copy I had was destroyed when Uncle's house was consumed.

This map is a surprisingly major commission for the young engraver to have received at the outset of his career. One might doubt Smillie's word, were it not for the fact that newspaper accounts of 1823 confirm his

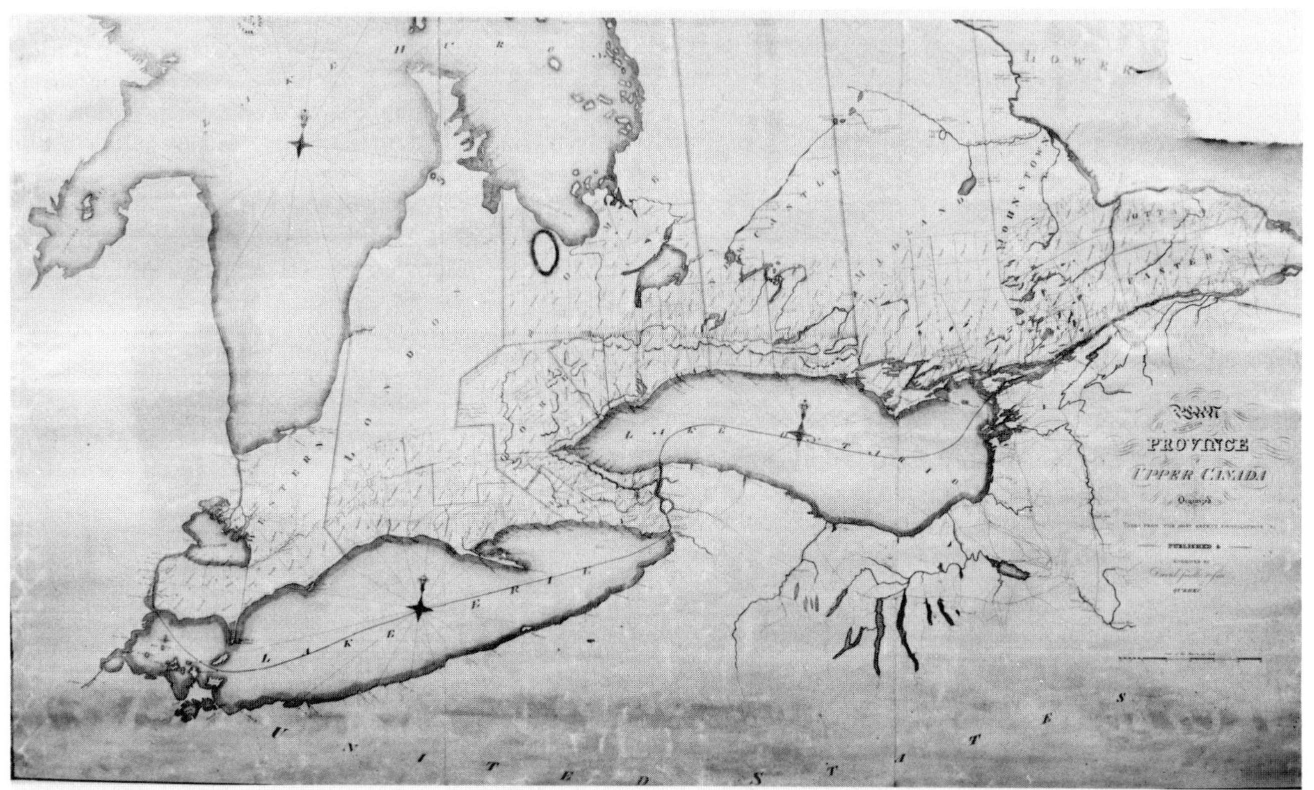

9 ASQ, Cartes et plans, tiroir 226A

remarks, and also that one impression of the map has survived (ASQ, Cartes et plans, tiroir 226A). The three sheets are joined, mounted on linen, watercoloured, and varnished.

The map etched by Smillie is an early version of the important map of Upper Canada compiled for the province by James G. Chewett (1793–1862) and eventually published by the Canada Company in 1825. The 1823 map gives an idea of the content of the manuscript map, now lost, which was in the House of Assembly at York (Toronto) in 1821/1822. The story of its unauthorized 1823 publication unfolds in a series of notices and letters in the *Upper Canada Gazette*.

On 3 April 1823 the surveyor general of Upper Canada, Thomas Ridout (1754–1829), placed a notice in the *Upper Canada Gazette* announcing that an authentic map of Upper Canada would be engraved in London within a few months and warning the public "from being imposed upon by a Surreptitious Copy" said to be on the eve of publication. A week later David William Smith (act. 1818–1825) placed a notice in the same paper advertising that he was having a correct map of the province engraved in Quebec, on a large scale (10 miles to 1 inch), and that it would be ready in June, at a price of two pounds ten shillings. He added that other promises to publish this map might not be fulfilled in the near future. These rival notices continued for over a year; Smith's ran until 17 June 1824, and the surveyor general's until November 1824.

A series of letters to the editor of the *Upper Canada Gazette* cast some light on this controversy. Smith, in a lengthy letter on 10 April 1823, refuted the charge that he was publishing a "Surreptitious Copy" of the surveyor general's map. He noted that when a manuscript map of the province had been delivered to the House of Assembly during its second session (late 1821 or during 1822), a member of the House had asked him to make a copy of it. He had borrowed the original map for about three months, completed the copy, and returned the original. He added that all this was done quite openly. In time, when the member of Parliament (who was never identified) did not ask for the copy he had ordered, Smith decided to make additions and improvements to his work and publish the map. He stated that the lieutenant governor had given his sanction to this venture, which was withdrawn later. He added that the map was being engraved in Quebec, by an artist from Edinburgh.

The surveyor general's reply, signed "Z.Y.," appeared on 17 April 1823. It defended the government's copyright and stated that no permission was ever given to Mr. Smith and that the first hint of his intention to publish the map was heard indirectly from a source in New York. Regarding additions to the map, the letter noted that Mr. Smith, who was a law student, was not qualified as a surveyor or draftsman. It also pointed out that Mr. Smith never publicly advertised his intended publication until challenged by the surveyor general's notice of 3 April 1823. The points were convincingly stated, and the editor, who had originally taken an impartial stance, refused to publish Smith's subsequent inflammatory letters and virtually indicted him as a "Map-Seizer." It was not until the controversy had run its course in Upper Canada newspapers that the surveyor general placed a notice in the *Quebec Mercury* regarding the illegal publication.

Little is known of David William Smith. He does not appear to have been related to the early surveyor general of Upper Canada, Sir David William Smith (1754–1837). He is recorded by the Upper Canada Law Society as entering law school in 1818. He was an active member of the Juvenile Advocates Society, of which Robert Baldwin (1804–1858) was a founder. On his admission to the bar in 1823, he was put forward by Attorney General Sir John Beverley Robinson (1791–1863). His name continues on law society records until 1825. Smillie does not seem to have known him well, for he refers to him as "a Mr. Smith;" however, Smillie did engrave a bookplate for him (Cat. No. 10).

Sixteen-year-old Smillie probably did not know that he was producing a pirated map when he accepted this commission. It is interesting to note that Smith's name is not on the map. Official opposition from Upper Canada would have virtually prohibited its sale in that province, and no impressions of it have been found in Ontario. The brief appearance of the 1823 map most likely hastened the printing of the authorized version. The government of Upper Canada sold the right to publish the map to the Canada Company sometime before August 1824. It was engraved in London and published in 1825 and 1826.

REFERENCES: Pilgrimage, p. 17; *Upper Canada Gazette*, 3, 10, 17, 24 April, 1, 15 May 1823; *Quebec Mercury*, 3, 6 May 1823; Canada Company Papers (arch. mat.); Penfold 1974, nos. 1395 1396; Upper Canada, House of Assembly 1818 1821, pp. 284–285, 288, 318–320, 414; Upper Canada, House of Assembly 1821–1822, p. 28; Joan Winearls, map librarian, John P. Robarts Research Library, University of Toronto, advice regarding contemporary Ontario maps, from her research on early maps of Ontario.

10. David William Smith Bookplate c. 1823
Etching and/or engraving
No impressions located
Inscribed in plate *David William Smith / J Smillie, Jun. Sc. Quebec*

This bookplate is described as having a crest. David William Smith is presumably the same law student from York, Upper Canada, who commissioned James Smillie to engrave a map of Upper Canada (see Cat. No. 9).

REFERENCES: Prescott 1919, p. 129.

11. Rev. L. C. Jenkins Bookplate c. 1823
Etching and engraving on laid paper; 9.4 × 6.9 (plate)
Inscribed in plate c. *SEMPER PARATUS* [motto with armorial] / *Rev:d L C Jenkins,*; u.l. *N:o*

James Smillie's manuscript note attached to the Scrapbook comments on the bookplate as follows:

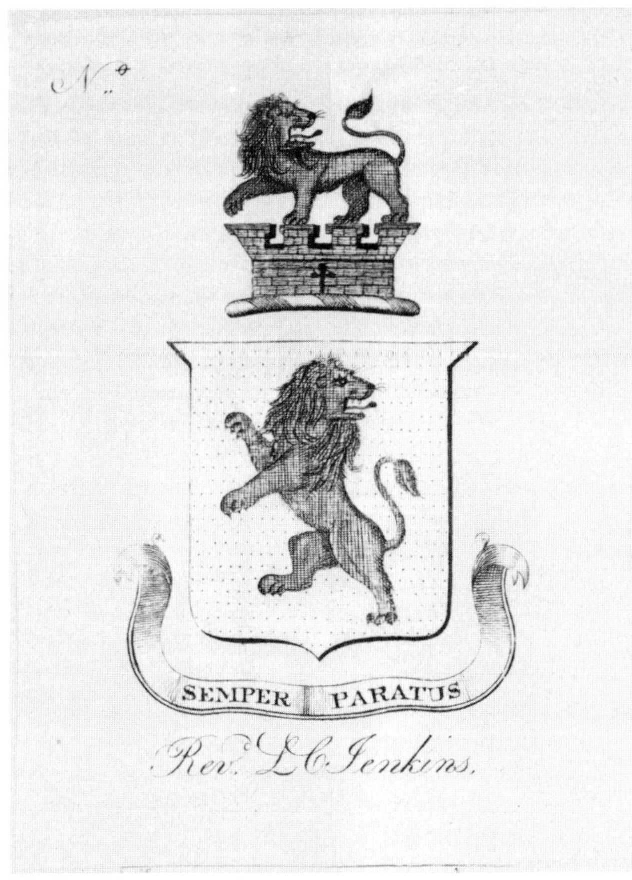

11

No. 7. My brother Willie in one of his summer expeditions visited Prince Edward Island. He there met a gentleman who, in the course of conversation learnt brothers name. He immediately asked him if he ever lived in Quebec. When answered in the affirmative the thought struck him that he must be the engraver of this plate. He gave him this impression expressing the desire that he would give to me with his compliments. Mr. Jenkins is now a very old man. He has lived in that locality nearly ever since the engraving of this plate about fifty years ago.

The Reverend Louis Charles Jenkins (1797–1884), a Church of England clergyman, was "Assistant and Preacher" to Protestant settlers in parts adjacent to Quebec from 1821 until 1823. He was also assistant secretary to the Diocesan Society for Promoting Christian Knowledge and co-chairman of the Quebec Immigrant Society.

REFERENCES: Scrapbook, no. 7; Millman 1959, pp. 60-61; *Quebec Almanac*, 1821–1823; MD 1822.

12. Plan of St. Gabriel 1824
Etching and engraving on onionskin; 39.0 × 23.0 (sheet)
Scale: Approximately 1 league to 1 inch
Inscribed in plate u.r. *Figurative Plan / OF / S:t GABRIEL / And the Adjacent Seigniories. / J. Smillie Sc:t*

This map is bound with a report of the House of Assembly of Lower Canada entitled *Eighth Report of the Committee of the House of Assembly on That Part of the Speech of His Excellency the Governor in Chief Which Relates to the Settlement of the Crown Lands, with the Evidence Taken before the Committee*. One impression noted is watermarked "JOHN LAYES / 1814."

REFERENCES: Lower Canada, House of Assembly 1824; Gagnon 1895, no. 1023; PAC 1976, vol. 2, p. 605 (B/325, H3/325).

13. Chasseur's Museum Entry Ticket
c. 1824–1826
Etching and engraving on card; 15.1 × 11.4 (sheet)
Inscribed in plate u.c. *Chasseur's / MUSEUM / Quebec*; c.l., in subject, *FOUNDED BY / P. CHASSEUR / 18 JULY 1824*; l.c. *Smillie, Quebec.*

Pierre Chasseur (1783–1842), a Quebec carver and gilder, founded a natural history museum in 1824. The press praised his three-hundred-specimen display in 1826, and by 1827 he was fundraising to provide addi-

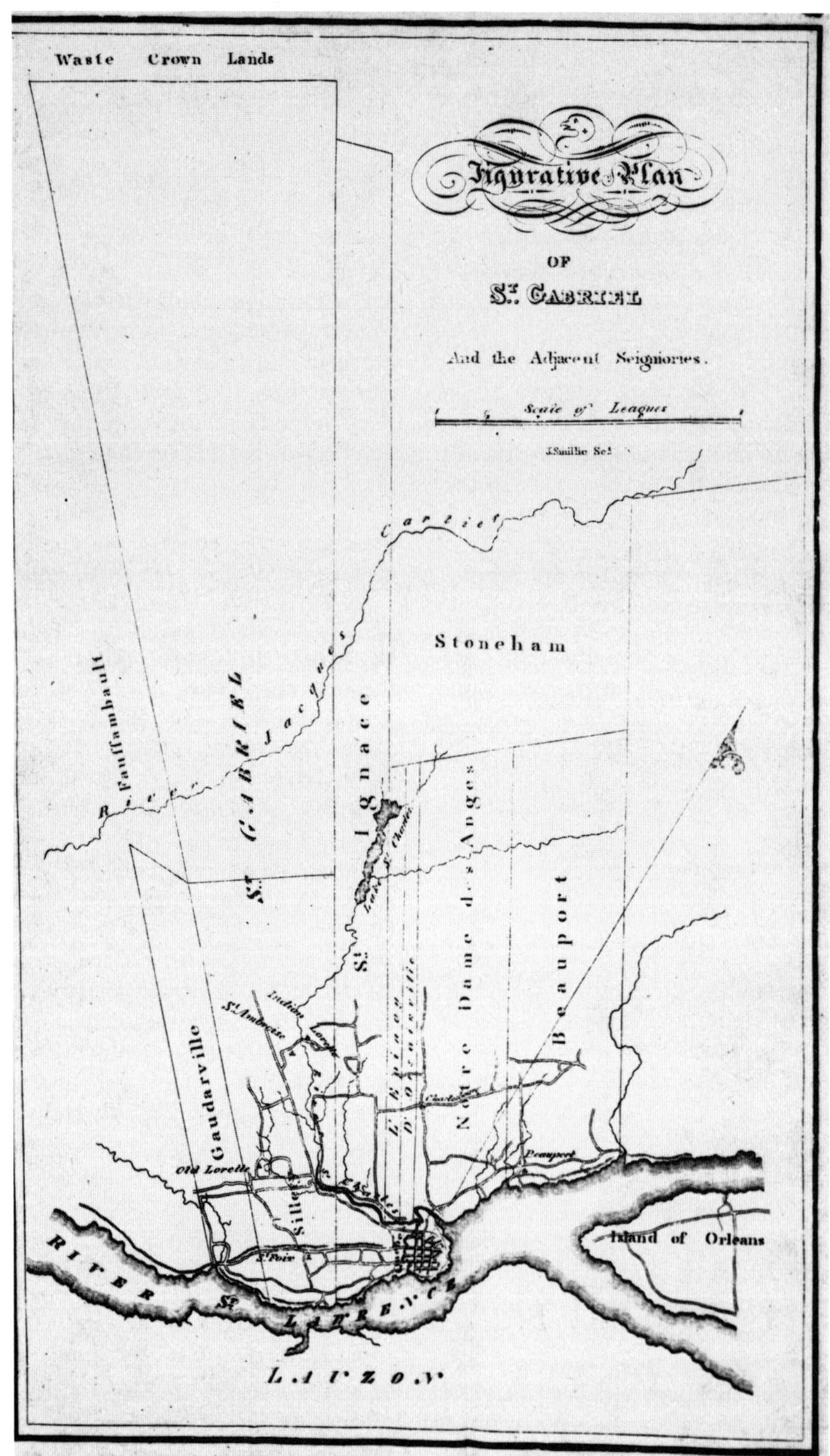

12 NA C121057

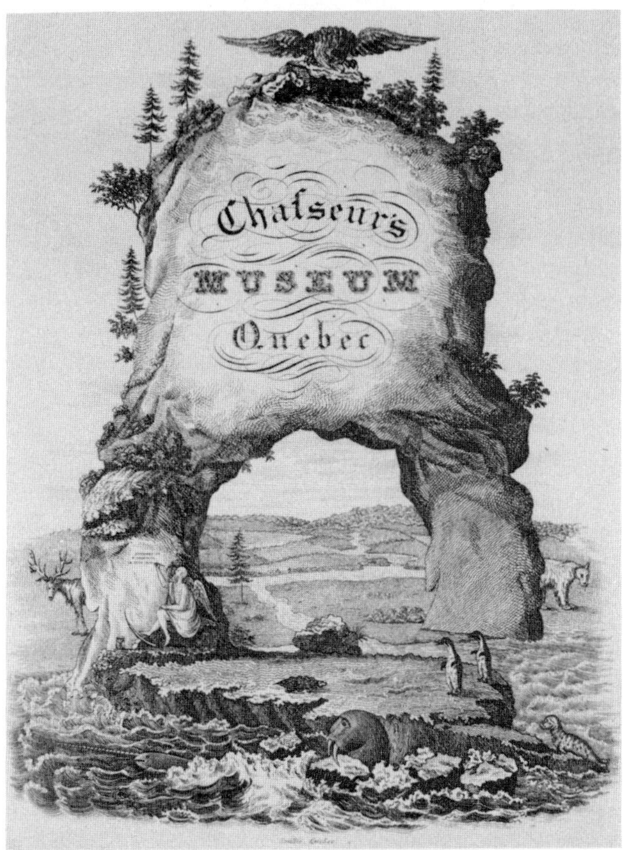

13 ASQ, Polygraphie 8, no. 46

tional exhibition space. Chasseur sold his collection to the government of Lower Canda in 1835. He died at Quebec on 21 May 1842.

The impression of the entry ticket illustrated (ASQ, Polygraphie 8, no. 46) bears on the reverse Chasseur's red wax seal and his manuscript authorization for perpetual free admission to the "Gentlemen of the Seminary of Quebec," dated 14 August 1826. Another impression bears the same manuscript date.

A biographical note about the activities of David Smillie, Sr., in Quebec links him with Pierre Chasseur. As William Cumming Smillie recalled:

> [David Smillie, Sr.] lingered six years, the last two entirely deprived of the use of his limbs. Two days previous to his loss of locomotion he had been appointed by the "Quebec Literary & Historical Society", to a position in its service designed to collect specimens of the minerals of the Country, as it was his favorite study—and as a skilled Taxidermist, to collect & preserve the Birds and quadrupeds of the Country, which Constituted the beginning of the Institute's collection; and in connection with his practise of this art, he had instructed a very deserving good man known in that day as a Carver & gilder, by the name of Chauseur, who was afterwards employed either [largely?] or on salary by the Lavall College, to collect & preserve for it, which was no doubt the foundation of the now large collection in the museum of the College in Quebec.

REFERENCES: Porter 1977; *La Gazette de Québec*, 18 May 1826; *La Bibliothèque canadienne* 3, no. 1 (juin 1826): 35; *Quebec Mercury*, 17 March 1827; Gagnon 1913, no. 2334; William Cumming Smillie Papers (arch. mat.), Memoranda and Agreements, p. 41; Gagnon 1896, pp. 108–109.

14. J. Hoffman Bookplate c. 1824–1829
Etching on wove paper; 8.8 × 6.2 (sheet)
Inscribed in plate u.c. *VIRTUTE NON ASTUTIA* [motto with armorial] / *J. Hoffman.*; l.c. J. *Smillie Jun:r sc:t Quebec.*

This bookplate was printed for Josias Hoffman (c. 1800–1829), a Quebec lawyer who died 12 July 1829, at the age of twenty-nine.

James Smillie probably etched many more bookplates than the six examples contained in his Scrapbook, but he did not always sign these plates. Among bookplates attributed to him are those of Daniel McCallum, Dr. William Marsden, Neilson & Cowan, and D. Daly (see Appendix L.11).

REFERENCES: Gagnon 1895, no. 4864; *Quebec Almanac*, 1824–1828; QD 1826; Gagnon 1895, nos. 4899, 4895, 4912; Gagnon 1913, no. 2693.

15. Mr. Ramage as Bob Logic 1825
Etching and engraving on wove paper; 22.9 × 14.9 (sheet)
Inscribed in plate l.c. *M:r Ramage as Bob Logic, / Royal Circus Quebec, / 1825*; l.l. *L. Triaud Del:t*; l.r. *J. Smillie Sc:t*

In a manuscript note attached to his Scrapbook, James Smillie describes this print.

> No. 5. Etched on a pewter plate. I printed a number of impressions from this plate, but being ignorant of the mode of cleaning the ink from the surface (as in printing music plates) I was obliged, after every five or six impressions, to burnish the surface all over, having made it so rough with the ink dabber that it became quite dark.
>
> I had to apply such power with my little wooden press that, on the production of every impression the plate came out bent half round.

During the 19th century, music was engraved on

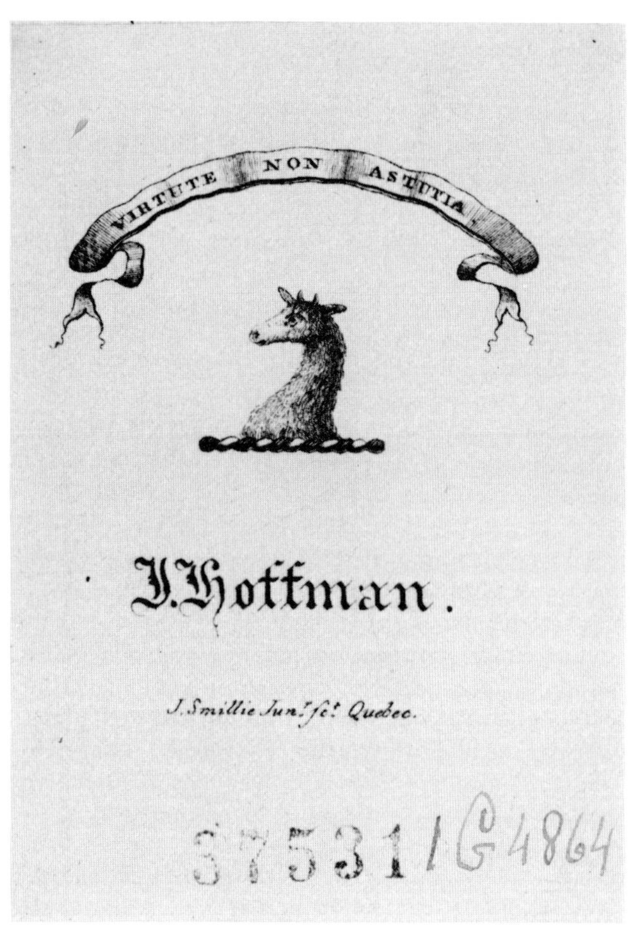

14 BVMG IG4864

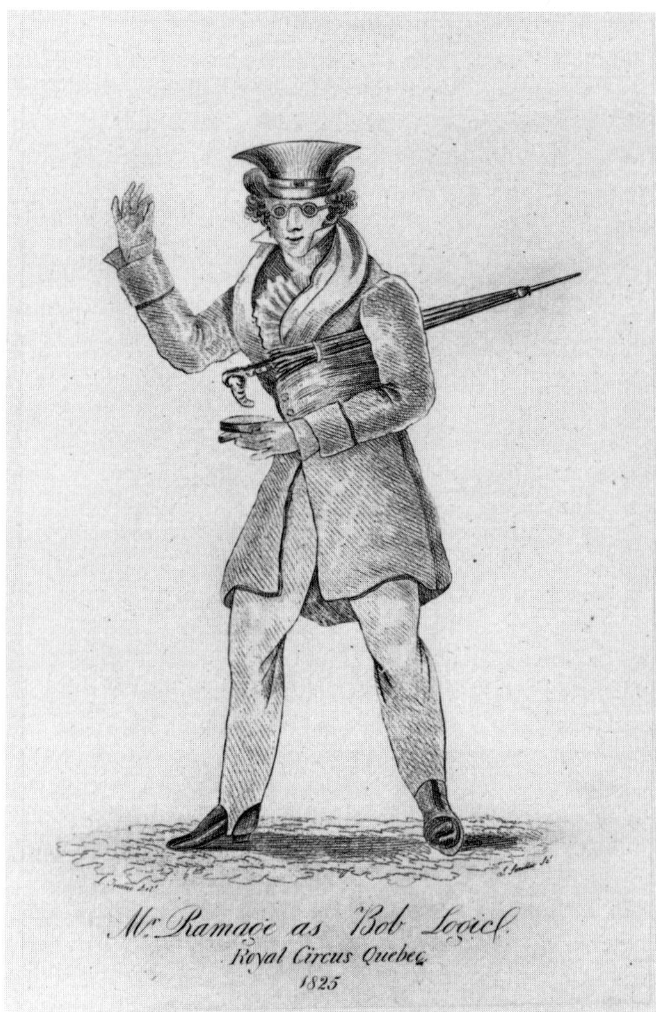

15

pewter plates, using a combination of punching and engraving. Smillie's mention of music printing and his use of a pewter plate suggest a familiarity with the process, but he is not known to have engraved music.

Ramage is depicted as Bob Logic, a character in *Tom and Jerry*, William Moncrieff's popular adaptation of Pierce Egan's *Life in London*, a novel of Regency high and low life. Ramage also played minor parts in *Hamlet* and *Romeo and Juliet* at the Theatre Royal, Montreal, during the season of 21 November 1825 to 8 May 1826.

Louis-Hubert Triaud (1794–1836), whose drawing Smillie used as a model for this print, taught painting and drawing at the Ursuline Convent. In 1820 he shared studio space with Jean-Baptiste Roy-Audy (1778–c. 1848), and they advertised themselves as "Peintres en portraits, miniatures et traits d'histoire." In 1832 Triaud assisted Joseph Légaré (1795–1855) in decorating a new Quebec theatre. Smillie included other Triaud drawings in the Scrapbook: an outline pencil, pen, and ink drawing of a theatrical figure inscribed "By Triaud of Quebec 1828" (facing Scrapbook no. 45) and a pencil drawing of the Dalhousie coat of arms, dated 1825 by Smillie (see Cat. No. 41).

REFERENCES: Scrapbook, no. 5; Calderisi 1981, p. 83; Tatham 1984, pp. 171, 174; Klein 1972, p. 158; *La Gazette de Québec*, 28 March 1820; Cauchon 1971, p. 55; *Quebec Mercury*, 14 February 1832; Porter 1978, p. 148.

16. Prisoner in Confinement 1825

Etching and engraving or etching and aquatint
No impressions located

In November 1825 the French and English language newspapers in Quebec announced that proof impressions of this print—said to be small—could be seen at their offices. The English review described the print as done "partly in the line and partly in the aquatint style" on copper, and the French review said that it was "en partie au burin et en partie à l'eau-forte." The abilities of the self-trained engraver were praised, and it was suggested that under the direction of an accomplished artist, this young man might reach the highest level of his profession.

At this stage in his career, James Smillie was probably copying an earlier engraving, such as plate 7 from William Hogarth's *The Rake's Progress*. No impression of Smillie's print is found in the Scrapbook; instead, Smillie pasted in an undated English language newspaper review of the work.

REFERENCES: Scrapbook, facing no. 11; *La Gazette de Québec*, 10 November 1825.

17. Notes of Exchange 1825
Etching and engraving on onionskin; 28.5 × 20.5 (sheet)
Inscribed in plate under each vignette *Smillie.*; c.l. *Published by W. A. Leggo, Quebec.*

Three notes of exchange appear on one sheet, printed from a single plate. Each note has the same vignette view of a steamboat towing two sailing vessels. The composition is similar to the illustration that James Smillie etched for James George (Cat. No. 76). The wording differs slightly for the first, second, and third notes. Smillie dated both Scrapbook impressions of this plate to 1825. For further information about William Augustus Leggo, see Cat. No. 22.

REFERENCES: Scrapbook, no. 6; Supplementary Scrapbook, no. 1.

18. The Virgin and Infant Saviour c. 1825
Engraving; approximately 12 inches × 18 inches [30.5 × 45.7]
No impressions located

In his autobiography James Smillie describes this engraving as being after a print by an Italian master, and says that it was his most daring undertaking and a wonderful work, on which he laboured for six months. When it was rejected by his patrons at the Ursuline Convent, he himself published a number of impressions and had them hand coloured, but he made little profit in their sale. His only impressions were destroyed in the fire that burned his uncle's house in Quebec.

REFERENCES: Pilgrimage, p. 20.

19. Fort Chambly c. 1825
Etching and engraving, with watercolour, on wove paper; 11.8 × 20.7 (image), 15.7 × 22.8 (sheet)
Inscribed in plate l.c. *Fort Chambly & part of the Great Camp 1814.*; l.r. *Smillie sc Quebec*

A manuscript note by James Smillie, attached to the Scrapbook, reads as follows: "No. 9. From an engraving. I was inspired with a desire to publish a series of views in Canada. This was the first plate, and the last too!—at that time." The Scrapbook impression is dated 1825 in pencil.

The source of Smillie's composition is the view drawn by Joseph Bouchette (1774–1841) and engraved in aquatint by William James Bennett of London (1787–1844), to illustrate Bouchette's 1815 publication. Smillie's linear rendering is much more naive than the tonal print that he copied. There are slight variations in the foliage, and Smillie leaves the sky blank. The subject is watercoloured and the margins are tinted beige.

REFERENCES: Scrapbook, no. 9; Bouchette 1815, facing p. 171.

20. Lindsay Trade Card c. 1825
Etching and engraving on wove paper; 6.7 × 10.7 (sheet)
Inscribed in plate c. *E. B. LINDSAY / Notary Public / near the Exchange / S! Peter Street / Lower Town. / QUEBEC*; l.l. *Smillie.*; l.r. *Quebec.*

One vignette illustrates boats sailing, and the other, a boat sinking. Errol Boyd Lindsay is listed in Quebec directories from 1824. In 1832 he received a government appointment from Lord Aylmer (1775–1850), which continued to at least 1866.

REFERENCES: Scrapbook, no. 11; *Quebec Almanac*, 1824; QD 1826–1850; *Blue Book* 1867, p. 71.

21. Jackson Trade Card c. 1825
Etching and engraving on wove paper; 6.6 × 9.1 (plate)
Inscribed in plate c.r. *R. Jackson / GUN MAKER / Montreal*; l.l. *J. Smillie Jun! Sc! Quebec.*; l.l. to r. *Manufactures all kinds of Rifles & Fowling Pieces on the most improved principle, Flints & Detonating Guns, / carefully altered, repaired or stocked. NB. Fine brass work cleaned, Bronzed and Lacquered.*

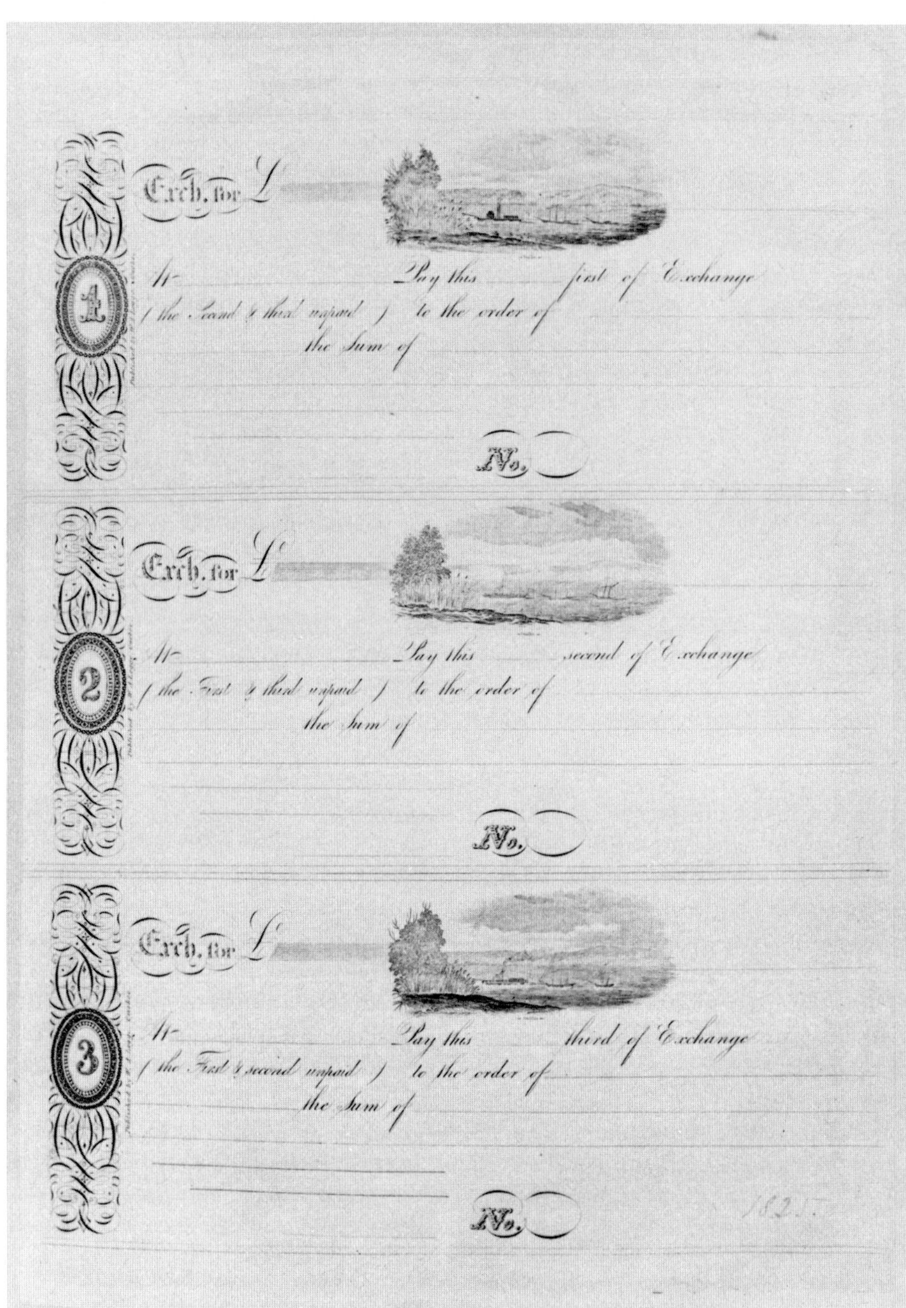

Exch. for £

At Pay this first of Exchange (the Second & third unpaid) to the order of

the Sum of

No.

Exch. for £

At Pay this second of Exchange (the First & third unpaid) to the order of

the Sum of

No.

Exch. for £

At Pay this third of Exchange (the First & second unpaid) to the order of

the Sum of

No.

1825

17

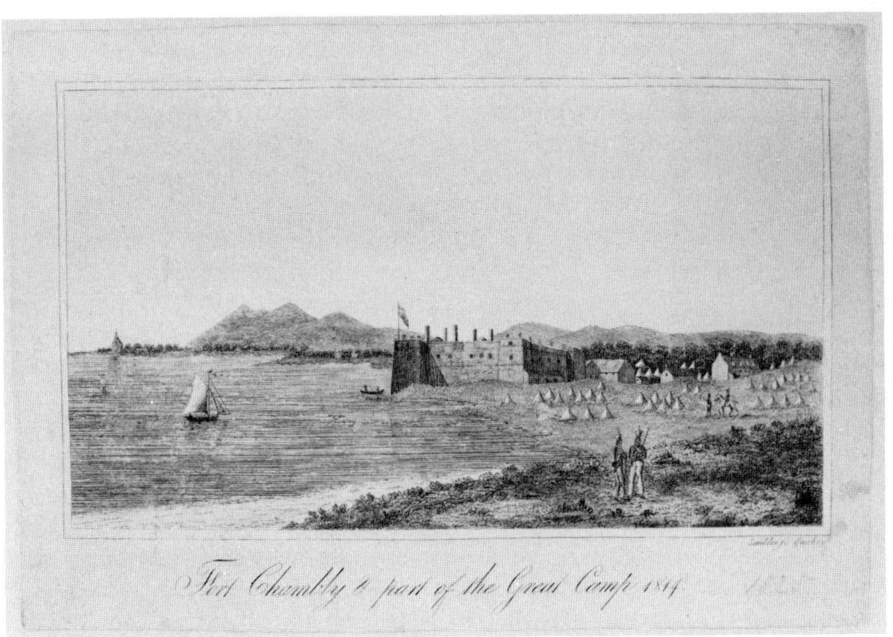
Fort Chambly & part of the Great Camp 1814

19

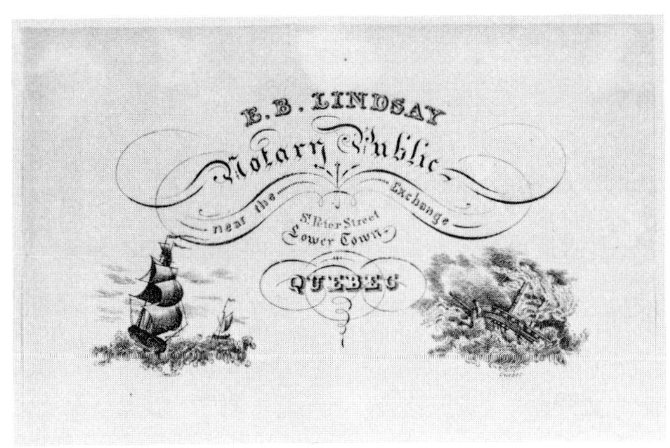
E. B. LINDSAY
Notary Public
near the Exchange
St. Peter Street
Lower Town
QUEBEC

20

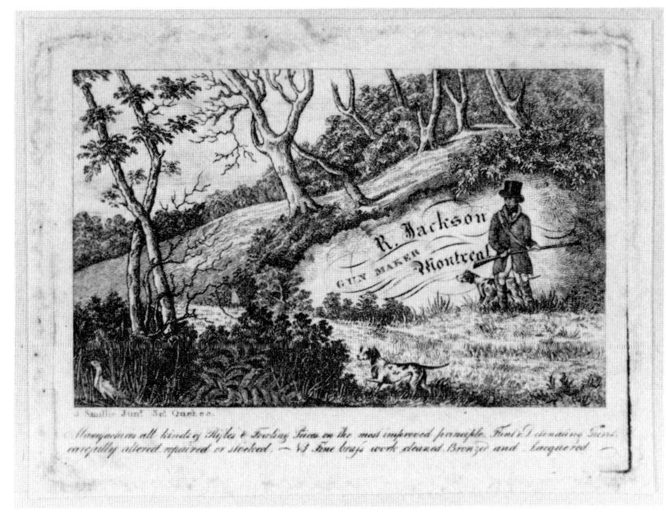
R. Jackson
GUN MAKER
Montreal
J. Smillie Junr. Sc. Quebec.
Manufactures all kinds of Rifles & Fowling Pieces on the most improved principle. Flint & Detonating Guns carefully altered repaired or stocked. — N.B. Fine brass work cleaned Bronzed and Lacquered —

21

Mr. Jackson may have been an emigrant member of the London gunmaking family; nothing is known, to date, of his business in Canada. This is one of James Smillie's most attractive cards, with an illustration probably copied from an English sporting print or trade card. It is also the only Smillie trade card that appears to have been commissioned from Montreal.

REFERENCES: Scrapbook, no. 12.

22. Leggo Bookplate c. 1825
Etching and watercolour on wove paper; 7.4 × 6.1 (plate)
Inscribed in plate c.r., on leaf, *W. A. LEGGO.*; l.c. *J. Smillie Jun! Sc.*

James Smillie comments on this bookplate in a manuscript note attached to the Scrapbook.

No. 13. Poor Leggo! He had the misfortune when young, to be shot in the face, loosing one eye and was otherwise very much disfigured in the face [these last three words crossed out]. He thought this device [a broken rose] (to paste in his book) a befitting emblem of himself.

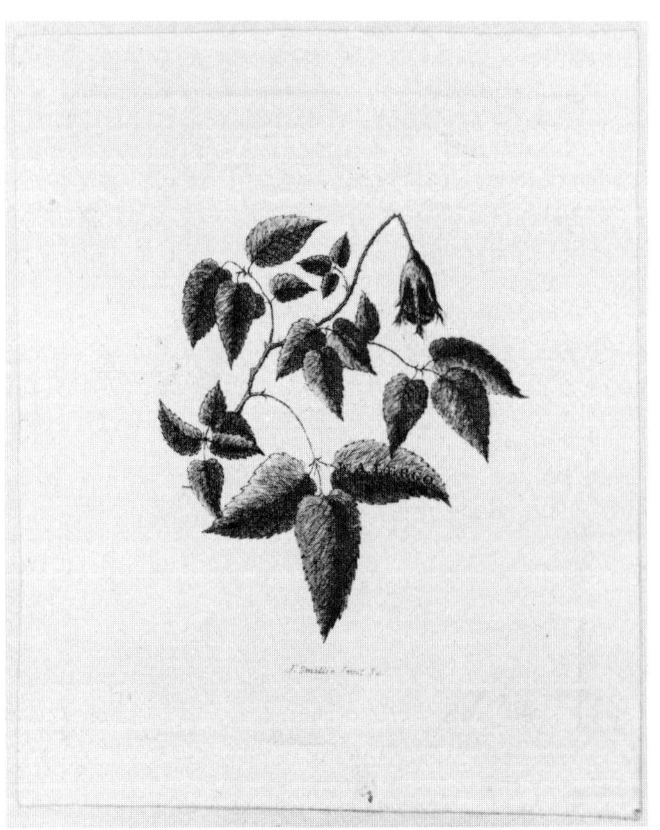

22

William Augustus Leggo (act. Quebec 1825–1855), a copper plate printer and ruler, is listed in Quebec directories from 1825 onwards. He also commissioned notes of exchange from Smillie (Cat. No. 17) and evidently printed some of Smillie's etchings; for example, he is mentioned as the printer of one of the maps for the House of Assembly in 1827 (Appendix L.1–2, 4, 6). Leggo's *General Table of New and Full Moons*, located by the authors just prior to publication, was also etched by Smillie in 1827 (BSQ, Carton, Table T, no. 174, p. 18). One of his sons, W. A. Leggo, Jr. (1830–1915), became well known as the inventor of the Leggotype, a commercial printing process.

REFERENCES: Scrapbook, no. 13; QD 1826, 1850, 1855.

23. J. Smillie, Sr., Trade Card c. 1825
Etching and engraving on card; 11.5 × 7.5 (sheet)
Inscribed in plate c., below image, *J. SMILLIE, JEWELLER / & LAPIDARY, / To His Majesty. / 16 / MOUNTAIN STREET. / QUEBEC.*; l.l. *Gold & Silver / Snuff-Boxes, / Necklaces, Bracelets, / Crosses, Earrings, / Rings, & Pins.*; l.r. *All sorts of Gems / Mounted to any Pattern / in the neatest style / and on the Shortest / Notice.*; l.c. *NB. Has always on hand a choice Collection of / Crystals and Pebbles, found in this Country. / The best price given for Old Gold and Silver.*; l.l. of vignette *J. Smillie Jun! sc.*

As a manuscript note by James Smillie, Jr., attached to the Scrapbook, records:

No. 14. At this time Uncle had just returned from England. He had secured the title of 'Jeweller to his Majesty' (George IV) of which he was very proud, and must needs get out a card making there and then quite a sensation.

The Scrapbook impression of this card is dated "1825" in pencil.

James Smillie, Sr., was appointed jeweller in ordinary and lapidary to King George IV by warrant dated 19 February 1824 (Introduction, p. 2). Unfortunately, no further references have been found to indicate what jewellery he supplied, nor is the date of his visit to England recorded.

In the windows of the shop can be seen the variety of goods that James Smillie, Sr., offered for sale. The display features hollow ware, presumably in silver and including candelabra, candlesticks, goblets, pitchers, tankards, teapots, sauceboats, cream and sugar containers, a covered tureen, and a cruet stand. An assortment of necklaces, bracelets, earrings, rings, brooches, hairpins, vinaigrettes, and unset gemstones is arranged

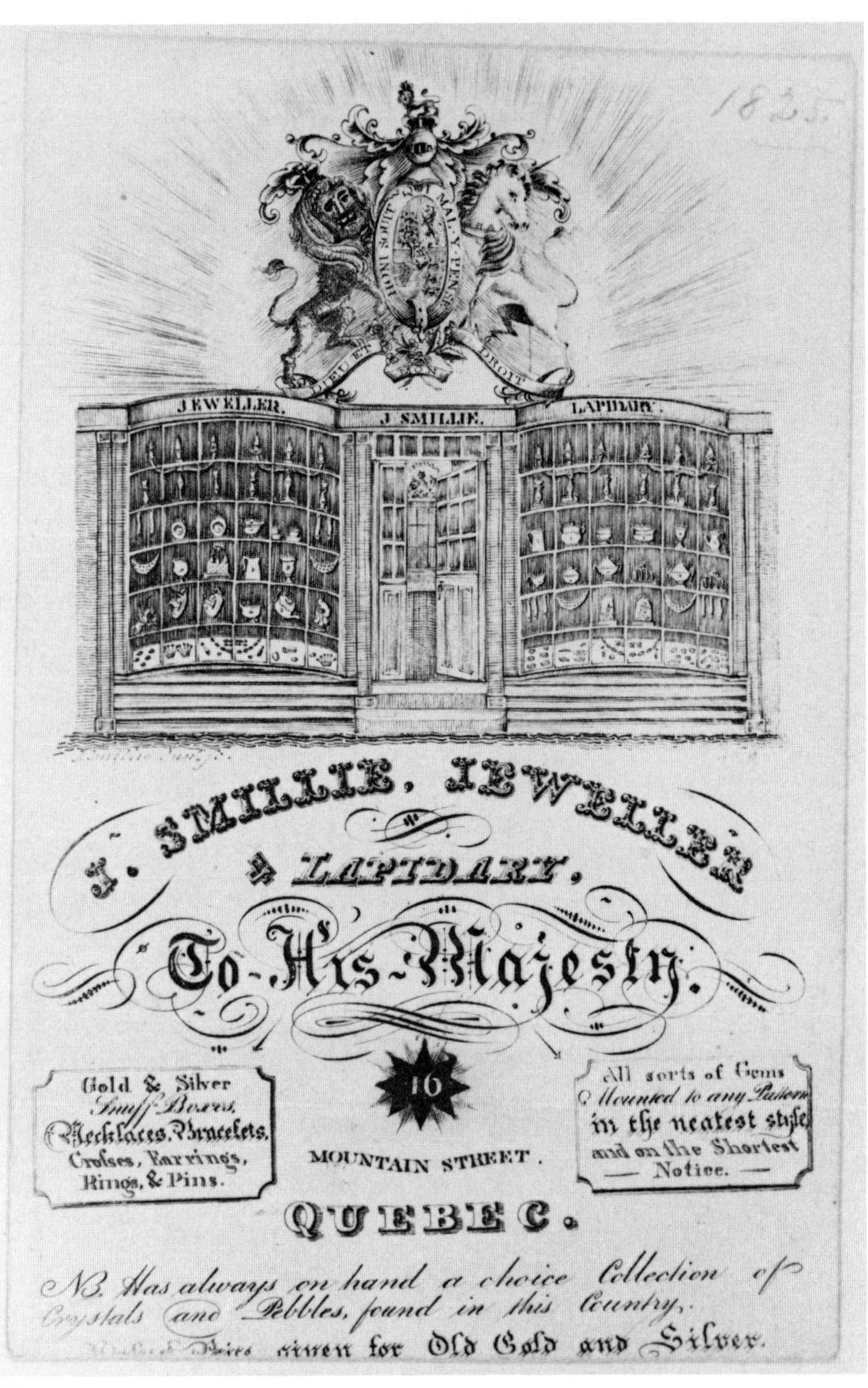
1825.
HONI SOIT QUI MAL Y PENSE
DIEU ET
DROIT
JEWELLER.
J SMILLIE.
J. SMILLIE, JEWELLER
& LAPIDARY,
To His Majesty.
16
Gold & Silver
Snuff Boxes,
Necklaces, Bracelets,
Crosses, Earrings,
Rings, & Pins.
MOUNTAIN STREET.
All sorts of Gems
Mounted to any Pattern
in the neatest style
and on the Shortest
— Notice. —
QUEBEC.
N.B. Has always on hand a choice Collection of
Crystals and Pebbles, found in this Country.
Price given for Old Gold and Silver.

23

along the bottom of the windows. There are also some figurines and possibly some harness decorations.

REFERENCES: Scrapbook, no. 14; Lord Chamberlain's and Lord Steward's Departments Papers (arch. mat.).

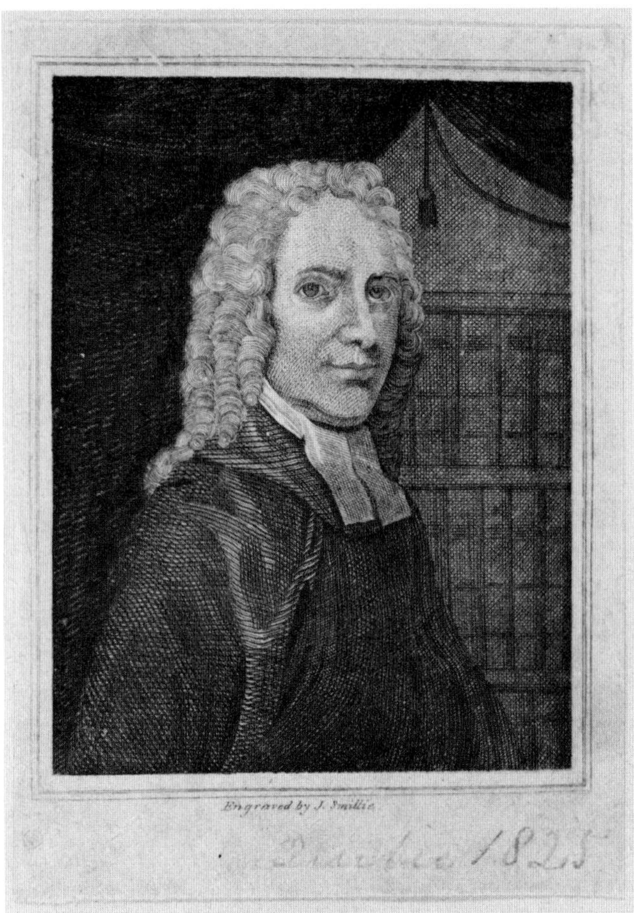

24

24. Isaac Watts c. 1825
Etching and engraving on calendered wove paper; 7.9 × 5.8 (sheet)
Inscribed in plate l.c. *Engraved by J. Smillie.*

James Smillie's manuscript note attached to the Scrapbook describes this print as "No. 14. Isaac Watts. My first attempt at portrait engraving. From an English plate in same style." The Scrapbook impression is dated "Quebec 1825" in pencil.

Isaac Watts (1674–1748), an English Nonconformist minister, was regarded as the father of English hymnody. The half-length image of Watts resembles the engraving by Robert Newton (act. London 1809–1835), after a drawing by John Thurston (1774–1822), published in 1822 and used as an illustration in the 1824 *Effigies Poeticae*. The Newton engraving, however, lacks the background bookcase and curtain. Both engravings must be based on an earlier print.

REFERENCES: Scrapbook, no. 15; O'Donoghue 1914, vol. 4, pp. 418–419; Procter 1824.

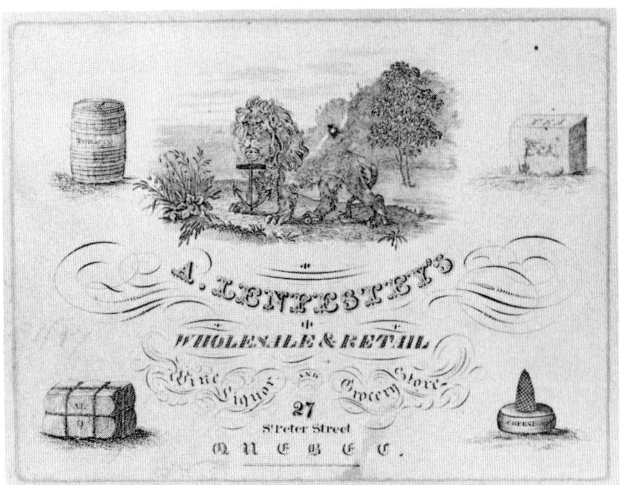

25

25. Lenfestey Trade Card c. 1825
Etching and engraving on card; 7.7 × 10.4 (sheet)
Inscribed in plate c. *Eng^{d} by J. Smillie. / A. LENFESTEY'S / WHOLESALE & RETAIL / Wine Liquor AND Grocery Store / 27 / St Peter Street / QUEBEC.*

In addition to the central image of the lion and the anchor, this trade card has vignettes of tobacco, tea, cheese, and a package addressed to "AL / Q" (A. Lenfestey / Quebec).

REFERENCES: Scrapbook, no. 19.

26. Dorion Trade Card c. 1825
Etching and engraving on wove paper; 11.8 × 7.7 (sheet)
Inscribed in plate l.c. *Drawn & Engraved by J. Smillie. / P. DORION'S / Ironmongery & Hardware Store, / N° 11 Buade S^{t}, Upper Town Market / QUEBEC. / NB. Always on hand an extensive & general supply of Ironmongery, Hardware, / Cuttlery & Plated Ware, from the first Manufacto-*

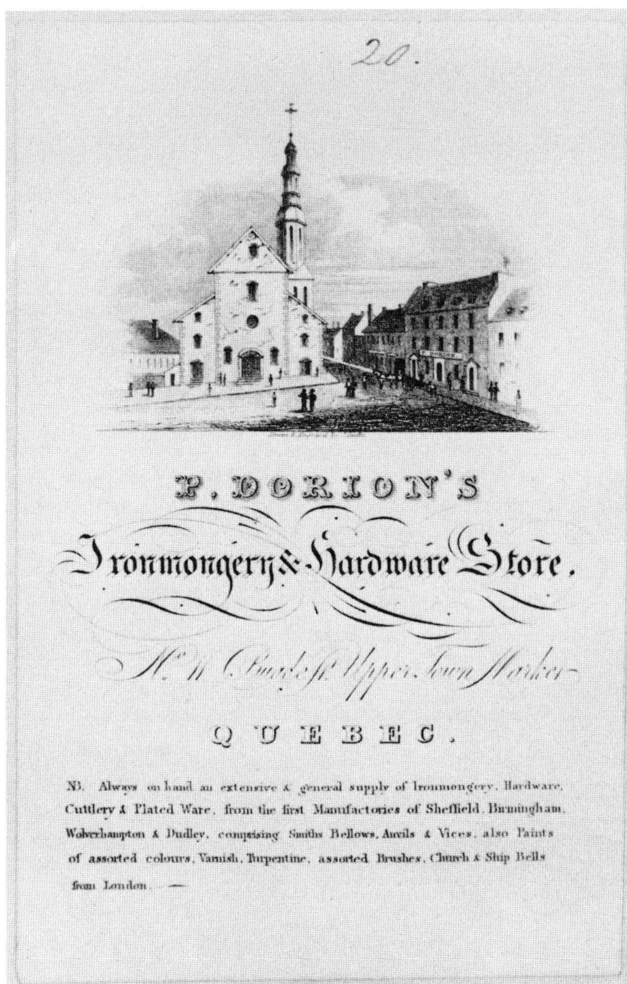

26

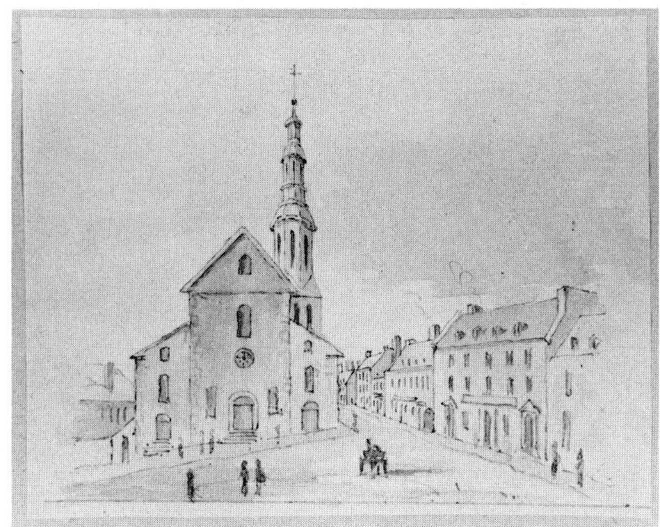

27

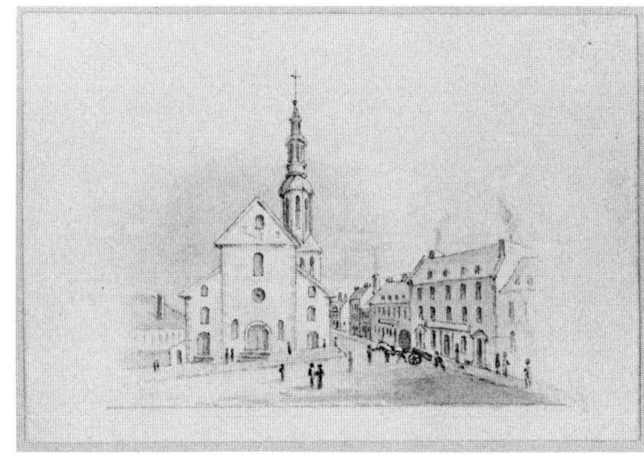

28

ries of Sheffield, Birmingham, / Wolverhampton & Dudley, comprising Smiths Bellows, Anvils & Vices, also Paints / of assorted colours, Varnish, Turpentine, assorted Brushes, Church & Ship Bells / from London.

The vignette illustrates the Upper Town market and church. On Buade Street, at the right, a wagon is unloading supplies for Dorion's hardware store. Cat. No. 28 is James Smillie's wash sketch for this composition.

REFERENCES: Scrapbook, no. 20; QD 1826.

27. Upper Town Market and Church c. 1825–1829
Brown wash on wove paper; 7.2 × 9.3

REFERENCES: Scrapbook, no. 86.

28. Upper Town Market and Church c. 1825–1829
Brown wash on wove paper; 5.2 × 7.7

James Smillie placed this wash sketch and Cat. No. 27 in the Scrapbook near the etching *Roman Catholic Church* from *Picture of Quebec* (Cat. No. 69h). They are closer in composition, however, to the vignette view on the Dorion trade card (Cat. No. 26). Of the two wash sketches, Cat. No. 28 most closely resembles the trade card.

REFERENCES: Scrapbook, no. 87.

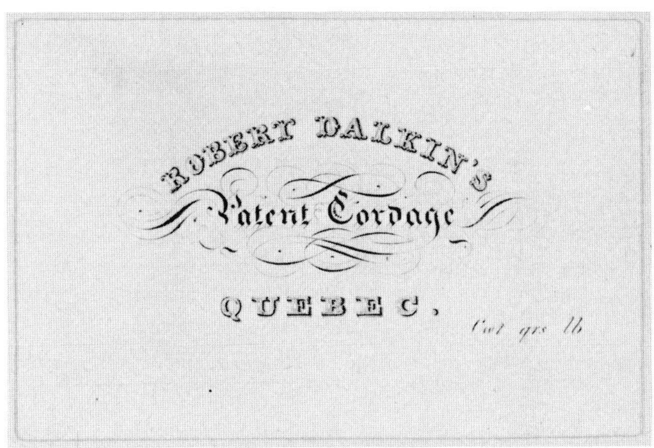
ROBERT DALKIN'S
Patent Cordage
QUEBEC,

29

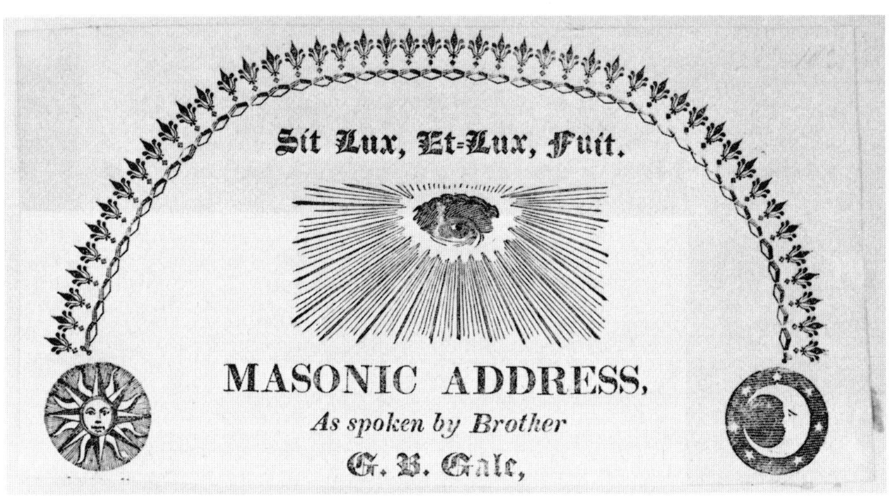
Sit Lux, Et-Lux, Fuit.
MASONIC ADDRESS,
As spoken by Brother
G. B. Gale,

30

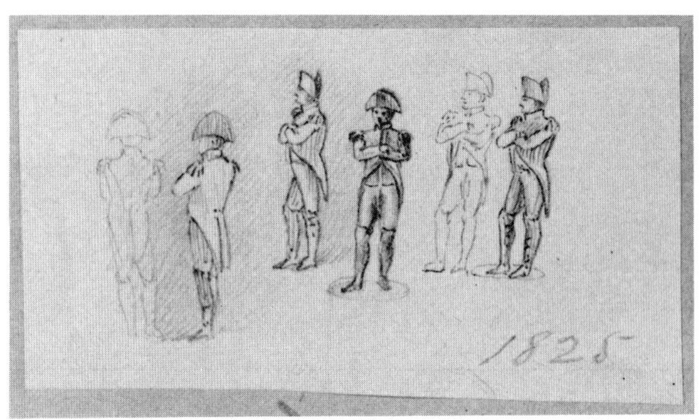
1825

31

29. Dalkin Trade Card c. 1825
Etching on card; 5.9 × 9.0 (sheet)
Inscribed in plate c. *ROBERT DALKIN'S / Patent Cordage / QUEBEC.*; l.r. *Cwt qrs lb*

Robert Dalkin, Jr., owned a staple rope warehouse and manufactory at 25 Cul-de-Sac Street in 1822. Robert Dalkin, Sr., of 23 Cul-de-Sac, is listed as a ship chandler in 1822 and 1826.

REFERENCES: Scrapbook, no. 21; QD 1822, 1826.

30. Masonic Address c. 1825–1827
Wood engraving on wove paper; 11.2 × 21.5 (sheet)
Inscribed in block u.c. *Sit Lux, Et=Lux, Fuit.*; l.c. *MASONIC ADDRESS, / As spoken by Brother / G. B. Gale,*

This decorative sheet heading is cut just below the title and dated 1825 in pencil. James Smillie's manuscript note attached to the Scrapbook comments, "No. 8. My first attempt at wood engraving." No other wood engravings by Smillie have been located.

George B. Gale was an actor, living in Quebec from 1825 to 1827 and from 1830 to 1831 (see Pilgrimage, n. 35).

REFERENCES: Scrapbook, no. 8.

31. Studies of Napoleonic Figure c. 1825
Graphite on wove paper; 3.7 × 7.0
Inscribed in pencil, at a later date, l.r. *1825*

James Smillie notes on the Scrapbook page that this drawing was taken "from a small brass figure." His sketches illustrate the sculpture from the front, side, and back.

REFERENCES: Scrapbook, facing no. 27.

32. The Quebec Driving Club 1826
Etching and aquatint on laid or wove paper; 31.9 × 48.1 (plate)
Inscribed in plate l.c. *The Quebec Driving Club meeting at*

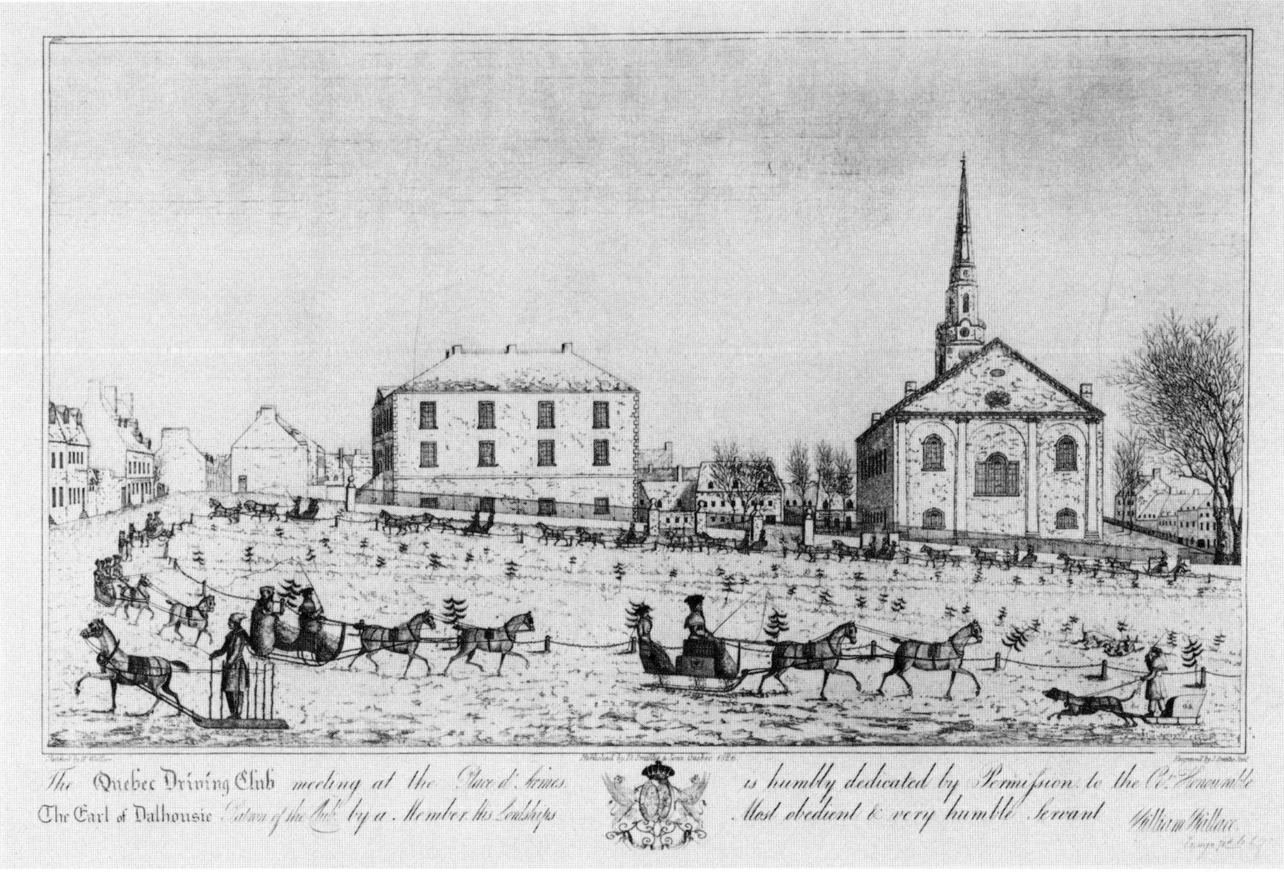

32 Private collection

the Place d'Armes, is humbly dedicated by Permission, to the R.t Honourable / The Earl of Dalhousie Patron of the Club, by a Member, His Lordships Most obedient & very humble servant / William Wallace, / Ensign 71st Lt. Infy; l.l. *Sketched by W. Wallace.*; l.c. *Published by D. Smillie & Sons, Quebec, 1826.*; l.r. *Engraved by J. Smillie Junr*; u.l. *April.*
State I: No pedestrian figures in centre of park (illustrated)
State II: Two pairs of pedestrians added to centre of park

The *Driving Club* is one of James Smillie's most successful and expressive etchings and the only located work in which he uses aquatint. The composition is rendered with a variety of subtle pictorial effects that, despite the stiffness of draftsmanship, contrast favourably with his later and more mechanical vocabulary.

The engraver included his father's shop sign "D. Smillie & Sons" on the family's home at 8 Garden Street, the house to the immediate left of the cathedral. The initials "G.S." on the dog sleigh in the right foreground may mean that the young driver is Smillie's brother George. Houses on St. Louis Street at the left are inscribed "St Georges" and "Commissariat." This print was issued uncoloured or watercoloured in a full range of tones or with a single yellow tint.

The artist, Ensign William Wallace (fl. 1824–1841) of the Seventy-first Regiment, Highland Light Infantry, is only known for this one composition. He arrived in Quebec in June 1824 and probably left the country in October 1829, when he transferred to the Ninety-eighth Regiment. Although the dedication of the print is made by Wallace, the Smillie firm seems to have retained the publication rights. In his autobiography Smillie notes that he made very little from its sale. The work was printed in two states and on variously watermarked papers ("J. WHATMAN / TURKEY MILL," dated 1821, 1824, or 1825), which suggests that it was issued at intervals or upon demand.

REFERENCES: Pilgrimage, p. 19; Allodi 1980, no. 24; *Army Lists*, 1826–1841.

33. Bust of Charles J. Fox 1826
Watercolour and graphite on card; 20.6 × 15.9
Inscribed in pencil u.r. *12th Augst 1826*; l.l. *JSmillie Junr*

A manuscript note by James Smillie, attached to the Scrapbook, identifies this work, "No. 36. Charles J. Fox, M.P. My first attempt from the round. The bust was painted black."

Charles J. Fox (1749–1806) was an English Whig statesman. The model that Smillie copied was probably a plaster replica of the 1805 marble bust (NPGL 3887) by Joseph Nollekens (1737–1823).

REFERENCES: Scrapbook, no. 36; Yung and Pettman 1981.

34. Edmund Kean as Richard III 1826
Graphite on card; 11.0 × 9.6
Inscribed in pencil l.c. *Drawn by J. Smillie Junr / Mr Kean, / as / Richard the Third.*

As James Smillie comments in a manuscript note attached to the Scrapbook:

No. 32. I made this drawing from an engraving. At this date (1827) the great tragedian was on a visit to Quebec. I called on him and showed him the production. He professed to be pleased. Hem!

Edmund Kean (1787–1833), the famous English actor, toured the United States and Canada in 1825/1826. He opened at Montreal's Theatre Royal on 31 July 1826. In Quebec, performances of *Richard III* and *Othello* were billed at the Royal Circus from 4 September 1826, and he remained in the city until at least 6 October 1826. The Scrapbook dating of the event to 1827 is a year out, which is understandable since Smillie's notes were made many years later.

This drawing is based on a stipple engraving by R. Page, a plate to volume 1, no. 4, of *The Drama or Theatrical Pocket Magazine* (August 1821), published by T. & J. Elvey.

Smillie's efforts may have been rewarded by an order for four silver medals, which Kean presented to the Huron chiefs at Indian Lorette. On 7 October 1826 the *Quebec Mercury* described the medals as "neatly executed by Mr. Smillie and bearing the following inscription": "Presented / BY EDMUND KEAN / the British Actor, / to ______ / A Chief of the Huron Indians / October 5, 1826."

REFERENCES: Scrapbook, no. 32; Hall 1931, nos. 146A, 156; O'Donoghue 1914, vol. 2, p. 670, no. 13; *Quebec Mercury*, 7 October 1826.

35. Hare and Foxes 1826
Graphite on card; 17.5 × 21.7
Inscribed in pencil l.c. *Drawn by J. Smillie Junr*; u.r. *10th October 1826*

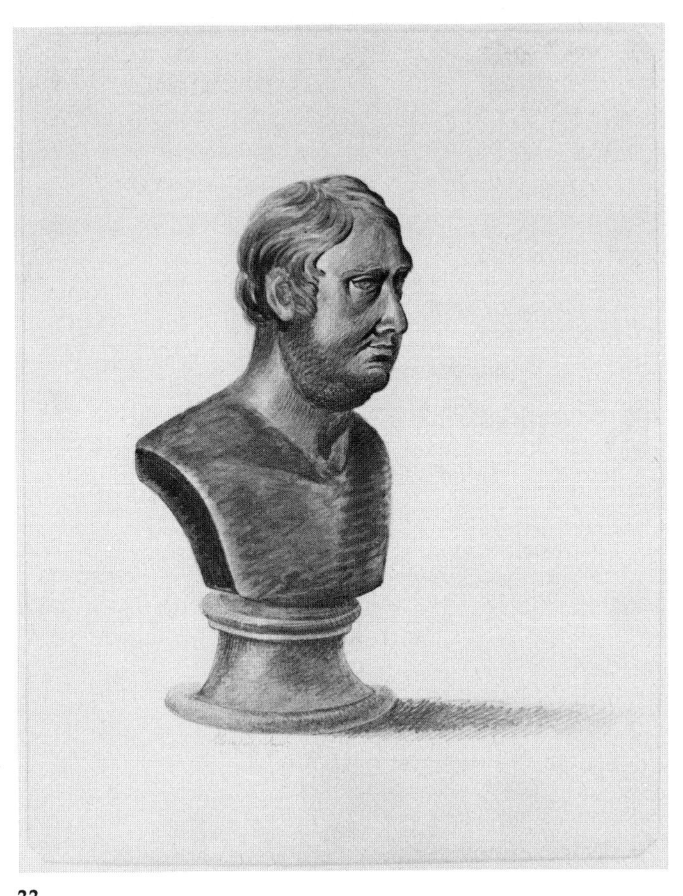

33

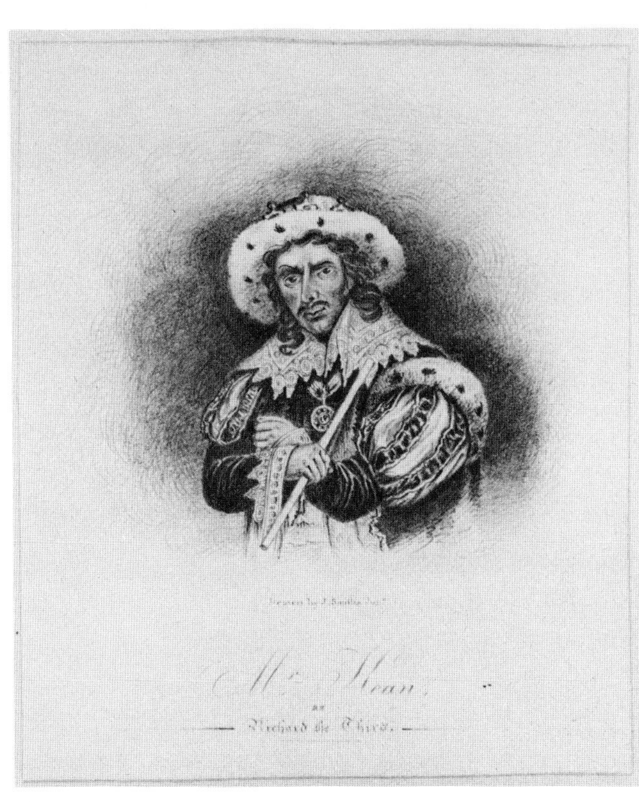

34

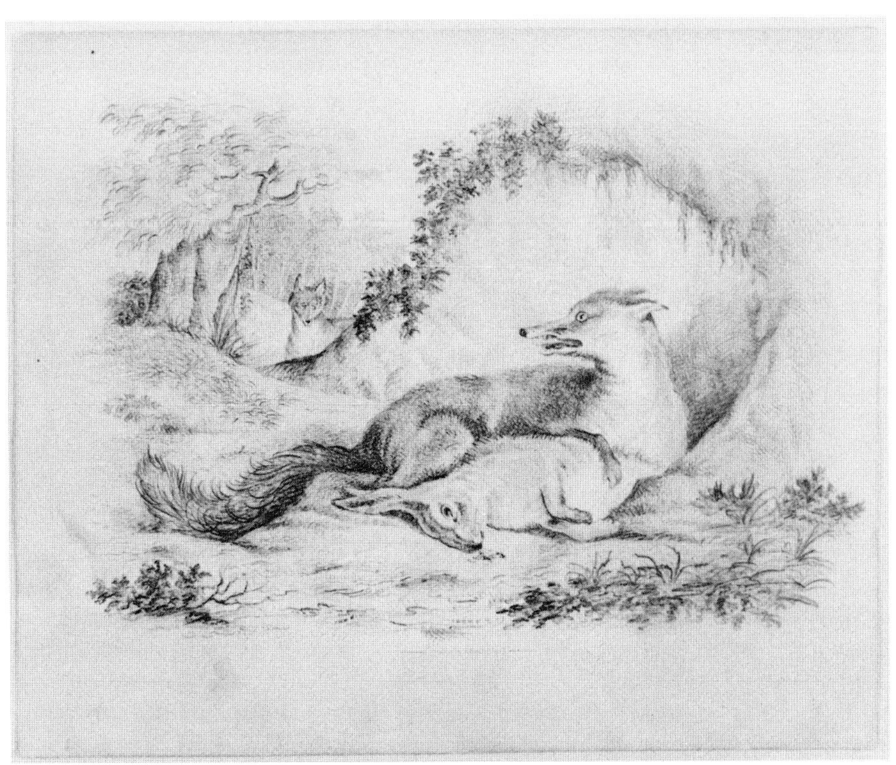

35

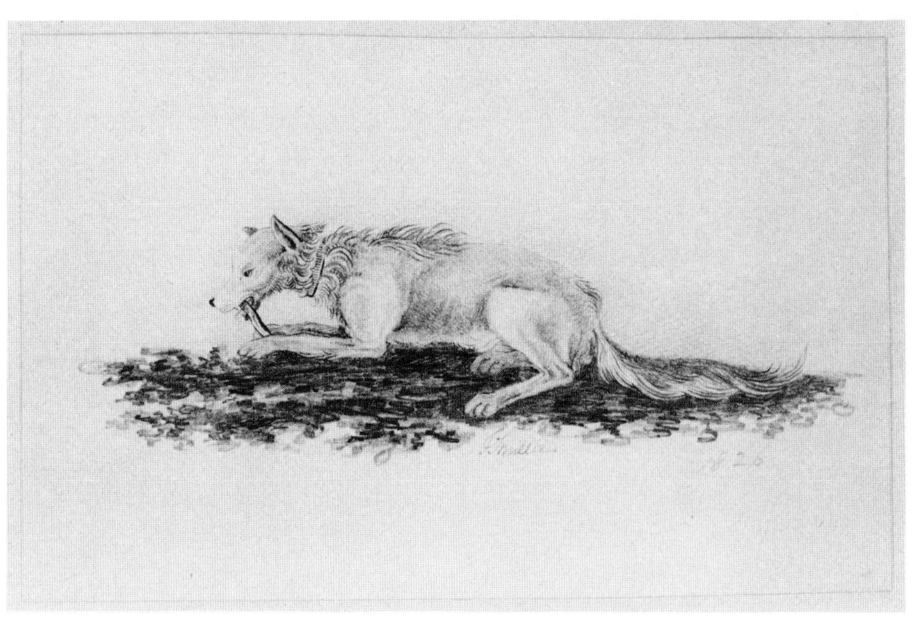
36

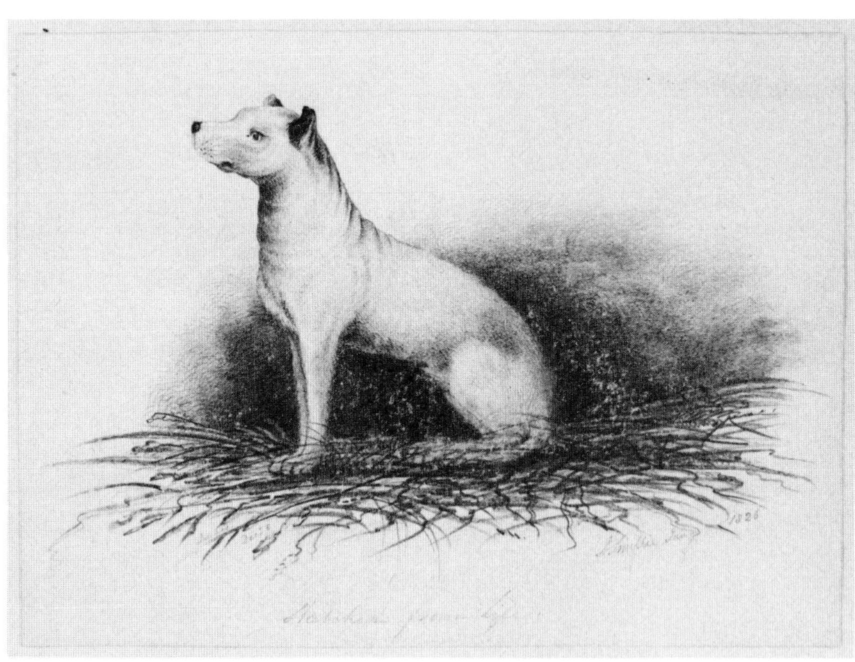
37

In a manuscript note attached the the Scrapbook, James Smillie described this drawing as "No. 34. after Landseer." This reference is probably to the most famous member of the artistic Landseer family, Sir Edwin Henry Landseer (1802–1873). Smillie met various members of the family when he travelled to London in 1827.

REFERENCES: Scrapbook, no. 34; Pilgrimage, pp. 22–23.

36. Dog Gnawing Bone 1826
Graphite on card; 11.0 × 17.5
Inscribed in pencil l.c. *J Smillie*; l.r. *1826*

James Smillie's manuscript note attached to the Scrapbook describes this drawing and Cat. No. 37, "Nos. 30, 31. Both from life!"

REFERENCES: Scrapbook, no. 30.

37. Dog 1826
Graphite on card; 11.8 × 16.1
Inscribed in pencil l.l. *Quebec / Dec.r 8*; l.c. *Sketched from Life*; l.r. *J. Smillie Jun 1826*

REFERENCES: Scrapbook, no. 31.

38. Skull of Colonel Despard c. 1826
Black wash, heightened with white, on wove paper; 17.0 × 17.5
Inscribed in ink u.c. *40*; r.c. *Smillie*; in pencil r.c. *1826*; l.r. *Portrait of Col....*

James Smillie's manuscript note attached to the Scrapbook identifies the subject as "No. 40. Skull of Col. Despard, a french traitor." Scrapbook no. 41, mounted on the same page, is an etched portrait of Despard published by James Gandee, Albion Press, London, 1 June 1810.

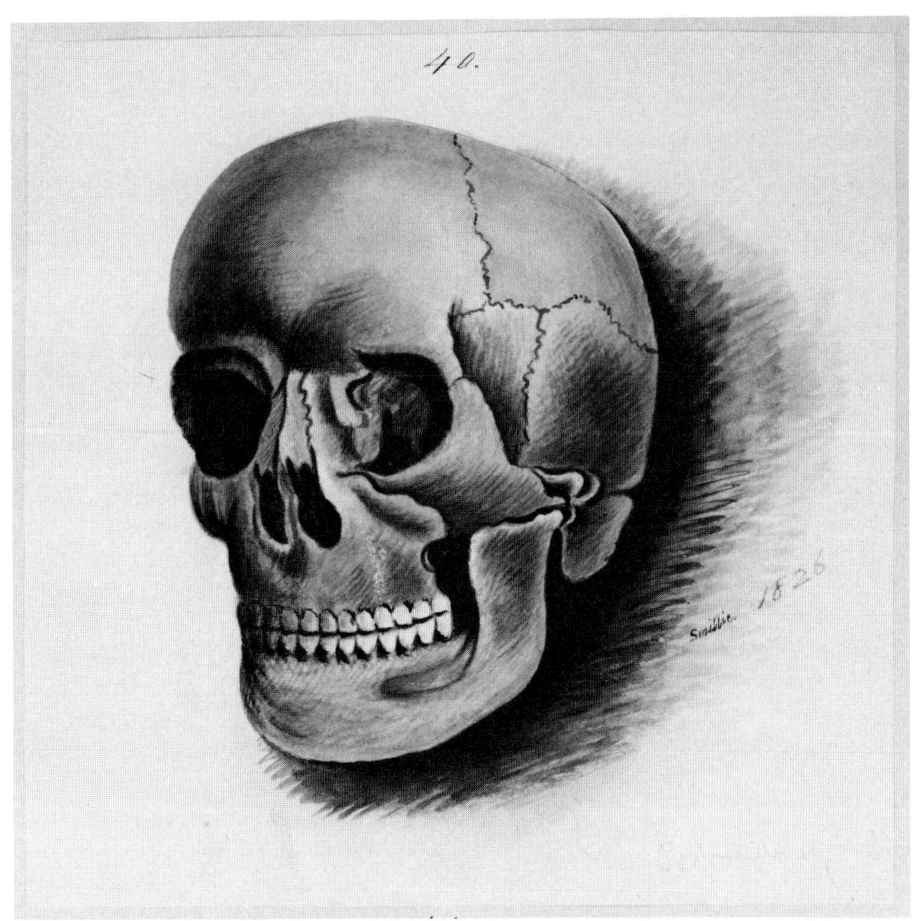

38

Edward Marcus Despard (1751–1803) was an Irish-born officer in the British armed forces who was charged with plotting to assassinate George III and executed in 1803. He was the last man to be hung, drawn, and quartered in England.

REFERENCES: Scrapbook, no. 40.

39. Langhorne's Poems c. 1826
Graphite on card; 13.7 × 9.6
Inscribed in pencil l.c. *Drawn by J. Smillie Junr.*; l.l. to r. *On his time smoothed staff reclined, / With wonder view'd the opening flower. / Langhorne's Poems.*

James Smillie states in a manuscript note attached to the Scrapbook, "No. 33. from an engraving." The subject depicts an old man leaning on a staff.

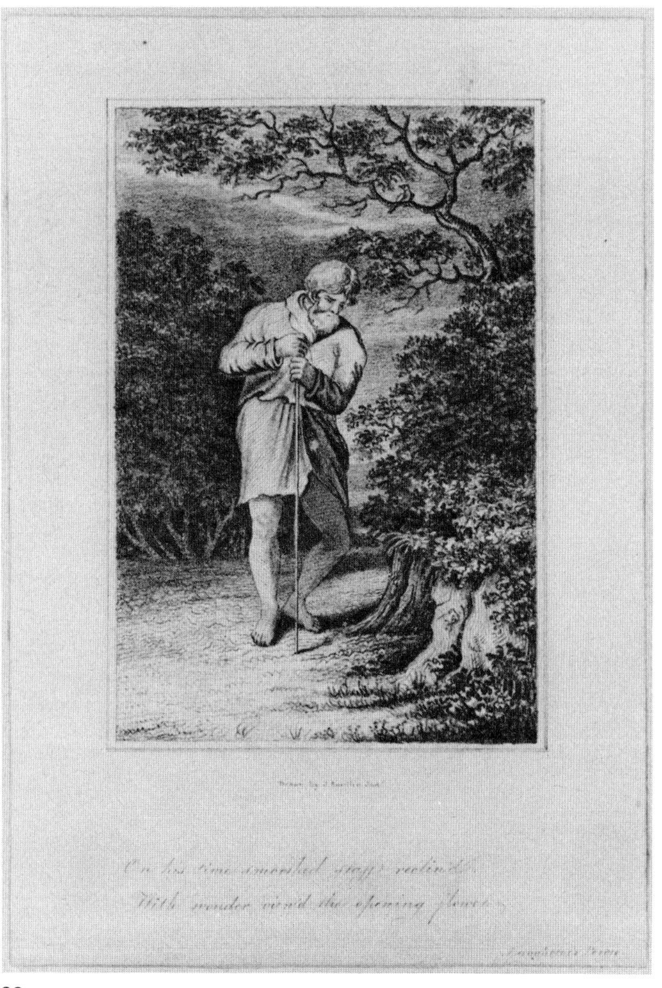

39

John Langhorne (1735–1779) was an English poet whose best-known work, "The Country Justice," gives a sympathetic treatment to the humble and unfortunate.

REFERENCES: Scrapbook, no. 33.

40. An Old Canadian c. 1826
Watercolour over graphite on card; 20.3 × 16.8
Inscribed in pencil u.l. *Died Novr. 1826*; in brush point l.r. *JS* [monogram]

James Smillie comments in a manuscript note attached to the Scrapbook, "No. 35. An old Canadian aged 100 years, perfectly hale and active. This is a copy from a drawing by Edd. Heaton of Yorkshire England."

Edward Heaton (fl. 1825–1828), an English artist who visited Quebec in 1825/1826, had a number of contacts with Smillie. His watercolour portrait of Smillie (cover) served as the model for a 1901 etching by Smillie's son James David (Pilgrimage, p. 12). Heaton also painted a watercolour portrait of Adam Kidd (MTL JRR 74), the poet for whom Smillie etched a book illustration (see Cat. No. 73).

The subject of this watercolour has not been identified. The only centenarian listed in Quebec obituaries of November 1826 was William Gordon, a veteran of the Battle of the Plains of Abraham, who died in Scotland, at the age of 106.

REFERENCES: Scrapbook, no. 35; Harper 1970, s.v. "Edwin Heaton"; *Quebec Mercury*, 11 November 1826.

41. Dalhousie Bookplate c. 1826
Etching and engraving on wove paper; 10.2 × 7.9 (plate)
Inscribed in plate c., on arms, *TRIA JUNCTA IN UNO / ICH DIEN / ORA ET LABORA*

James Smillie inscribed his impression of this bookplate in pencil "Engraved for Lord Dalhousie / Quebec 1829." The date is incorrect, for Dalhousie had left Quebec the previous year. This etching may be based on a pencil drawing of the Dalhousie arms by Louis-Hubert Triaud (1794–1836) that Smillie preserved in the Scrapbook and dated 1825. Smillie's 1826 etching *The Quebec Driving Club* also includes the Dalhousie coat of arms (Cat. No. 32).

REFERENCES: Scrapbook, no. 93.

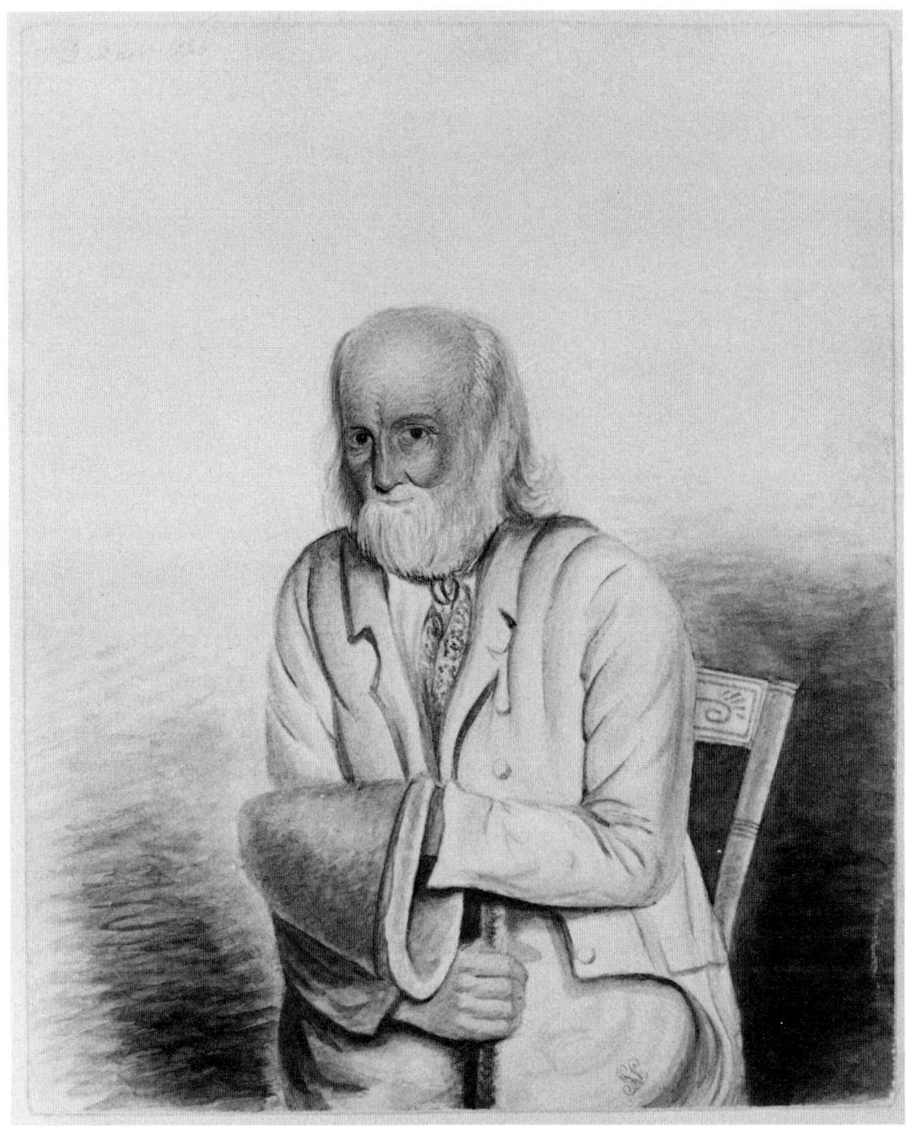

40

42. Maule Bookplate c. 1826
Etching on wove paper; 6.8 × 5.5 (sheet)
Inscribed in plate l.c. *CLEMENTIA ET ANIMIS / Fox Maule Esq.r*

Fox Maule, second Baron Panmure (1801–1874), served as aide-de-camp to his uncle, the Earl of Dalhousie, in Quebec from August 1821 until September 1828. He eventually succeeded to the title as eleventh Earl of Dalhousie.

James Smillie dated his impression of this bookplate "1829" in pencil. This dating is probably incorrect, for Smillie was absent from Quebec from October 1827 until August 1828, and Maule and Dalhousie left Quebec in September 1828.

REFERENCES: Scrapbook, no. 54; Supplementary Scrapbook, no. 6.

43. Quebec Fire-Assurance Company c. 1826
Etching on onionskin; 10.1 × 22.5 (sheet)
Inscribed in plate u.c. *By the Quebec Fire-Assurance Company*

James Smillie dated his Scrapbook impression "1826" in pencil. See Cat. No. 59 for a later version of this policy form.

REFERENCES: Scrapbook, no. 43.

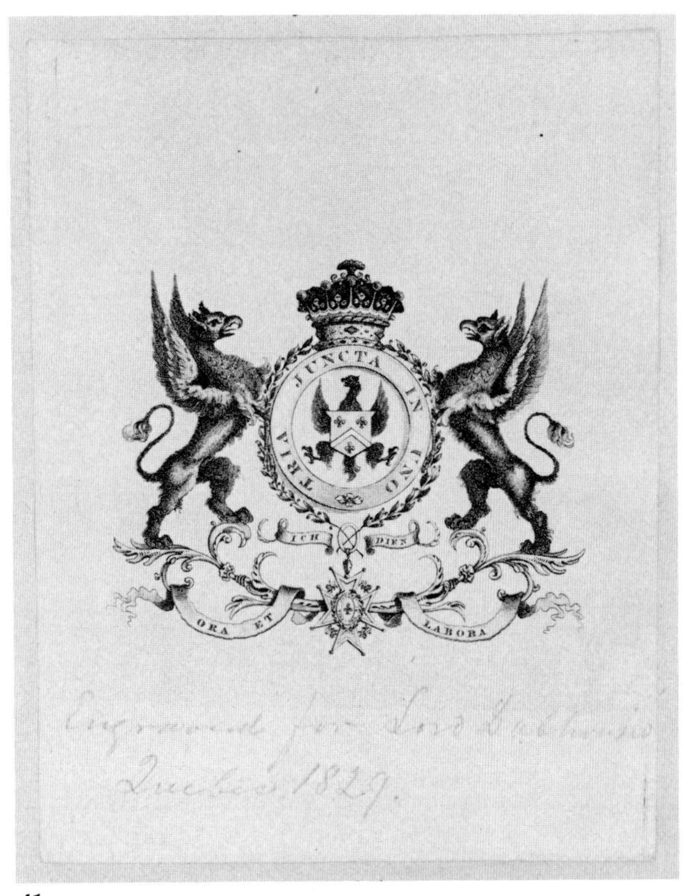
JUNCTA IN
UNO
VIRTUTE
ICH DIEN
ORA ET LABORA
Engraved for Lord Dalhousie
Quebec 1829.

41

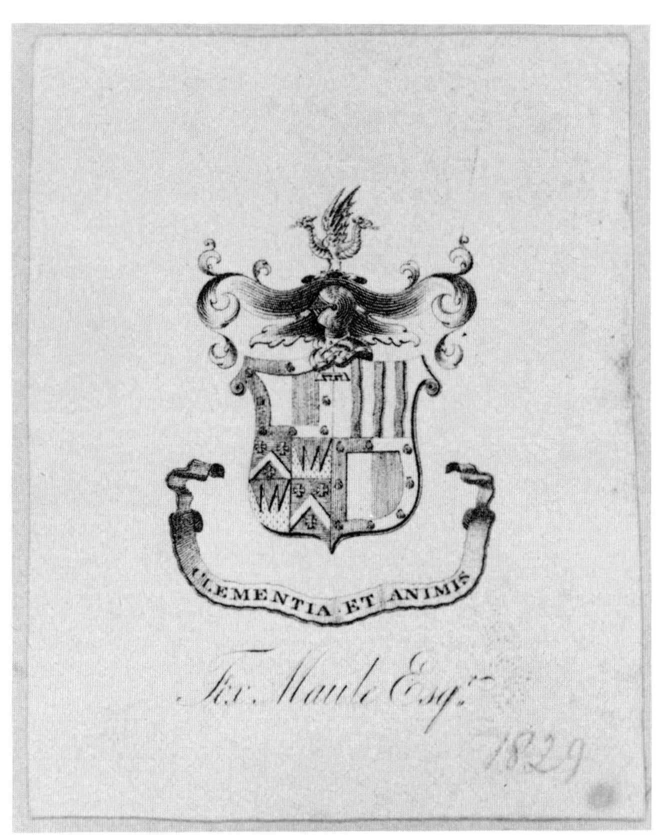
CLEMENTIA ET ANIMIS
Fox Maule Esqr.
1829

42

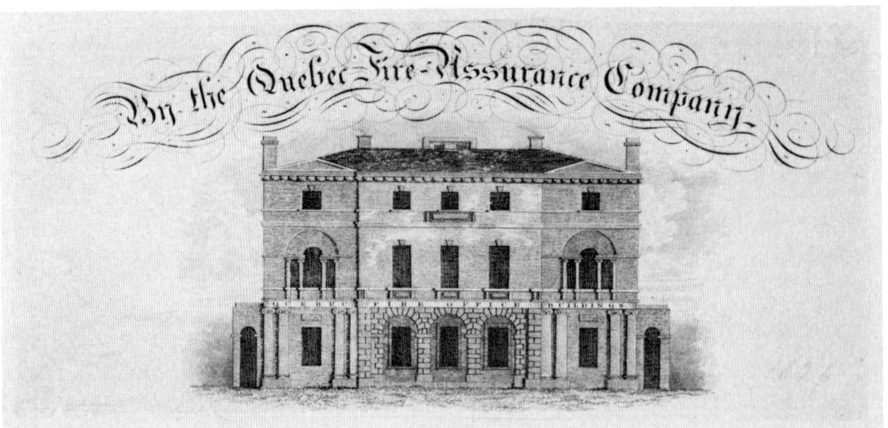
By the Quebec Fire-Assurance Company.

43

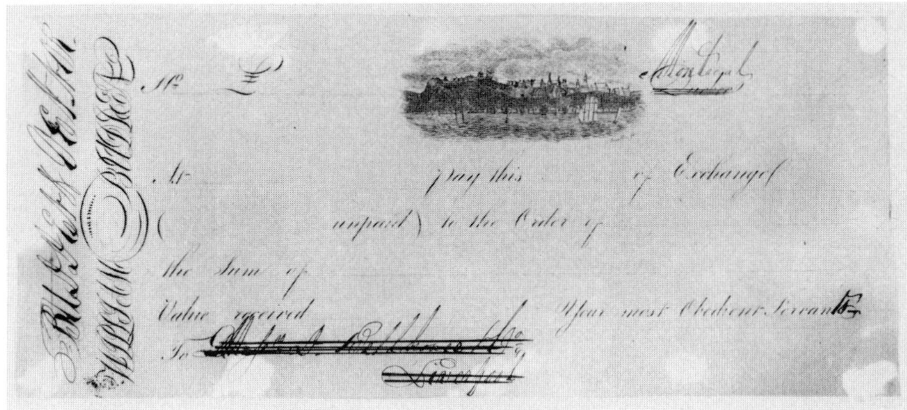

44

44. Note of Exchange c. 1826
Etching and engraving on laid paper; 9.6 × 22.9 (sheet)
Inscribed in plate u.c., under vignette, *Smillie sc.*; c.l. *WILLIAM BUDDEN*

This single note of exchange is embellished with a vignette view of Quebec, seen from Lévis. William Budden was a merchant at 11 St. Peter Street, Quebec. The only impression located is inscribed at centre left in ink "BUDDEN. . . ."

REFERENCES: Scrapbook, no. 44; QD 1822, 1826.

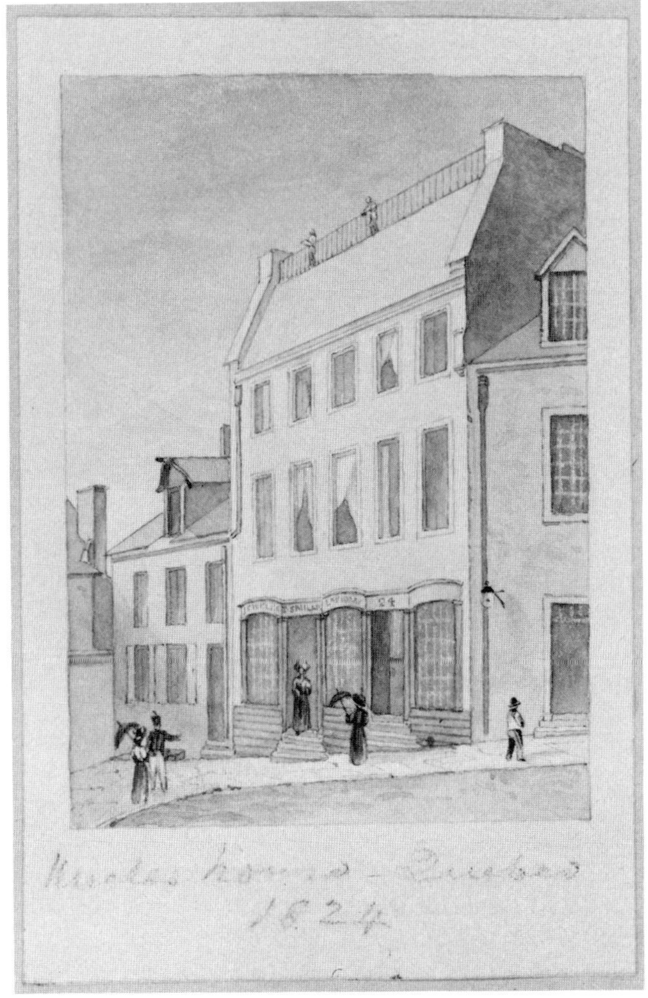

45

45. Uncle's House, Quebec c. 1824–1826
Brown wash over graphite on wove paper; 11.5 × 7.5
Inscribed in pencil l.c. *Uncles house—Quebec / 1824*

James Smillie's manuscript note attached to the Scrapbook describes this view and its companion (Cat. No. 46).

No. 37. Uncle James' house, in which also father's family lived for a time. From its roof, the view on the opposite page No. 38 was taken. Looking south down the bay, taking in the site of the falls of Montmorenci. 1826.

Smillie has quoted two different dates of execution, of which 1826 is more probable (see Cat. Nos. 46–48).

The sketch illustrates the house and shop of James Smillie, Sr., at 16 and 24 Mountain Street, where David Smillie, Sr., and his family lived when they first arrived in Quebec. This house was destroyed in the tragic fire of 4 February 1841.

Smillie's brown wash paintings of Quebec street scenes are similar in style to the work of Captain John Crawford Young (1788–c. 1859), who took an interest in the young engraver's artistic development.

REFERENCES: Scrapbook, no. 37.

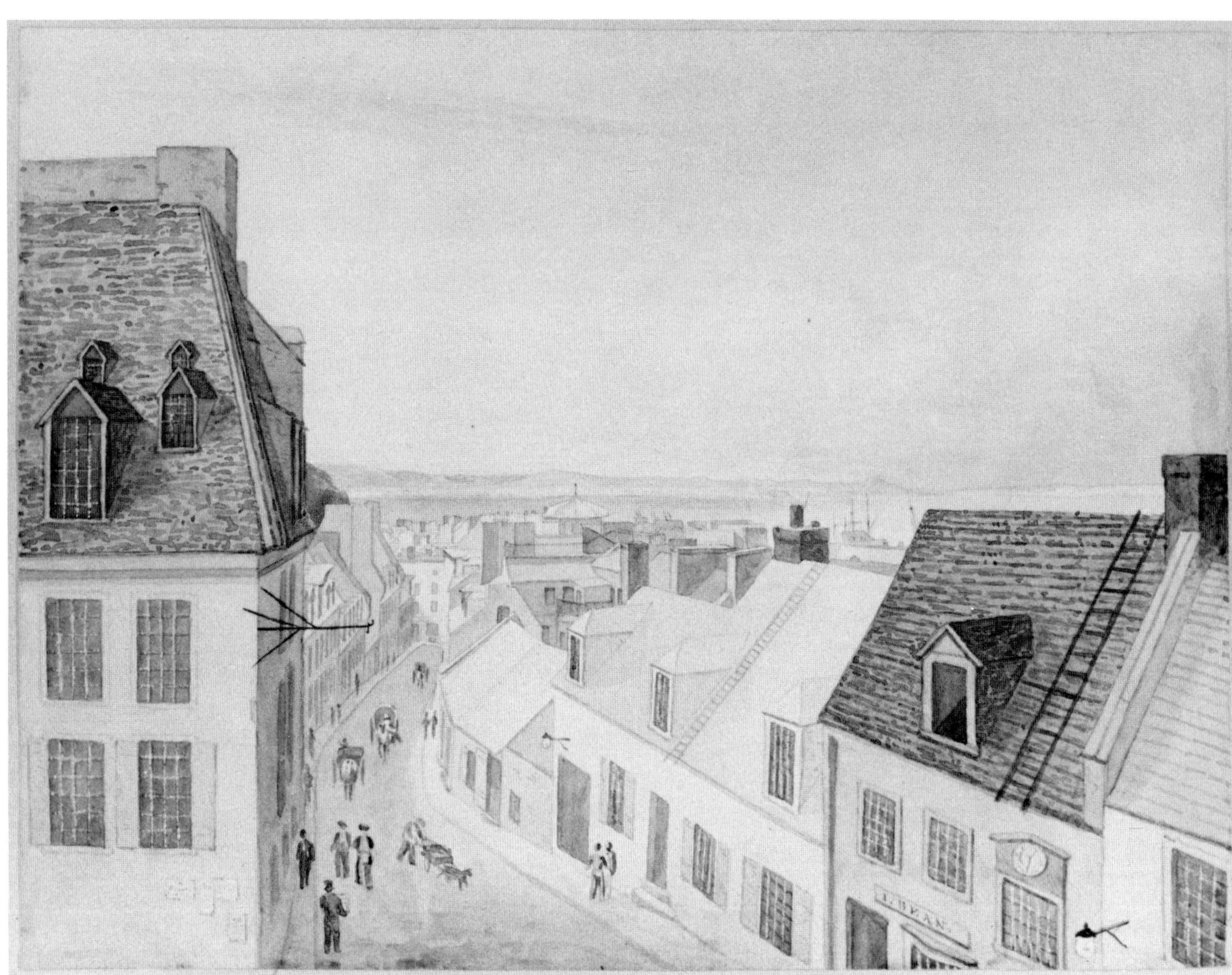

46

46. Looking from Mountain Street towards Montmorenci Falls c. 1826
Brown wash over graphite, with scraping, on wove paper; 22.7 × 30.2

This view was taken from the roof of the house belonging to James Smillie, Sr., described in the artist's note attached to the previous entry (Cat. No. 45). The house at the right has a sign that reads "J. Bean." John Bean was a watchmaker living at 21 Mountain Street in 1822 and at 13 Mountain Street in 1826. He was a family friend and witnessed the contract signed between James Smillie, Jr., and the Reverend George Bourne in 1829 (Appendix G).

REFERENCES: Scrapbook, no. 38; QD 1822, 1826.

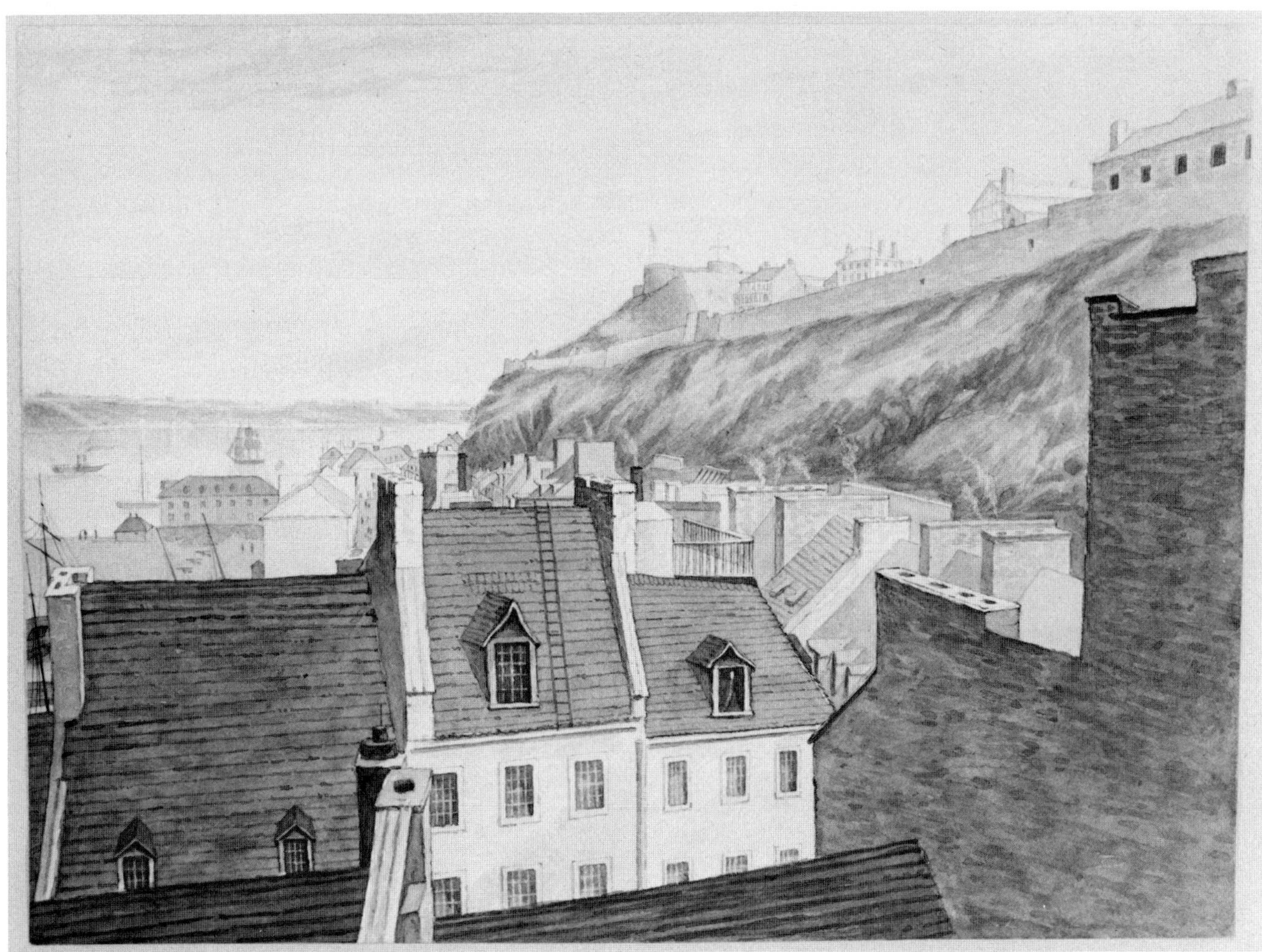

47

47. Looking from Mountain Street towards Cape Diamond c. 1826
Brown wash over graphite, with scraping, on wove paper; 20.5 × 27.9

In a manuscript note attached to the Scrapbook, James Smillie identifies the view, "No. 39. From top of the same house, looking north, giving a view of Cape Diamond, with citadel and telegraph for vessels. 1826." See Cat. No. 46 for another view taken from the roof of his uncle's house.

REFERENCES: Scrapbook, no. 39.

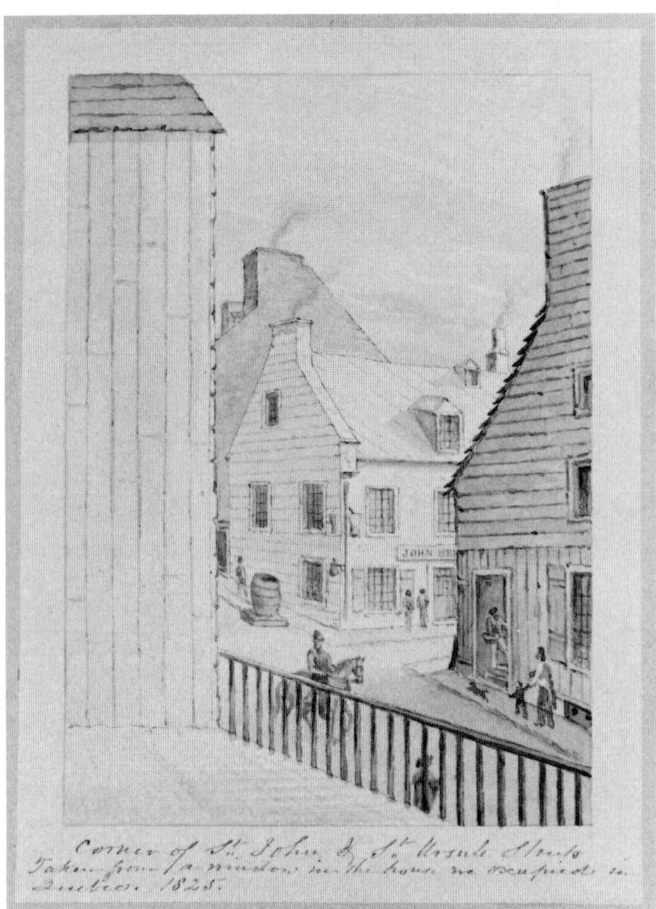

48

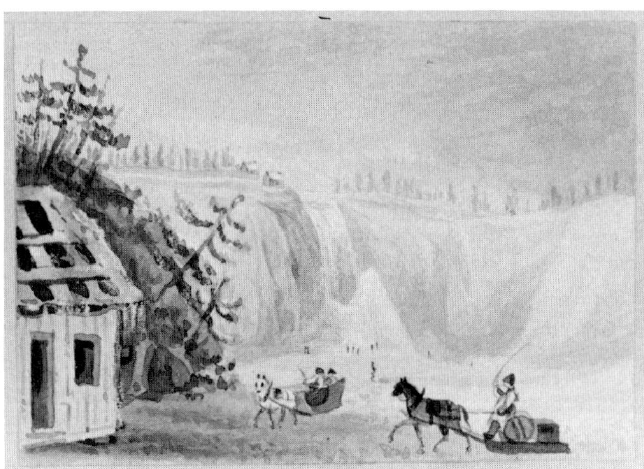

49

48. Quebec Street Scene c. 1825–1826
Brown wash on wove paper; 13.8 × 10.2
Inscribed in ink l.c. *Corner of S.t John & S.t Ursule Streets / Taken from a window in the house we occupied in / Quebec. 1825.*

The intersection of St. John and St. Ursule streets would not have been visible from any of James Smillie's known addresses (Pilgrimage, n. 14). The inscription on the view may have been made at a later date. Stylistically the work corresponds with his Quebec views (Cat. Nos. 45–47).

REFERENCES: Scrapbook, no. 46.

49. Falls of Montmorenci in Winter c. 1825–1828
Brown wash, with scraping, on wove paper; 7.8 × 11.3

James Smillie refers to this view in a manuscript note attached to the Scrapbook as "The falls of Montmorenci in winter with ice cone."

REFERENCES: Scrapbook, no. 47.

50. Habitant in Winter Landscape c. 1825–1828
Brown wash over graphite on wove paper; 11.2 × 8.0
Inscribed in pencil l.r. *J Smillie Jr.*

Cat. Nos. 49 and 50 are probably copies of sketches by garrison artists. The dating is suggested by James Smillie's placement of these drawings in his scrapbook.

REFERENCES: Scrapbook, no. 53.

51. Picturesque Views of Canada 1827
Graphite on card; 16.5 × 12.5
Inscribed in pencil u.c. *PICTURESQUE VIEW'S / OF / CANADA.*; l.c. *QUEBEC. / Published by D. Smillie & Sons / June 1827.*; l.l. of vignette *Designed by J. Smillie Jun.r*; l.r. of vignette *Quebec 18 Feb.y 1827*; r., on tree trunk, *JS*

James Smillie's manuscript note attached to the Scrapbook identifies this drawing as "No. 29. Once more taken with the fever of publishing a series of views in Canada, but got no further than to make a drawing of the title page. In 1827."

The vignette depicts a Niagara-like waterfall, with an Indian encampment in the foreground. The tepee and overhanging tree with surface roots are similar to those

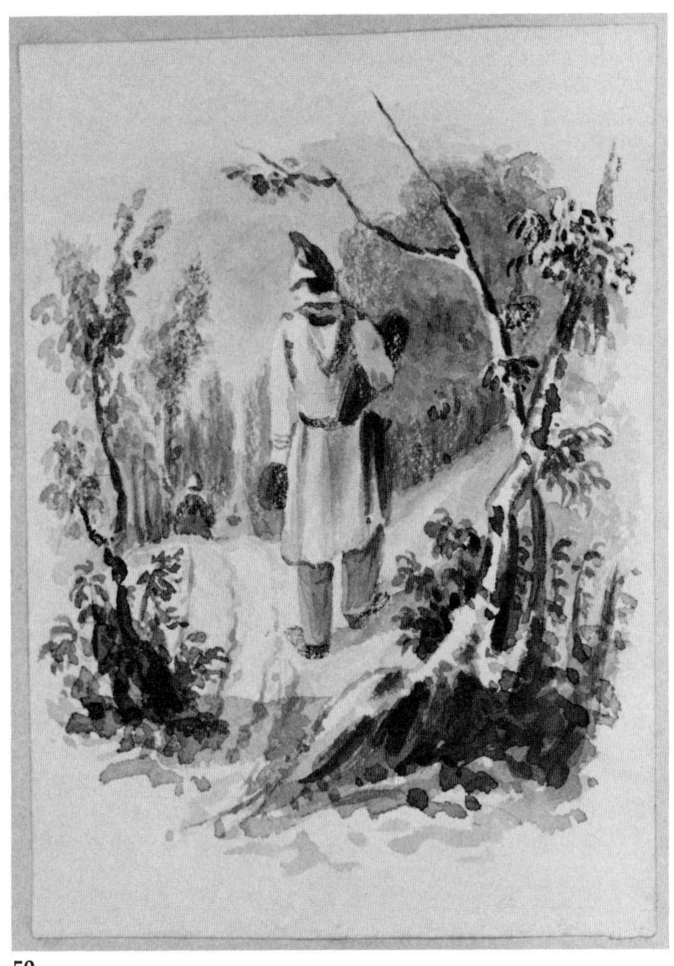

50

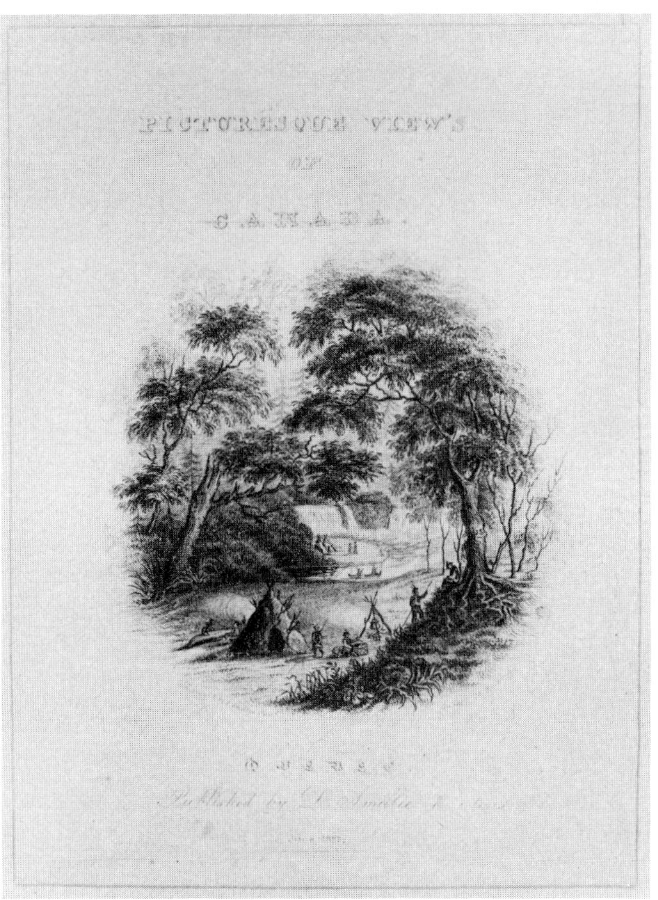

51

seen in the inset view of the 1827 map of the Saint John River Valley (Cat. No. 54).

REFERENCES: Scrapbook, no. 29.

52. Section of Country Lying between the Old Seigniorial Settlements on the River St. Lawrence and Southern Boundary of the Province 1827
Etching and engraving on wove or japan paper; 26.0 × 31.7 (plate)
Surveyor: Joseph Bouchette
Scale: Approximately 15 miles to 1 inch
Inscribed in plate l.l. *PLAN / Shewing that Section of Country / lying between the Old Seig.r Setlem.ts / on the River S.t Lawrence and Southern / Boundary of the Province. or Mars Hill / Highlands. / Joseph Bouchette, / Surv.r Gen.l / Quebec April 1827. / A. this point is nearly opposite to the highest peak of Mars Hill / 40 miles due North of the Monument at the Source of the S.t Croix ~ / Eng.d by J. Smillie Jun.r*

State I: Note "A" below title (illustrated)
State II: Omits note "A" of inscription

James Smillie's manuscript note attached to the Scrapbook records the following: "No. 42. Engraved to illustrate statistics published by the House of Assembly, 1827."

This map is bound with the 1827 *Journals of the House of Assembly of Lower Canada*. In the assembly's Minutes of Evidence, the committee chairman, Dr. François Blanchet (1776–1830), asked for the expense of compiling a map of the country between the old settlements of the south shore of the St. Lawrence and the southern boundary of the province, embracing the Saint John River, and a second map of the same country, reduced in scale and printed with a lithographic press to furnish the committee with two hundred copies. Surveyor General Joseph Bouchette (1774–1841) estimated that this work could be done for a gross sum of "55 Pounds Currency." Correspondence between David and James Smillie in 1827 and 1828 shows that Blanchet ordered the printing of an additional one hundred impressions of one of James Smillie's 1827 maps, and that Smillie, then in Britain, was hoping to receive the plate, so that he could have some impressions printed on his own account (Appendix L.2, 4, 6).

A second state of the map was published in the *Star and Commercial Advertiser* on 23 April 1828. This state omits the line giving Joseph Bouchette's name, the date, and note "A" below the title. Some impressions of the map are watermarked "BALSTON & CO / 1825."

REFERENCES: Scrapbook, no. 42; Gagnon 1895, no. 4412; Lower Canada, House of Assembly 1827a; *Star and Commercial Advertiser*, 23 April 1828; PAC 1976, vol. 10, p. 605 (H3/1001–1827).

53. Plan de la Rivière du Saguenay 1827
Etching and engraving on wove or laid paper; 42.0 × 53.2 (plate)
Surveyor: A. Larue
Scale: Approximately $4^1/_2$ leagues to 1 inch
Inscribed in plate u.r. *Plan De la Riviere du Saguenay, Lac's, Rivieres & Ruisseaux. / ainsi que la qualité du Sol du Terrein et des Bois situés / de chaque coté de la dite Riviere du Saguenay, fait / d'apres une Esquise et Informations données par / PASCAL TACHÉ ECUIER, SEIGNEUR DE KAMOURASKA, / apres avoir résidé durant l'espace de Vingt deux Années a / faire le Commerce des Pelleteries a la Pointe-Bleu, Shékut- / imitsh et Tadousac, fait par le Soussigné Clerc Arpenteur. / Quebec 27th Dec*[r] *1825. / (Signé) A. Larue. // Reduced to one half the scale of the*

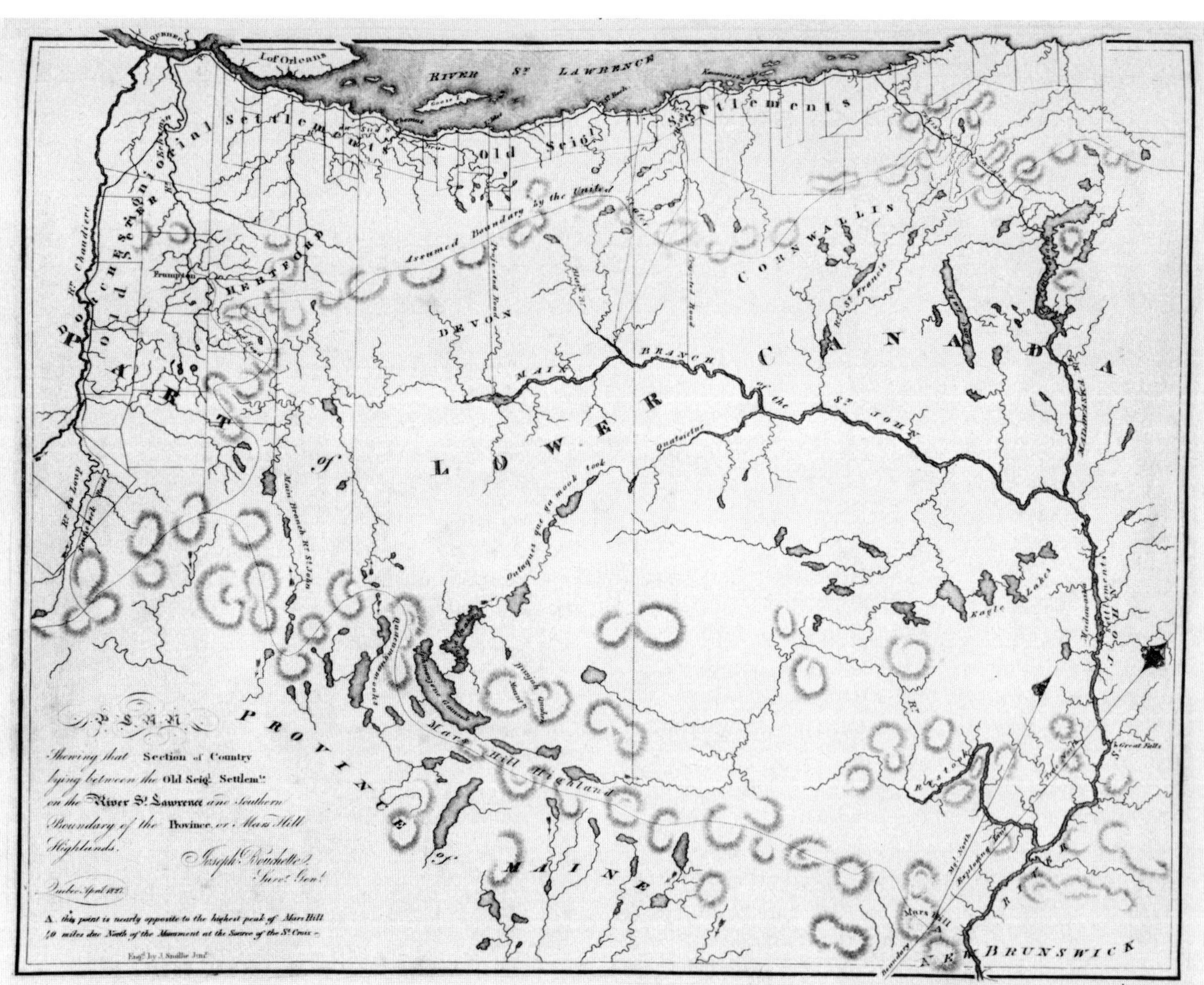

52

Origin! plan of A. Larue by Wm. Sax. Land Survr. / Quebec April 1827. / Engd. by J. Smillie Junr.

This map is bound with the 1827 *Journals of the House of Assembly of Lower Canada*. It was also issued separately with *Rapport d'un comité de la Chambre d'Assemblée sur l'opportunité d'ouvrir des chemins de colonisation dans la Province de Québec, ayant siège pendant l'année 1827; Rapport des commissaires pour explorer le Saguenay*; and the *Star and Commercial Advertiser* for 1 August 1829.

The *Star and Commercial Advertiser* described its publication of the map at length.

We publish on the other side of this paper the Map of the Saguenay Country, for the assistance of the public in forming an opinion of the benefit that may be derived from settling that important section of the Province. It was originally engraved by order of the Legislature; and with the view of following up their very liberal intentions, and for the accommodation of our readers, we have been at the expense of getting these additional copies thrown off.

The particular reason for publishing it at this time, is to illustrate the labours undertaken last year, and still continued this season, for the more full exploration of the tract of country in question. While the mother country is annually fitting out expeditions for making discoveries in Africa, for ascertaining the north coast of America, or visiting the Pole of the earth; it is befitting that Canada should explore the regions that are peculiarly her own, but which have hitherto remained a *Terra incognita septentrionalis*. She has thus obtained for herself the credit of providing settlements for her own future resources; and of these honours she cannot be deprived.

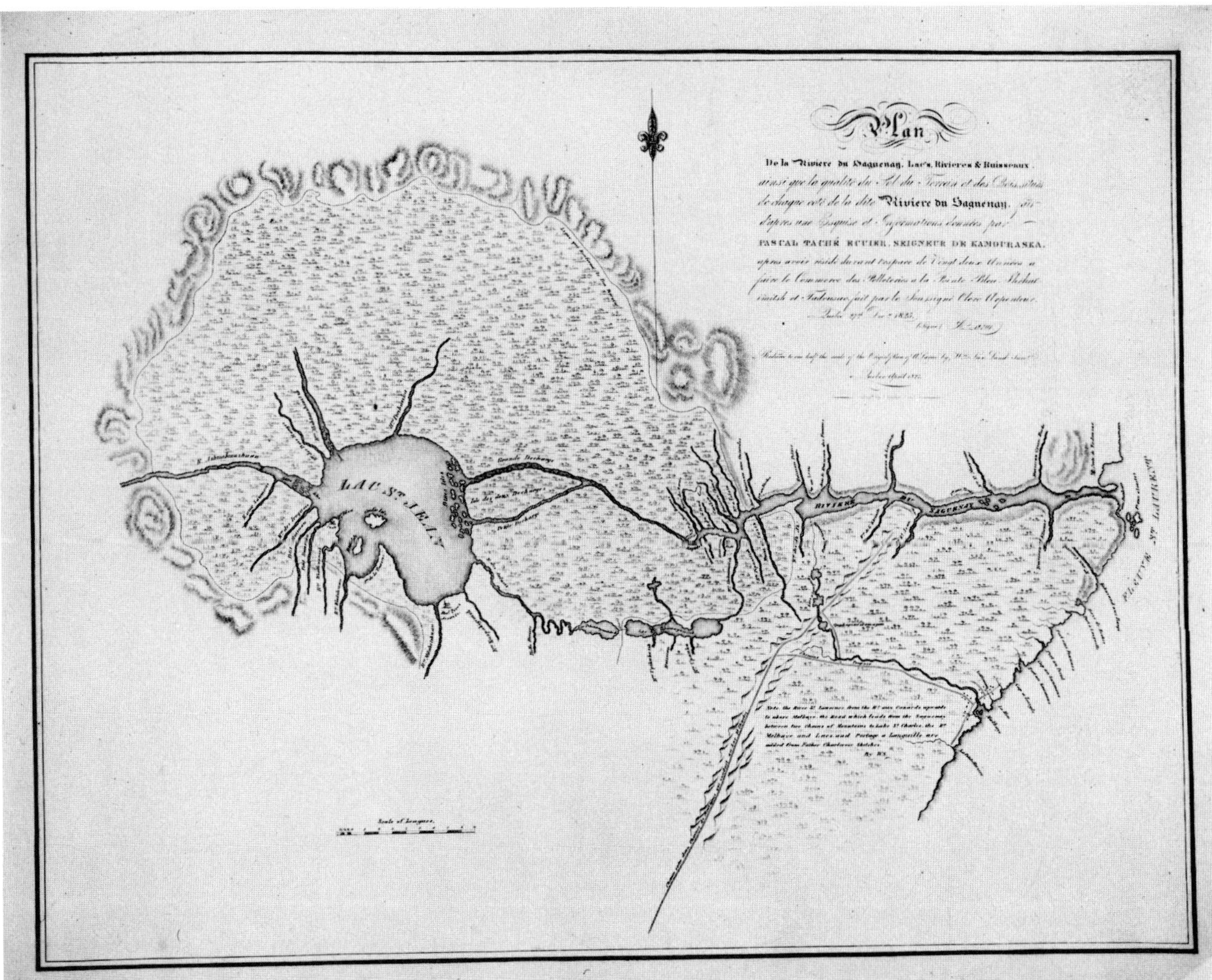

53

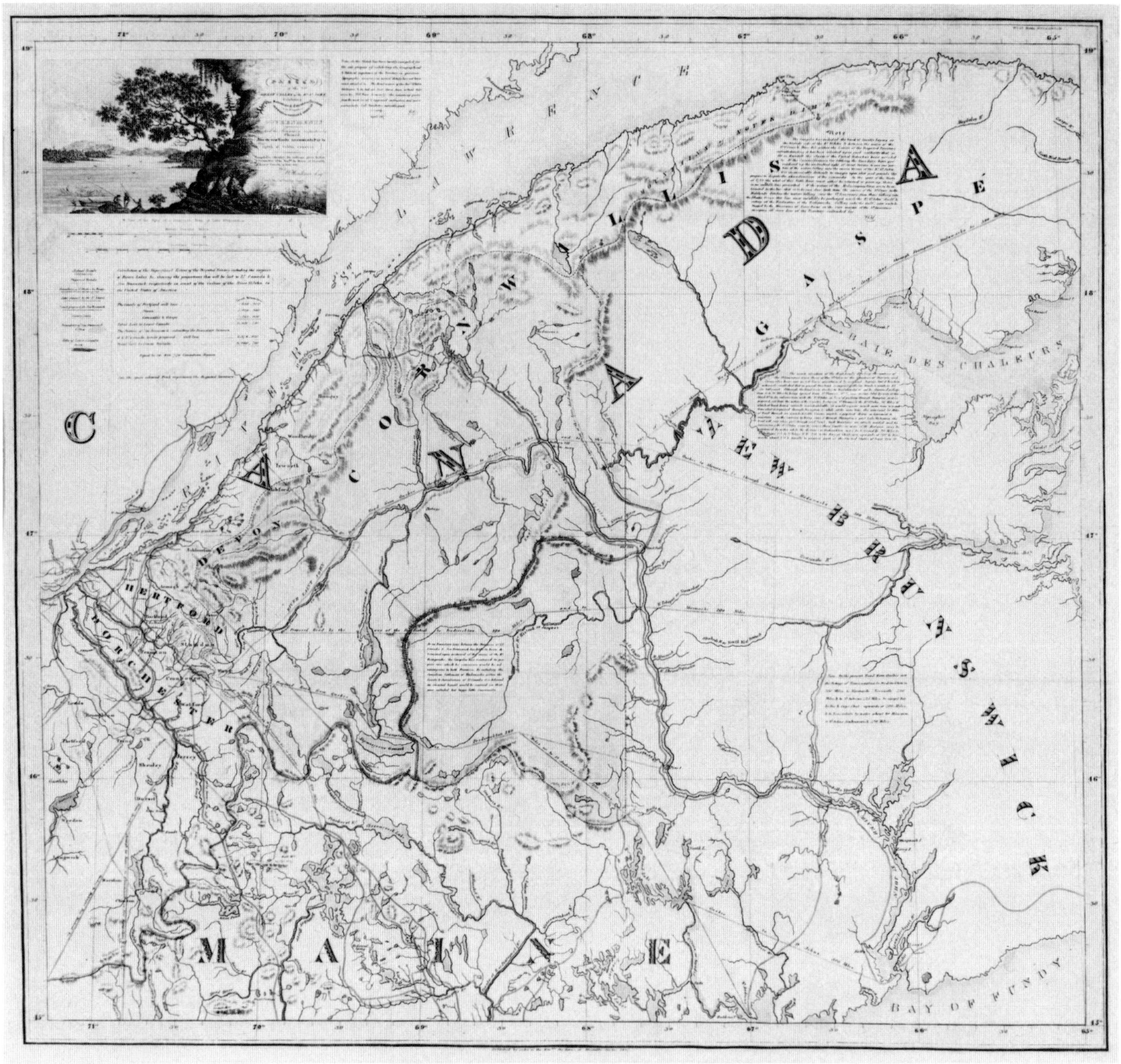
71°
70°
69°
68°
67°
66°
65°
49°
48°
47°
46°
45°
MAINE
GASPÉ
BAIE DES CHALEURS
BAY OF FUNDY
DEVON
HERTFORD
DORCHESTER

54

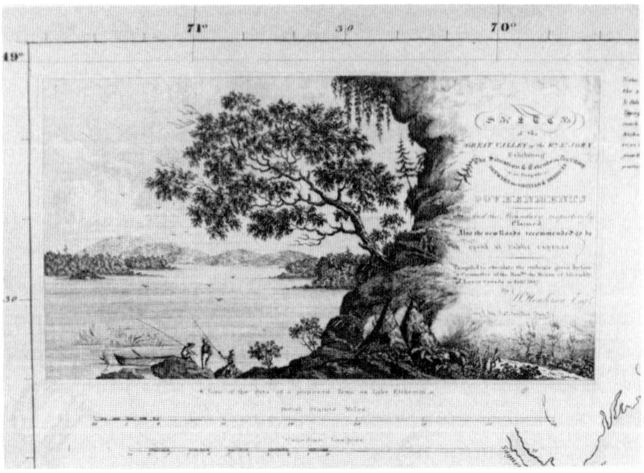
71°
70°
49°

detail

"The report of the Commissioners for exploring the Saguenay", with its accompanying documents, presented to the House of Assembly last Session, and ordered by them to be printed, extends to 208 pages....

Some impressions of the map are on laid paper, watermarked "BALSTON & CO / 1825."

REFERENCES: Lower Canada, House of Assembly 1827a, 1827b, 1829b; *Star and Commercial Advertiser*, 1 August 1829; Gagnon 1895, nos. 809, 3124.

54. Sketch of the Great Valley of the River St. John 1827

Etching and engraving on wove or laid paper; 47.7 × 52.8 (plate)
Surveyor: William Henderson
Scale: British miles, 20 miles to 1¼ inches; Canadian leagues, 5 leagues to 1 inch
Inscribed in plate u.l., within borders of inset view, *SKETCH / of the / GREAT VALLEY of the R.r S.t JOHN. / Exhibiting the Situation & Extent of the Territory / in Dispute / BETWEEN the BRITISH & AMERICAN / GOVERNMENTS // And the Boundary respectively / Claimed. / Also the new Roads recommended to be / opend at Public expence. // Compiled to elucidate the evidence given before / the Committee of the Hon.ble the House of Assembly / of Lower Canada in Feb.y 1827. / By W. Henderson Esq.r / Eng.d by Ja.s Smillie Jun.r*; u.l., below borders of inset view, *View of the Site of a proposed Town on Lake Etchemin.*; l.c. *Published by order of the Hon.ble the House of Assembly, Quebec, 1827.*; u.c., note on surveys, *W.H. / April 1827*

This map is bound with the 1827 *Journals of the Legislative Assembly of Lower Canada*. It was also issued separately with the special committee report *Rapport d'un comité de la Chambre d'Assemblée sur l'opportunité d'ouvrir des chemins de colonisation dans la Province de Québec, ayant siège pendant l'année 1827*. Some impressions of the map are watermarked "J. WHATMAN / TURKEY MILL" or "AP / 1825."

For the engraving of this map James Smillie was awarded the first-prize medal by the Society for the Encouragement of the Arts and Sciences in Canada on 6 March 1828 (Appendix L.8).

REFERENCES: Pilgrimage, p. 19; Gagnon 1895, nos. 809, 4451; Lower Canada, House of Assembly 1827a, 1827b; *Star and Commercial Advertiser*, 19 March 1828.

55. Quebec and Its Environs c. 1827–1830

[James Pattison Cockburn], *Quebec and Its Environs: Being a Picturesque Guide to the Stranger* (Quebec: Printed by Thomas Cary & Co., Freemason's Hall, Buade Street, 1831), 42 pages, 7 plates; 13.2 × 19.4 (sheet, size varies)

Although James Pattison Cockburn (1779–1847) modestly omitted his name from the title page of this guidebook, he is acknowledged as the author of the text and six of the illustrations. (The seventh plate, or frontispiece, by Thomas George Marlay [1809–1837] is found in some, but not all, copies of the guide).

Cockburn has not previously been known as a printmaker, but Smillie clearly credits him with a knowledge of etching and the Scrapbook contains two etchings of Swiss scenery, which are inscribed in pencil by Smillie "Etched by Col. Cockburn, Royal Artillery" (Appendix D).

James Smillie described his collaboration in this work as technical assistance in biting and finishing plates that had already been drawn on copper by Cockburn (Cat. Nos. 55c–d, f) and the execution of some plates himself, "with the intention of starting a publication" (Cat. Nos. 55a–b, e). At the outset Cockburn may not have had a guidebook in mind: on 10 June 1829 the *Star and Commercial Advertiser* announced that "It is understood that Col. Cockburn, R.A., intends to give a picturesque Series of slight etchings on a small scale, by himself, of the two Canada's and adjacent parts of the United States." Smillie had evidently hoped to publish the plates himself, but on 25 October 1830 his brother David wrote to him in New York, "Coll. Cockburn sent for his plates a few days ago as he could not let them go on your terms—selfish again" (Appendix L.11). Although Smillie remembered Cockburn's interest in his welfare with gratitude, he seemed to forget or be unaware when writing his autobiography that these plates were eventually published.

The dating and attribution of the individual etchings is problematic. For this reason they are presented in published order, with a general dating of c. 1827 to c. 1830. The dating of the individual prints will be discussed in the entries.

Of all the impressions of the six views kept in the Scrapbook, only the *Falls of Montmorenci* bears the title in the plate, etched in Smillie's hand. It is possible that the remaining titles were added by another engraver after Smillie left Quebec. There is no evidence that this second engraver made any changes to the images of the Cockburn/Smillie plates.

REFERENCES: Pilgrimage, p. 20; Bell and Cooke 1978.

55a. View from the Ramparts c. 1828–1829
Etching on wove paper; 8.7 × 14.3 (image)
Inscribed in plate l.c. *View from the Ramparts*.

A manuscript notation by James Smillie attached to the Scrapbook describes Cat. Nos. 55a and b as "Nos. 48, 49. . . .a series of views of Quebec, which I attempted to publish from drawings by Col. Cockburn of the Royal Artillery. 1828." The only known watercolour by Cockburn similar to this print is *From the Ursuline Bastion, Quebec*, 1829 (ROM 951x205.13).

REFERENCES: Scrapbook, no. 48 (proof before letters); Supplementary Scrapbook, no. 4 (imp. on same sheet with Cat. No. 55b, proof before letters); Pilgrimage, p. 20.

55b. Wolfe's and Montcalm's Monument
c. 1828–1829
Etching on wove paper; 9.8 × 14.4 (image)
Inscribed in plate l.c. *Wolfe's and Montcalm's Monument*.

This monument was designed by John Crawford Young (1788–c. 1859). He submitted his design and specifications on 10 October 1827 (NGC 29238, 29239), and the foundation stone was laid a month later. Construction was completed in September 1828.

The watercolour by James Pattison Cockburn closest in composition to this print is *Monument to Wolfe and Montcalm*, 1829 (ROM 951x205.20).

REFERENCES: Scrapbook, no. 49 (proof before letters); Supplementary Scrapbook, no. 5 (printed on same sheet with Cat. No. 55a, proof before letters); Pilgrimage, p. 20.

55c. Near No. 1 Tower c. 1830
Etching on wove paper; 9.7 × 13.9 (image)
Inscribed in plate l.c. *Near N° 1 Tower*

The proof impression in the Supplementary Scrapbook is inscribed in pencil "View of Cape Diamond from the Plains of Abraham / Col. Cockburn—1830." Some impressions of this subject are watermarked "Harris / 1825" or "[Prince of Wales crest] / HB / 1829."

A drawing by James Pattison Cockburn entitled *Near No. 1 Tower*, n.d. (NA I-30), bears the following inscription by the artist.

> This pen Sketch is reversed for the purpose of engraving—The view is taken from under No. 1 Tower looking to the Citadel, and the Church of Aubigny on the Point Levy shore—1830—J. Cockburn.

James Smillie noted that Cockburn began to etch this print himself, which may account for the fact that the image was not etched in reverse on the plate. Other watercolours by Cockburn of similar views (but not reversed) are *Cape Diamond from Below No. 1 Tower*, 1823 (NA I-65), and *Cape Diamond from Below No. 1 Tower*, 1828 (NA C-40018).

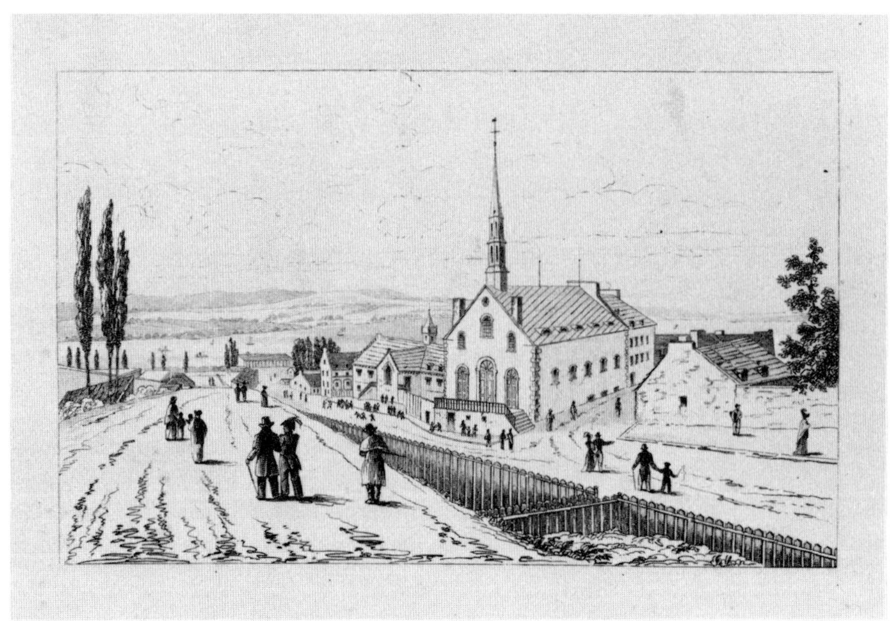

55a

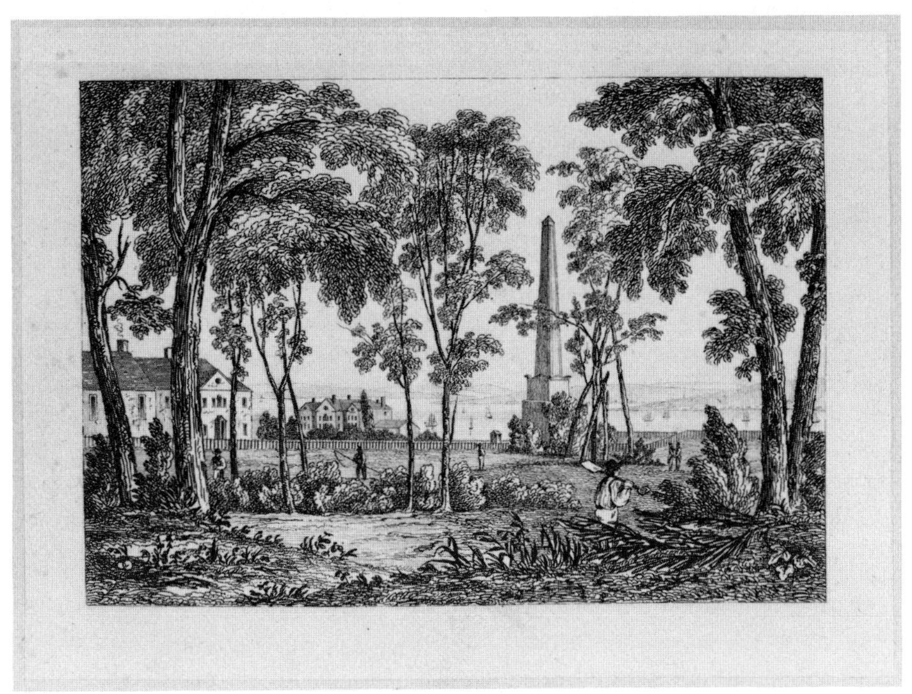

55b

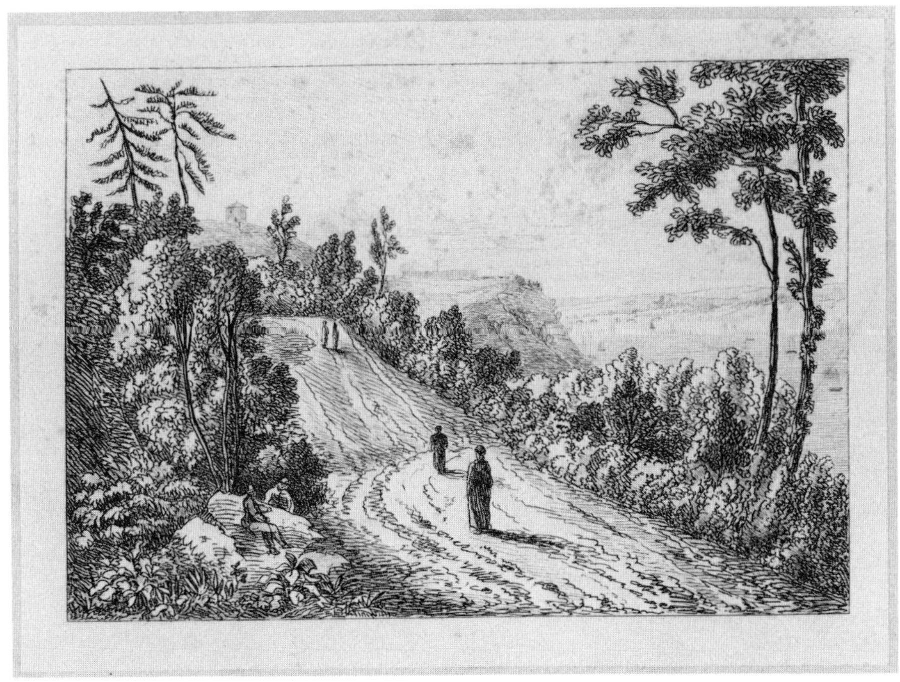

55c

REFERENCES: Scrapbook, no. 50 (proof before letters); Supplementary Scrapbook, no. 12 (proof before letters); Pilgrimage, p. 20.

55d. Quebec from Point à Pizeau 1830
Etching on wove paper; 9.2 × 14.2 (image)
Inscribed in plate l.c. *Quebec From Point à Pizeau.*

The proof impression in the Supplementary Scrapbook is inscribed in pencil "Distant view of Cape Diamond / 1829," with the date corrected to read 1830.

This was a popular view with James Pattison Cockburn. He did several versions of the subject, including the watercolours *Quebec from Point à Pizeau*, 1831 (NA I-10); *Quebec from Point à Pizeau*, 1831 (NGC 17663); and *Cape Diamond and Wolfe's Cove from Point à Pizeau*, c. 1831 (ROM 940x27.1); and the aquatint *Cape Diamond and Wolfe's Cove from Point à Pizeau*, 1833, published by Ackerman & Co., London.

REFERENCES: Scrapbook, no. 51 (proof before letters); Supplementary Scrapbook, no. 11 (proof before letters); Pilgrimage, p. 20.

55e. Falls of Montmorenci c. 1827
Etching on wove paper; 7.1 × 11.8 (image)
Inscribed in plate l.c. *Falls of Montmorenci.*
State I: No birds in sky (illustrated)
State II: Birds in sky
State III: With letters

James Smillie attached the following manuscript note to the Scrapbook, "No. 57. Falls of Montmorenci. Etched by myself. 6th of the series. Here the work ended, when I left for London, 1827. The views never were published."

Of the two impressions in the Scrapbook, the first state is lightly etched and printed in brown ink, and the second state is more heavily etched and printed in black. The etched title is in Smillie's hand.

Other versions of this subject by Cockburn include *Falls of Montmorency*, n.d., pencil and brown wash (NA I-16); *Picnic at Montmorency*, n.d., watercolour (ROM 940x27.2); and *The Falls of Montmorency (Quebec in the Distance)*, 1833, aquatint, published by Ackerman & Co., London. The first work cited is closest to Smillie's etching.

REFERENCES: Scrapbook, nos. 57 (i/iii, proof before letters), 58 (ii/iii, proof before letters on calendered wove paper); Pilgrimage, p. 20.

55f. Pigeon Net c. 1829
Etching on wove paper; 10.6 × 12.7 (plate)
Inscribed in plate l.c. *Pigeon net.*

James Smillie's manuscript note attached to the Scrap-

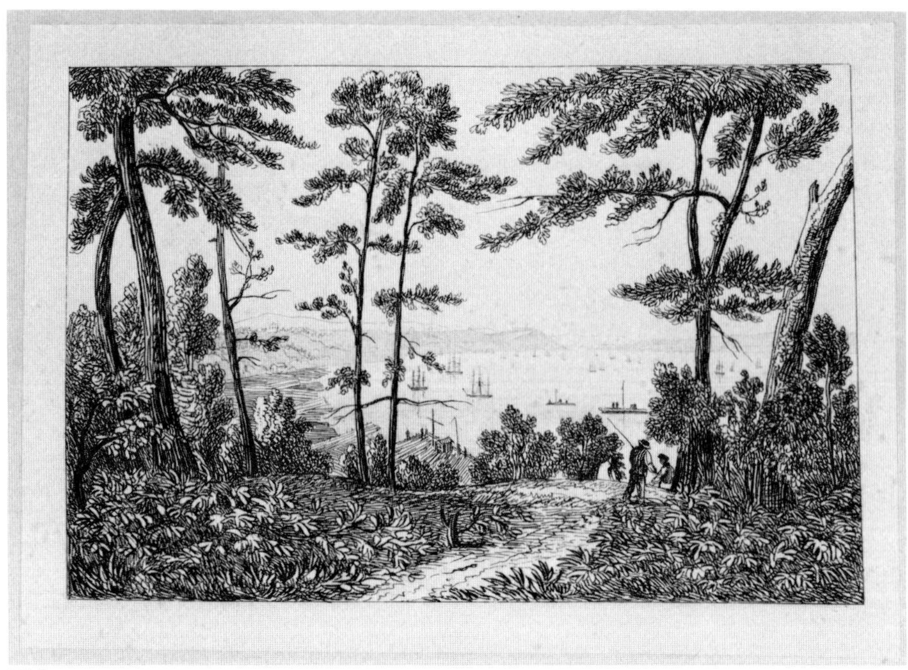

55d

book describes the print, "No. 56. Pigeon net. etched by Col. Cockburn R.A. 5th of the series." The proof before letters in the Supplementary Scrapbook is inscribed in pencil "Pigeon net. / J.S. 1829." The only known work by Cockburn similar to the etching is *Pigeon Net*, 20 September 1829, watercolour, pen and brown and black ink (NA I-75).

The plate measurement is taken from Smillie's proof impression. All other impressions examined have been trimmed within the plate. Some impressions of this subject are watermarked "C Anse[ll] / 1822."

REFERENCES: Scrapbook, no. 56; Supplementary Scrapbook, no. 9 (proof before letters); Pilgrimage, p. 20.

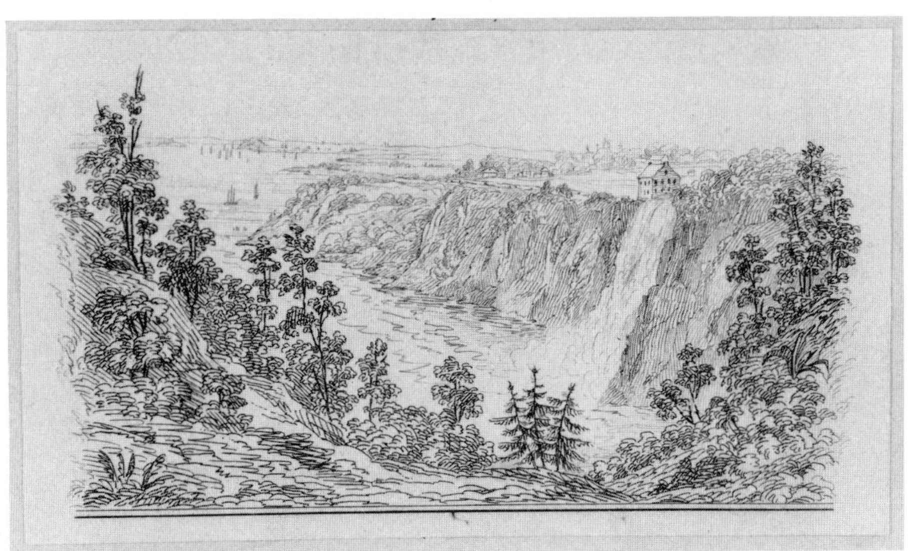

55e

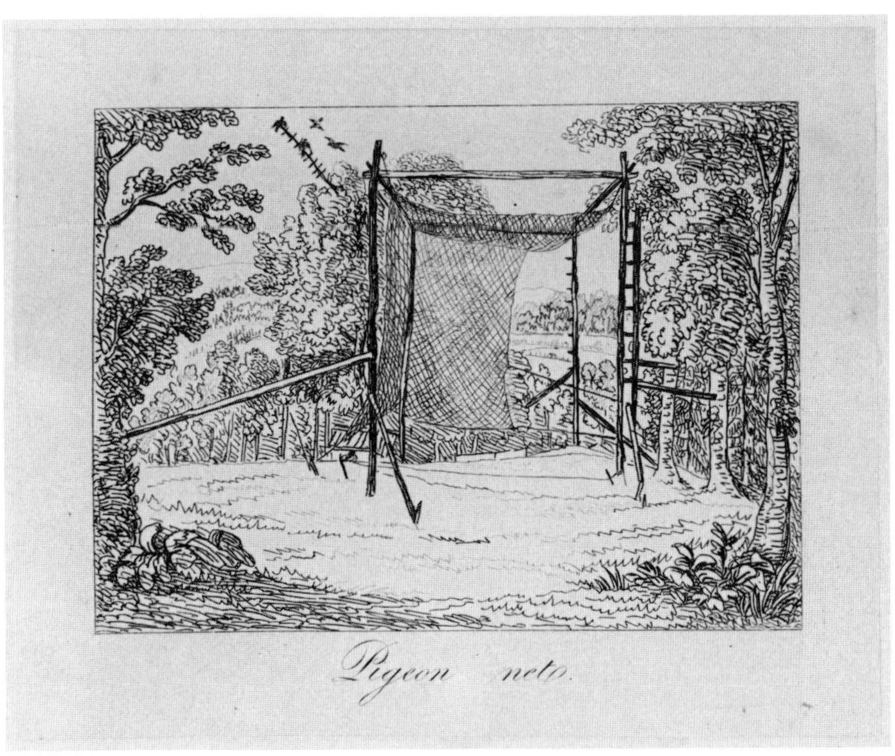

55f

56. London and Its Vicinity 1828

James Smillie, Jun., *London and Its Vicinity to the Extent of About Twenty Miles* (Quebec: D. & J. Smillie, August 1828); set of five etched views stitched with title wrapper; 28.9 × 22.7 (each sheet)

While James Smillie was studying engraving under Andrew Wilson in Edinburgh in 1828, he and fellow pupil Colin Campbell were set to etch copies of engravings from *Views in London and Its Vicinity* by George Cooke (1781–1834). Cooke's publication was issued in twelve parts between 1826 and 1834 and contained forty-nine engravings after drawings by various established artists.

With an eye for business, Smillie decided that these study pieces might sell in Quebec. He bought two plates from Campbell, added three of his own, and had them printed with a title wrapper by the firm of James & John Johnstone (Appendix E). All five plates were inscribed with the month of execution and as being engraved by James Smillie, Jr. Some impressions were printed on wove paper, others on chine collée. A Canadian publication line and date were added from a second plate, possibly after Smillie's return to Canada.

Smillie wasted no time in publicizing this venture. He arrived back in Quebec on a Saturday, and by Monday morning his advertisement appeared in the *Quebec Mercury*. He announced that this was to be the first of a series of sets of such prints, but lack of response ended the project. An editorial in the *Quebec Mercury* recommended that Smillie "turn his attention to views of Canada; any landscape painter or draughtsman might put his work into Mr. Smillie's hands with every certainty of justice being done to them."

The order of the plates in this catalogue is taken from the stitched set in the National Gallery of Canada, Ottawa.

REFERENCES: Scrapbook, nos. 61, 63–67; Supplementary Scrapbook, no. 14; Pilgrimage, pp. 25–26; Ray

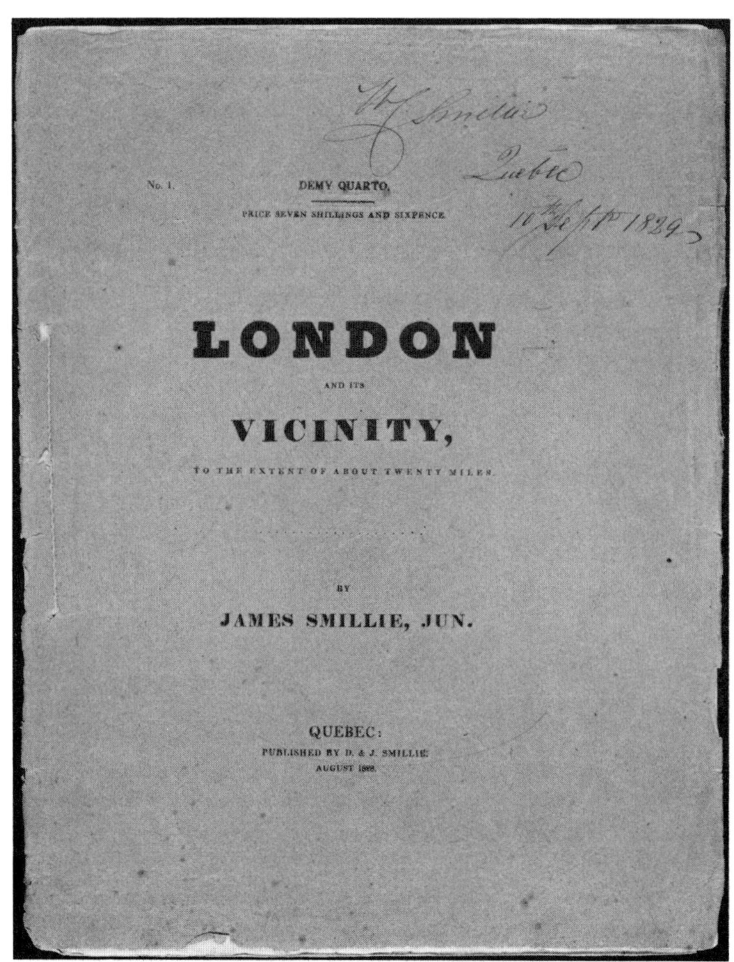

No. 1. DEMY QUARTO,

PRICE SEVEN SHILLINGS AND SIXPENCE.

LONDON

AND ITS

VICINITY,

TO THE EXTENT OF ABOUT TWENTY MILES.

BY

JAMES SMILLIE, JUN.

QUEBEC:

PUBLISHED BY D. & J. SMILLIE:

AUGUST 1828.

56a NGC, Rare Book Collection

1976, pp. 22–23; *Quebec Mercury*, 12 August 1828; *Star and Commercial Advertiser*, 13 August 1828; *La Bibliothèque canadienne* 7, no. 3 (août 1828): 118–119.

56a. London and Its Vicinity (wrapper) 1828
Letterpress printing on buff laid paper; 28.9 × 22.7 (sheet)
Inscribed in plate *NO. 1. / DEMY QUARTO. / PRICE SEVEN SHILLINGS AND SIXPENCE. / LONDON / AND ITS / VICINITY, / TO THE EXTENT OF ABOUT TWENTY MILES. / BY / JAMES SMILLIE, JUN. / QUEBEC: / PUBLISHED BY D. & J. SMILLIE. AUGUST 1828.*

James Smillie's manuscript note attached to the Scrapbook describes this venture.

No. 61. Cover of 1st No. of "Cookes London", being practice plates while under Mr Wilsons tuition. I had 150 sets printed in Edinburgh with the hope that I might dispose of them in Quebec on my return, but it was an utter failure.

References: Scrapbook, no. 61; Pilgrimage, p. 26.

56b. Hornsey Church 1828
Etching on wove paper or chine collée; 12.6 × 16.0 (Plate 1), 13.2 × 16.4 (Plate 2)
Inscribed in plates l.r. *Eng^{d} by Ja^{s} Smillie Junr*; l.l. *Edinburgh. Jany 1828.*; l.c. *HORNSEY CHURCH / Vicinity of London. / Quebec Published by D. & J. Smillie. Augst 1828.*
State I: Incomplete
State II: Completed (illustrated)

James Smillie comments on this work in a manuscript note attached to the Scrapbook, "No. 63—William Miller, the famous landscape engraver, recommended me to adopt this work as the foundation of my study. He considered Cookes etchings unequaled." William Miller (1796–1882), a Scottish engraver and painter in watercolour, had studied under George Cooke in London.

References: Scrapbook, no. 63 (imp. on wove paper); Supplementary Scrapbook, no. 14 (imp. on chine collée); Pilgrimage, p. 25.

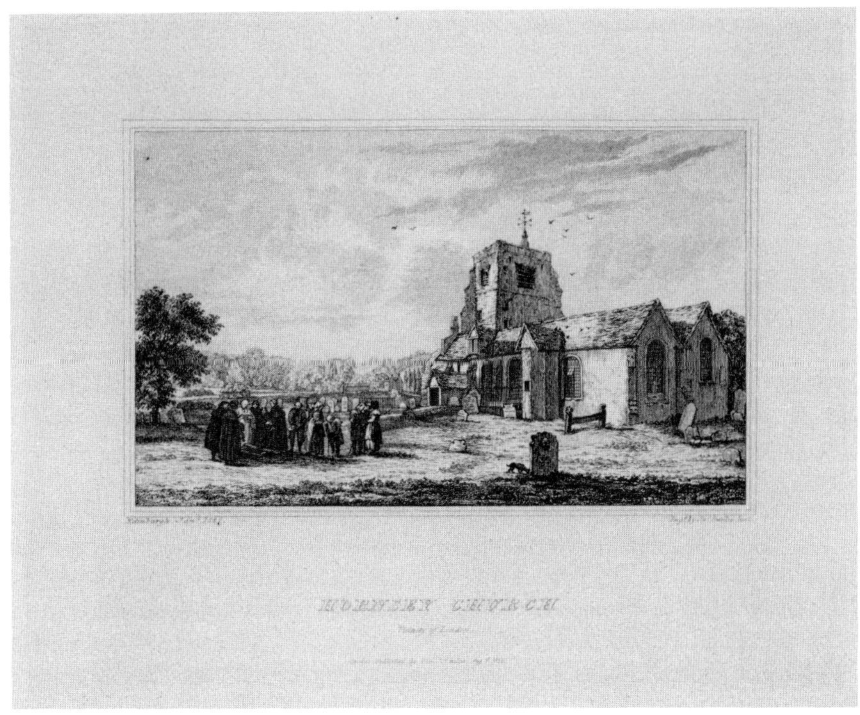

56b NGC, Rare Book Collection

56c. Ship Breaking opposite Wapping 1828
Etching on wove paper; 12.7 × 17.8 (Plate 1), 13.4 × 18.4 (Plate 2)
Inscribed in plates l.r. *Engraved by Ja^s. Smillie Junr.*; l.l. *Edinburgh March 1828.*; l.c. *SHIP BREAKING / opposite Wapping. / Quebec Published by D. & J. Smillie. August 1828.*
State I: Sky blank
State II: Sky completed (illustrated)

REFERENCES: Scrapbook, no. 64 (2 imps.; States I, II); Pilgrimage, p. 26.

56d. Sessions House, Clerkenwell Green 1828
Etching on wove paper; 14.0 × 20.0 (Plate 1), 14.5 × 20.4 (Plate 2)
Inscribed in plates l.r. *Engrav'd by James Smillie Junr.* ~; l.l. *Edinburgh April 1828.*; l.c. *SESSIONS HOUSE / Clerkenwell Green. / Quebec Published by D. & J. Smillie August 1828.*
State I: Sign at left background unlettered
State II: Sign lettering completed (illustrated)

This view is one of the subjects etched by Colin Campbell.

REFERENCES: Scrapbook, no. 66 (2 imps.; States I, II); Pilgrimage, p. 26.

56e. Tooting Church, Vicinity of London 1828
Etching on wove paper; 14.2 × 18.5 (Plate 1), 15.0 × 18.9 (Plate 2)
Inscribed in plates l.r. *Engrav'd by James Smillie Junr.*; l.l. *Edinburgh May 1828.*; l.c. *TOOTING CHURCH / Vicinity of London. / Quebec Published by D. & J. Smillie August 1828.*
State I: Sky blank
State II: Sky completed (illustrated)

This view was etched by Colin Campbell.

REFERENCES: Scrapbook, no. 65 (2 imps.; States I, II); Pilgrimage, p. 26.

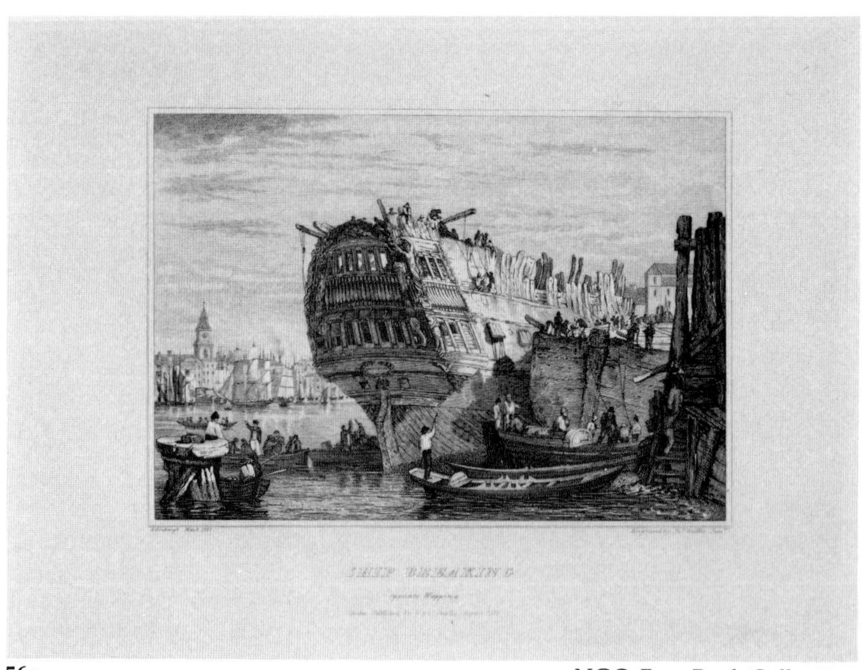

56c NGC, Rare Book Collection

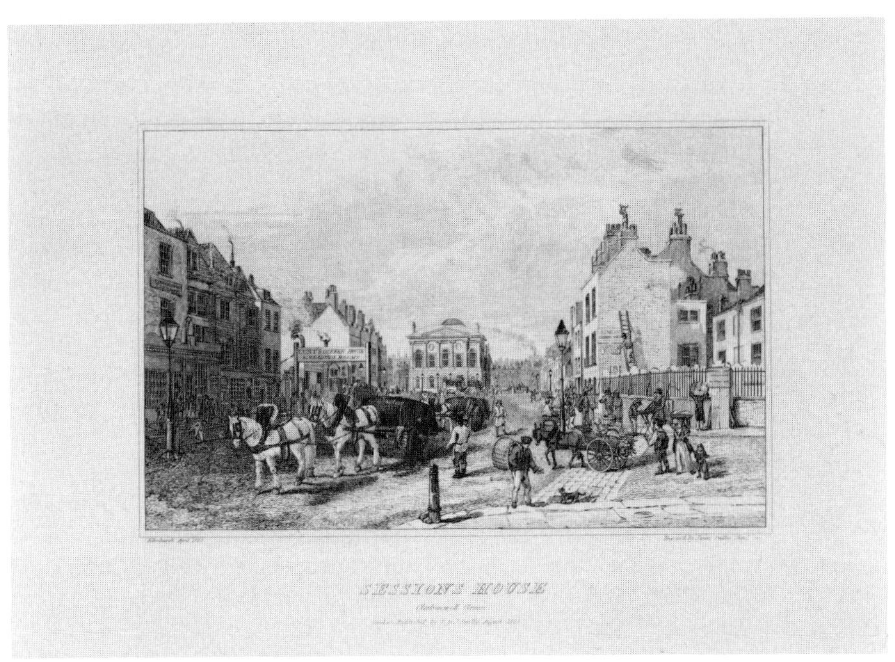

56d NGC, Rare Book Collection

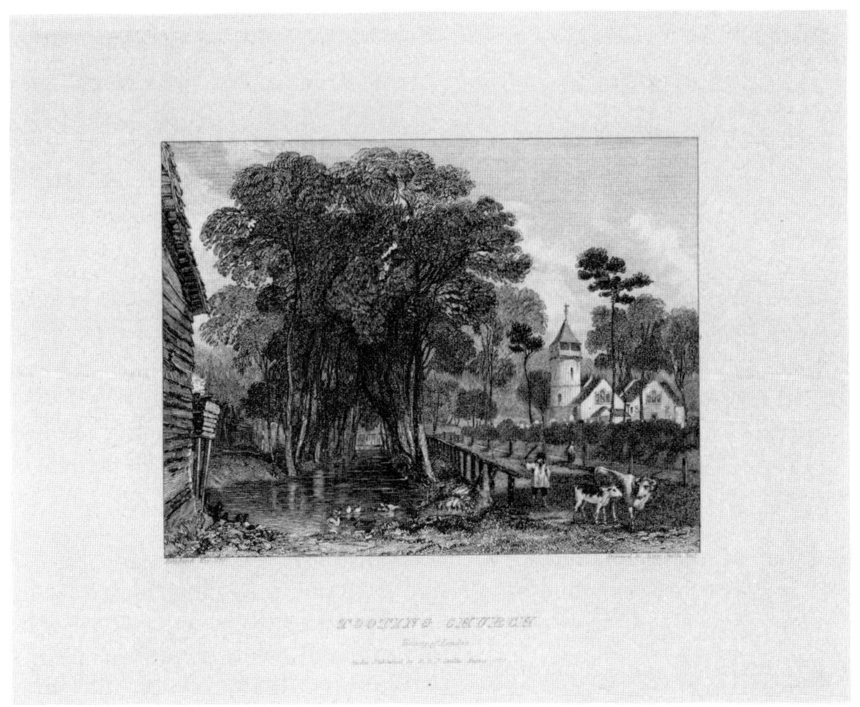

56e NGC, Rare Book Collection

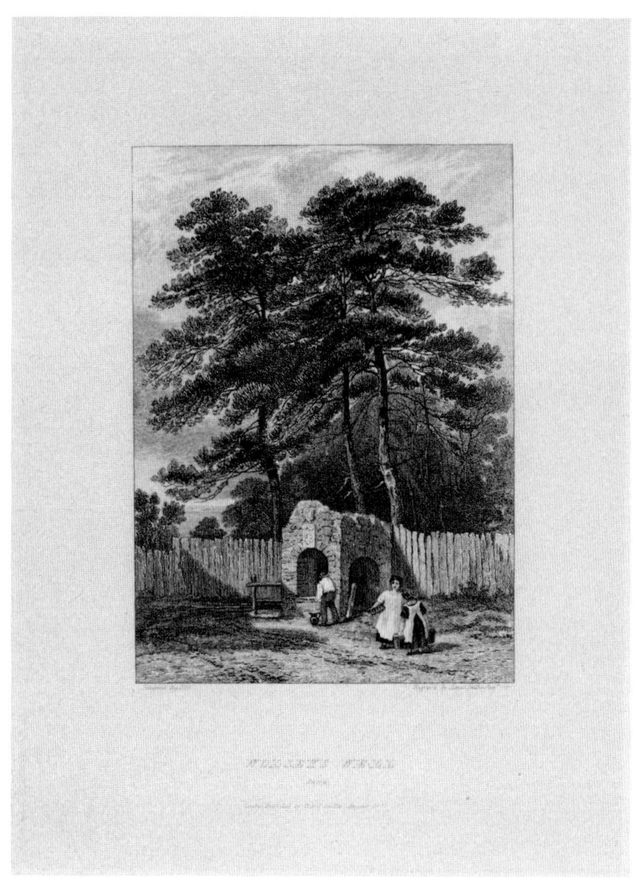

56f NGC, Rare Book Collection

56f. Wolsey's Well, Surrey 1828
Etching on wove paper; 18.2 × 13.5 (Plate 1), 18.7 × 14.0 (Plate 2)
Inscribed in plates l.r. *Engrav'd by James Smillie Jun.r ~*; l.r. *Edinburgh May 1828*; l.c. *WOLSEY'S WELL / Surry. / Quebec Published by D. & J. Smillie. August 1828.*; l.r., in subject, *J. Smillie*
State I: Incomplete
State II: Completed (illustrated)

REFERENCES: Scrapbook, no. 67 (2 imps.; States I, II); Pilgrimage, p. 26.

57. Letterhead with Angel 1828
Graphite on wove paper; 12.0 × 9.8
Inscribed in pencil u.c., over vignette, *To my Mother*; in ink l.r. *Edinburgh, Feby. 10th 1828*; l.l. *My Dear Mother*, [remaining text cut off]

REFERENCES: Scrapbook, no. 62.

58. Sir William Temple 1828
Etching and engraving on wove paper; 15.1 × 11.7 (sheet)
Inscribed in plate l.c. *Sir Wm Temple / Engraved by J. Smillie Jun.r, Edin.r, Feby. 1828.*

While taking instruction with Andrew Wilson in Edinburgh, James Smillie chose to copy portrait engravings as well as landscape compositions, so that he could choose to specialize in either field of subject matter. He had this portrait and Cat. No. 60 printed by James & John Johnstone of Edinburgh (Appendix E). His proof impression before letters is inscribed in pencil "Sir William Temple—Edinburgh 1828—with Andrew Wilson, No. 13 Hill Street, Edinburgh / unfinished."

Sir William Temple (1628–1699) was a British politician and author. The British Museum catalogue lists nine engraved portraits of him, all after a painting by Sir Peter Lely (NPGL 152).

REFERENCES: Scrapbook, no. 72; Supplementary Scrapbook, no. 8 (proof before letters); Pilgrimage, p. 25; O'Donoghue 1914, vol. 4, pp. 257, 405; Yung and Pettman 1981.

59. Quebec Fire Assurance Company 1828
Etching and engraving on wove paper; 17.0 × 25.0 (sheet)
Inscribed in plate u.c. *BY THE Quebec Fire Assurance COMPANY*; l.c. *Ja.s Smillie Jun.r, Quebec. / Incorporated by Act of Parliament.*; l.l. *Edinburgh March 1828*

James Smillie's manuscript note attached to the Scrapbook records, "No. 69. This is an order I took from Quebec and engraved in Mr. Wilson's establishment. This with the portraits No. 71 & 72 [Cat. Nos. 58, 60] filled up my engagement." This plate was printed by the firm of James & John Johnstone of Edinburgh (Appendix E).

Smillie had etched another policy heading for the same assurance company c. 1826 (Cat. No. 43). The 1828 policy heading shows a different building façade and adds figures to the foreground, which are reminiscent of those in genre sketches by John Crawford Young (1788–c. 1859). The building fronted on two streets in Lower Town, being located at 44 Sault-au-Matelot and 38 St. Peter Street.

REFERENCES: Scrapbook, no. 69; QD 1822.

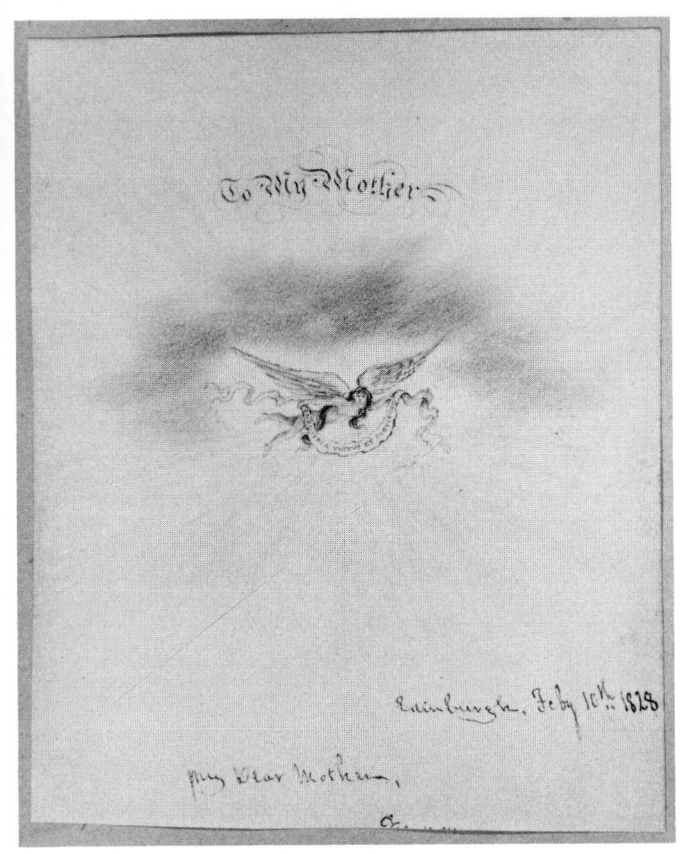
To My Mother
My Dear Mother,

57

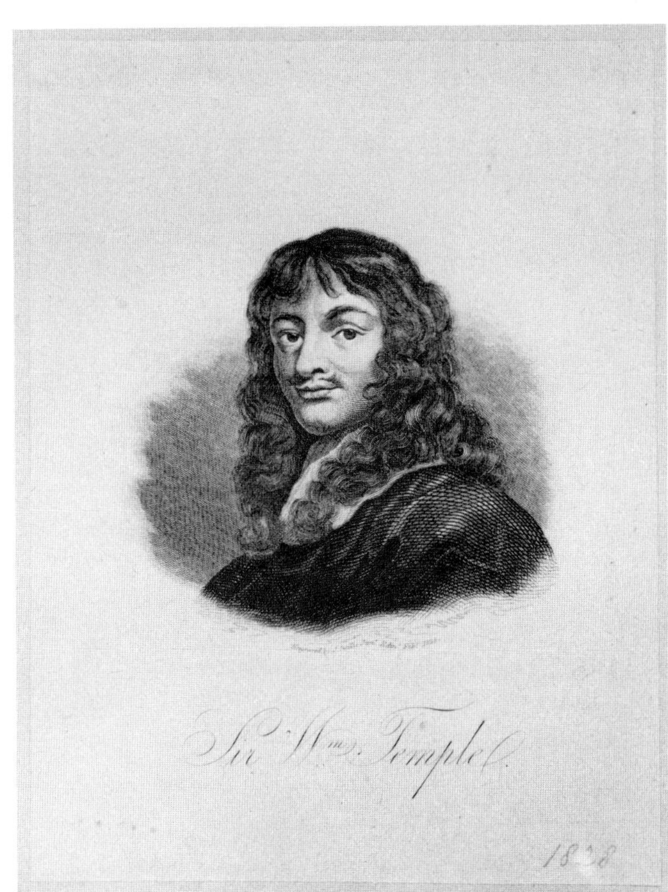
Sir Wm Temple

58

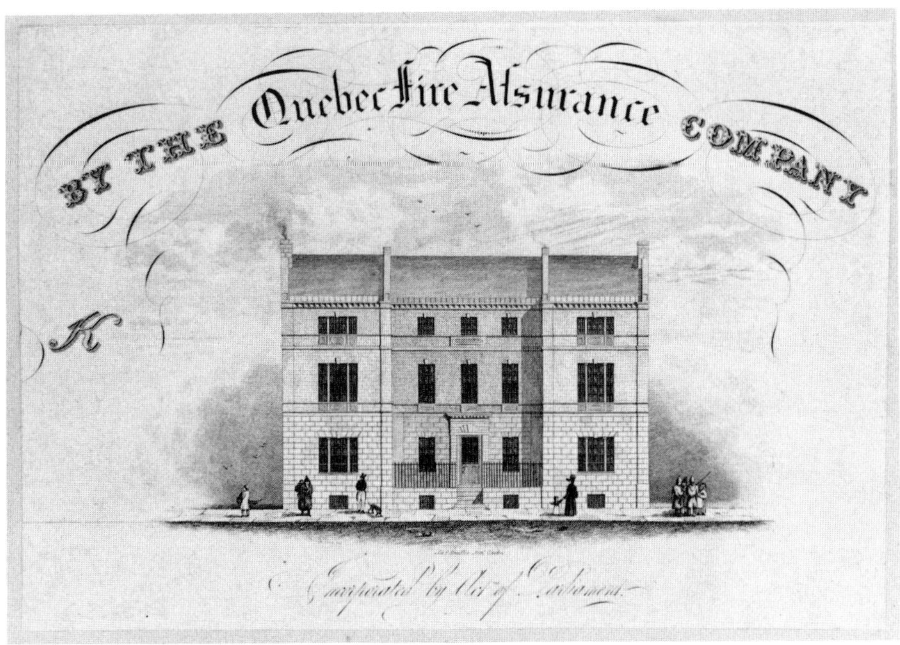
BY THE Quebec Fire Assurance COMPANY
Incorporated by Act of Parliament

59

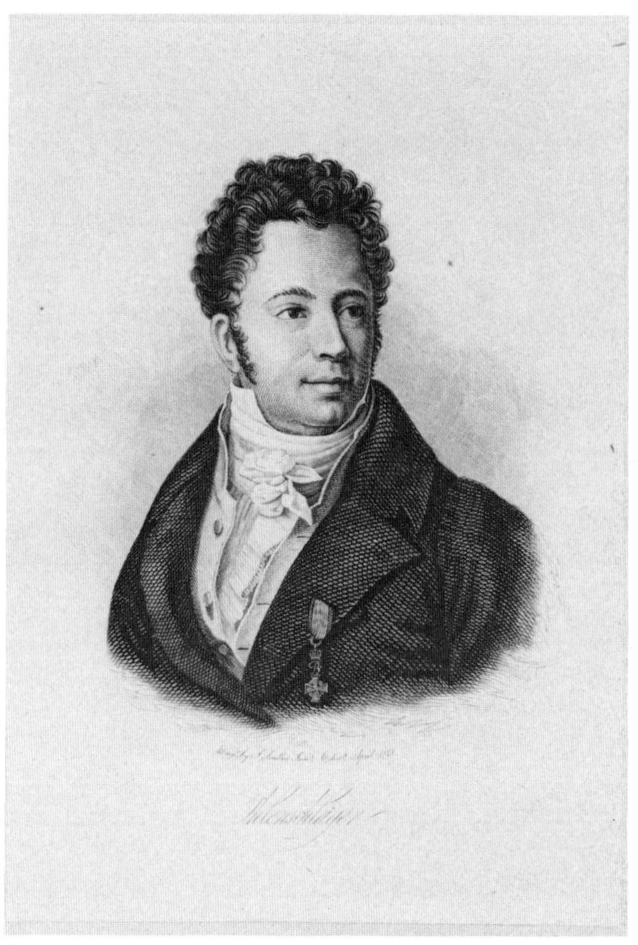

60

60. Adam Gottlob Öhlenschläger 1828
Etching and engraving on wove paper; 15.8 × 11.2 (plate)
Inscribed in plate l.c. *Eng.d by J. Smillie Jun.r, Edin.r, April 1828. / Ohlenschlager*

James Smillie copied a print based on the oil portrait by Friedrich Carl Gröger (1766–1838) in the Nationalhistoriske Museum, Frederiksborg, Denmark. This plate was printed by the firm of James & John Johnstone of Edinburgh (Appendix E). See also Cat. No. 58.

Adam Gottlob Öhlenschläger (1779–1850) was a Danish poet and one of the pioneers of the romantic movement.

REFERENCES: Scrapbook, nos. 70 (unfinished proof before letters), 71; Pilgrimage, p. 26.

61. William Smillie 1828
Black crayon, heightened with white, on buff wove paper; 31.8 × 26.9
Inscribed in pencil l.l. *Mr. William Smillie / uncle to my father.*; l.r. *Edin.r, May 1828 / JSmillie Jun.r, Del.t*

This small portrait, the most accomplished of James Smillie's drawings, may have been copied from another artist's work. An Uncle William living in Scotland is mentioned in family letters in 1827 (Appendix L.4).

REFERENCES: Scrapbook, between nos. 71 and 72.

62. Thomas Drysdale Trade Card 1828
Etching on wove paper; 5.6 × 7.8 (plate)
Inscribed in plate c. *Thos Drysdale / Watch Maker & Jeweler / 4 Lothian Street / Edinburgh / Every description of Watches & Clocks cleaned & repaired.*

In his autobiography, James Smillie mentions Thomas Drysdale (act. 1821–1849) as a friend who gave him some lettering commissions in Edinburgh in 1828. Smillie's brother David also mentioned Drysdale as an old family friend (Appendix L.8). When Smillie's Uncle

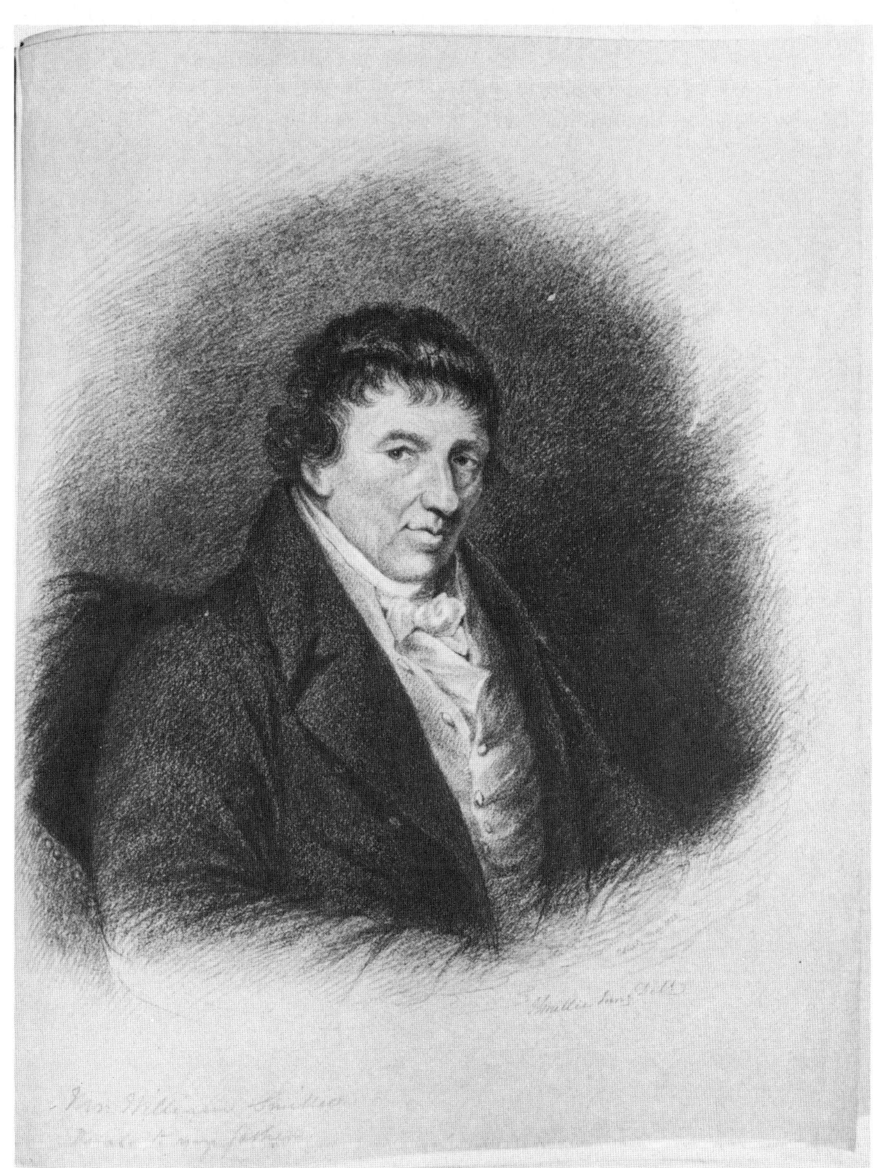

61

Thos. Drysdale
Watch-Maker & Jeweller
4. Lothian Street
Edinburgh
Every description of Watches & Clocks cleaned & repaired.
1828.

62

James died in the fire that consumed his house at 24 Mountain Street, Quebec, in February 1841, newspaper accounts refer to one Thomas Drysdale as his son-in-law and a jeweller, who also lived on Mountain Street. Drysdale is probably the same person as the watchmaker listed as active in Quebec from 1844 to 1849. When Smillie visited Quebec City in July 1873, he was not able to see his cousin Mrs. Brown (formerly Mrs. Drysdale [Appendix L.17]), but met her sons, Walter and Thomas Drysdale.

REFERENCES: Scrapbook, no. 68; Pilgrimage, p. 26; Quebec Mercury, 4, 6 February 1841; Langdon 1966, 1976; James David Smillie Diaries (arch. mat.), microfilm roll 2850.

63. Man's Head c. 1828
Etching and graphite on japan paper; 5.7 × 4.6 (plate)
Inscribed in pencil l.l. *J. Smillie Sc*

REFERENCES: Scrapbook, no. 55.

64. Cape Diamond, Quebec c. 1828
Etching on calendered wove paper; 15.7 × 11.6 (image), 19.3 × 13.9 (sheet)
Inscribed in plate l.c. *CAPE DIAMOND, QUEBEC, / From Sillery Cove.*; l.l. *M. Y. del*.; l.r. *Jayess sc.*

In a manuscript note in his Scrapbook, James Smillie records the following:

Nos. 74, 75, & 76 [read 77 instead of 76]. A new series in a more advanced style than the former, engraved previous to my going to Edinburgh. The drawings were furnished by Col. Cockburn and Capt. Young, both of the Royal Artillery. The fate of this series was like that of their predecessors, they never were published. When I removed to New York I put the plates into the hands of an Auctioneer who lost them, and in a year or two after he allowed me five dollars a piece for them! 1829. Royal Gurley, Auctioneer 1830.

In his autobiography Smillie notes that James Pattison Cockburn (1779–1847) urged him to publish views of Canada, and Cockburn and John Crawford Young (1788–c. 1859) were apparently prepared to provide

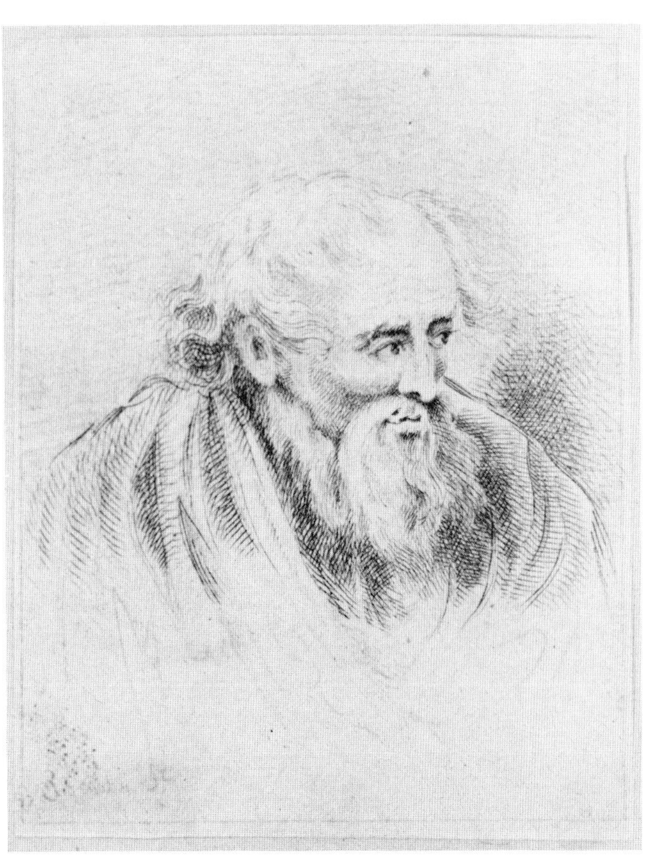

63

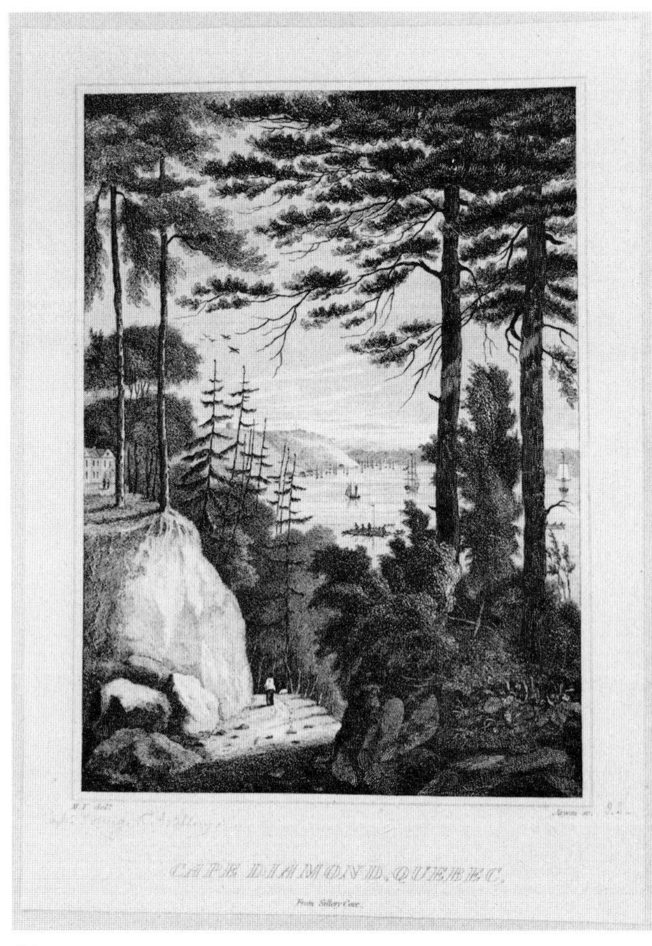

64

him with drawings. The project fell through, although Smillie worked on three plates and some prints were pulled (Cat. Nos. 64–66). The etching *Cape Diamond, Quebec*, after Young, is listed in the Millen Collection. The etching *Quebec from the Old Mill* (Cat. No. 66), after Cockburn, is found in various collections (MTL D1-100d; NYPL, Mss. Division, Emmet Collection, 4553).

Both Cockburn and Young abbreviated their names to initials. In keeping with this spirit of anonymity, Smillie has used "Jayess" to stand for his initials. He explained this cipher by annotating his Scrapbook impression in pencil on the lower left "Capt Young, R. Artillery." and on the lower right "J.S."

REFERENCES: Scrapbook, no. 74; Supplementary Scrapbook, no. 10 (proof before letters); Pilgrimage, p. 27; Godenrath 1938, no. 69.

65. Castle St. Lewis c. 1828
Etching on calendered wove paper; 15.5 × 11.5 (image), 18.8 × 13.9 (sheet)
Inscribed in plate l.c. *CASTLE, St LEWIS, QUEBEC, / From the south west end of Champlain St.*; l.l. *M.Y. del.*; l.r. *Smillie Sc.*; on house-sign within subject *J. Golin / House & Ship / Joiner*; l.r., on broadside within subject, . . . *Captn / Young / Del*

A brown wash sketch of this subject by John Crawford Young was formerly in the collection of the Earl of Dalhousie (NGC 29214.24). From his new posting, Young wrote to James Smillie at Quebec, and his letter illustrates the care that went into this collaboration.

Isle aux Noix
30th Novr. 28
I dont like the prospectus you sent me. I should write one & send it in the course of a few days—however it is quite time enough—the plates of the first series shd at least be ready to be exhibited, before an appeal is made to the public. I was very much pleased with the first Plate it does you infinite credit. Let this stimulate you to further execution & remember the success of the work will greatly depend on the talent exhibited in the first number—so dont spare care and attention to have the plates executed with beauty & spirit & be extremely careful to cut the figures with ease, grace, & bold effect. The general view of Quebec will *require all your skill*.

I would wish you to send me impressions of it, & the one you are now at *in every stage of advancement* as I can then correct any thing I may not like. Enclose them in an envelope and request either Col. Couper or Sir Noel Hill to forward them to me. Dont fail to send me one of the view from above Wolfe's Cove. I hope you have made every arrangement respecting the press & paper to be sent out by the first spring ships. I shall send some more views in the course of a week or two. I hope to have good account of your diligence & that all the plates are well advanced if not finished.
Very truly J.C.Y.

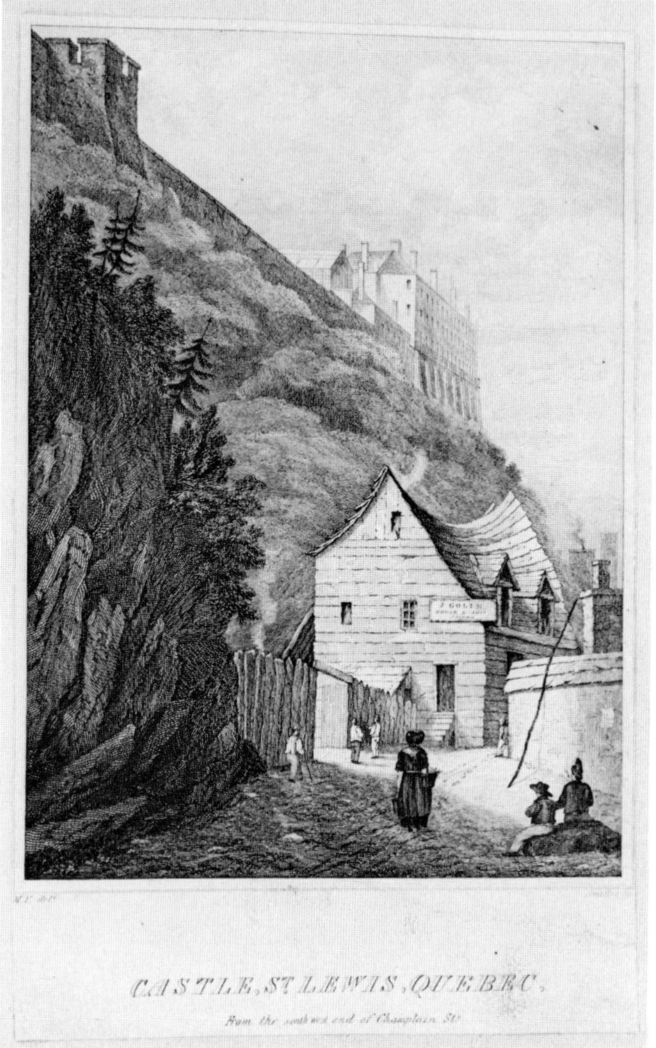

65

See also Cat. No. 64. At this date Lieutenant Colonel George Couper was aide-de-camp to Lord Dalhousie, and Sir Thomas Noel Hill (1784–1832) was deputy adjutant general at Quebec.

REFERENCES: Scrapbook, nos. 75, 73 (letter); Pilgrimage, p. 27.

66. Quebec from the Old Mill c. 1828–1830
Etching on chine collée or wove paper; 11.4 × 16.2 (image), 19.5X 25.9 (sheet)
Inscribed in plate l.c. *QUEBEC, FROM THE OLD MILL, / River St Charles.*; l.l. *J.C. del.*; l.r. *Jayess sc.*

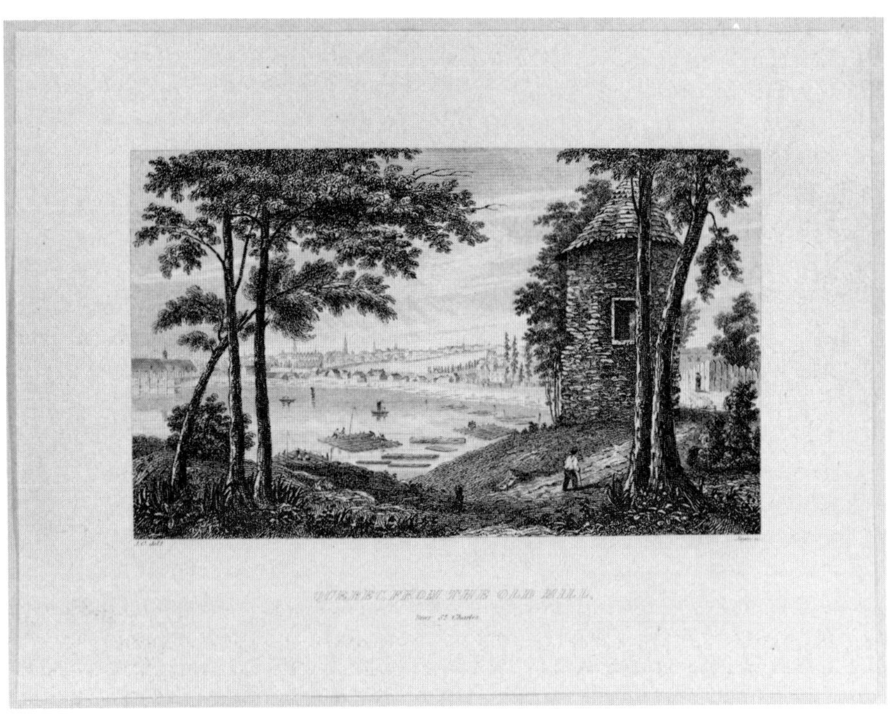

66

Watercolours of this subject by James Pattison Cockburn include *Quebec from the Round Tower on the Saint Charles River above Dorchester Bridge*, n.d., sepia, pen, and ink (NA C-40012); *Quebec from the Round Tower on the Saint Charles River above Dorchester Bridge*, n.d., watercolour (ROM 953.131.6); and *Quebec from the Saint Charles River*, 1832, watercolour (NA 1947-5). The first work cited is the closest to James Smillie's etching.

A clipping from the *Star and Commercial Advertiser* of 24 April 1830, mounted in the Scrapbook on the same page as Cat. No. 64, describes an extensive publication plan between Cockburn and Smillie.

Mr. Smillie, Junior, the young gentleman who long ago gave proof of eminent future abilities as an engraver, and who lately established his claim to distinguished ability by the publication of the *Convent Gate of Palestrina* [etched in New York in 1830 after a painting by Robert W. Weir (1803–1889)], has been sometime engaged on some etchings of views of Lower Canada and particularly of the Vicinity of Quebec, drawn by Col. Cockburn, commanding the Royal Artillery in the Canadas. The original of these views are in water colours and in the elegant taste of Col. Cockburn, already well known as the painter and writer of some valuable descriptions and views of Switzerland and other places, which were published in London by the first engravers and Lithographers. Several of these etchings are already finished. The text by Col. Cockburn is in preparation and about forty of the etchings will, it is supposed, be ready for publication in two or three months.

Mr. Smillie is also engaged on engravings of the New Catholic Church of Montreal, drawn by O'Kill [Cat. No. 74].

REFERENCES: Scrapbook, no. 77; Supplementary Scrapbook, no. 7; Pilgrimage, p. 27; *Star and Commercial Advertiser*, 24 April 1830.

67. Rocks and Fossils of Lower Canada 1829
Four etchings

James Smillie etched illustrations of rocks and fossils on four separate copper plates. These were printed on one sheet (43.0 cm × 27.0 cm), for binding with "Report of the Commissioners for Exploring the Saguenay" in the 1829 *Journals of the Legislative Assembly of Lower Canada*. The plates illustrate the report by Lieutenant F. H. Baddeley, R.E. (act. 1821–1831), entitled "Geognostical Section through a part of the Saguenay Country."

In April 1829 the same plates were issued with an article by Baddeley, "Fossil Organic Remains in the Rocks of Canada," which was published as a pamphlet and sold for five shillings for the benefit of the Quebec Ladies Bazaar Committee. The plates were issued a third time that year as illustrations for another article by Baddeley, entitled "On the geognosy of a part of the Saguenay Country," which appeared in the *Transactions of the Literary and Historical Society of Quebec*.

REFERENCES: Lower Canada, House of Assembly 1829a, Appendix V, 14 January 1829; *Quebec Mercury*, 14 April,

2 May, 14 November 1829; *Literary and Historical Society*, pp. 79–166.

67a. Fossil from Lake St. John 1829
Etching on wove paper; 18.5 × 14.0 (plate)
Inscribed in plate l.c. *AN UNKNOWN FOSSIL ORGANIC REMAIN / from Lake S.t John, Lower Canada. / Drawn the natural size.*; l.l. *L.t P. Ditmus del.t*; l.r. *J. Smillie sc.t*; u.l. *Pl. VIII.*

James Smillie's manuscript note attached to the Scrapbook states, "Nos. 27, 28. These two subjects bear the name of Lieut. P. Ditmus as draughtsman but I engraved them direct from the petrifications [Cat. Nos. 67a–b]."

The *Transactions of the Literary and Historical Society of Quebec* describes the plate.

For the accompanying very accurate drawing of this fossil, (pl. 8.) we are indebted to Lieut. Ditmus, 66th Regt., ample justice to which has been done by the engraver, Mr. Smilie."

The "unknown remain" has been identified by David Rudkin of the Department of Invertebrate Palaeontology, ROM, as the siphuncle of a nautiloid cephalopod, probably an actinocerid.

REFERENCES: Scrapbook, no. 27; Supplementary Scrapbook, no. 2; *Literary and Historical Society*, p. 127.

67b. Gigantic Trilobite 1829
Etching on wove paper; 18.5 × 14.0 (plate)
Inscribed in plate u.c. *GIGANTIC TRILOBITE.*; l.c. from *Lake S.t John, Lower Canada. / Drawn the natural size from the specimen in the writers possession.*; l.l. *L.t P. Ditmus del.t*; l.r. *J. Smillie sculp.t*; u.r. *PL. IX*

This plate is described in *Transactions of the Literary and Historical Society of Quebec*.

The accompanying copper-plate impression is by Mr. Smillie, from another accurate drawing with which we were favoured by Lieut. Ditmus. In both cases the engraver had also the advantage of consulting the specimens.

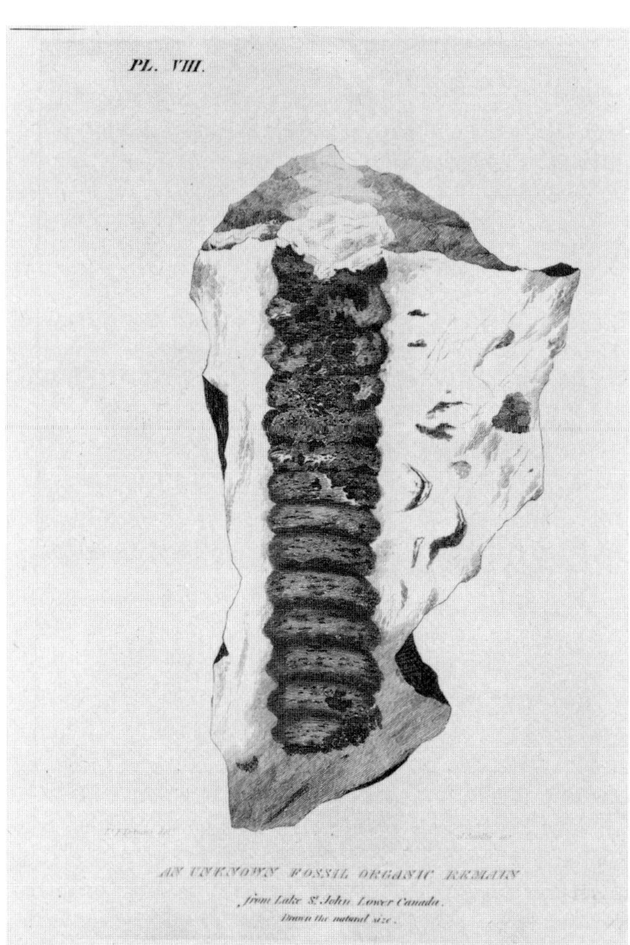

67a

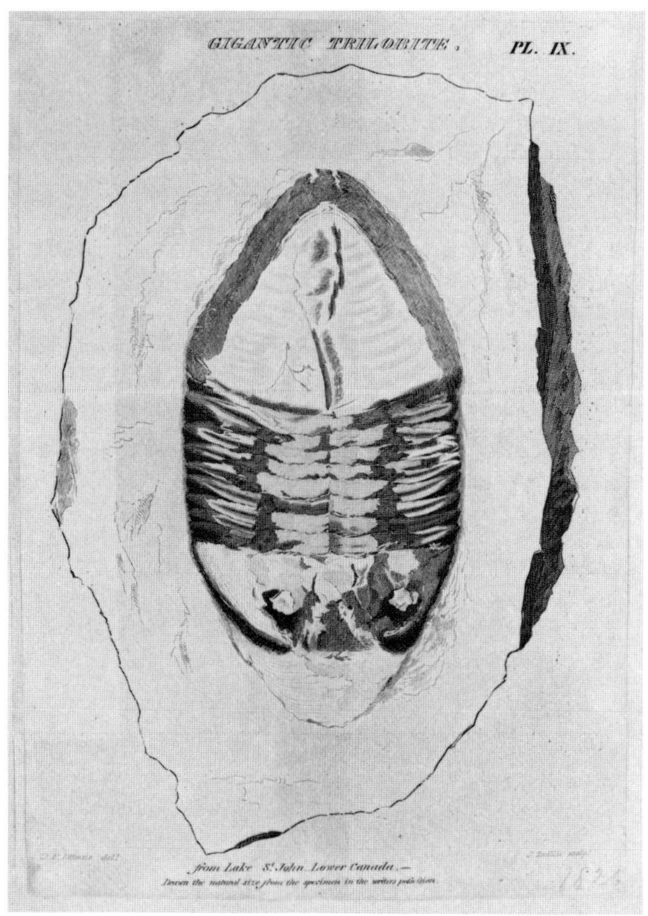

67b

See also Smillie's comments, Cat. No. 67a.

REFERENCES: Scrapbook, no. 28; Supplementary Scrapbook, no. 3; *Literary and Historical Society*, p. 133.

67c. Granite Formations 1829
Etching on wove paper; 22.0 × 13.5 (plate)
Inscribed in plate u.c. *Fig; 1.*; c. *Fig; 2.*; l.c. *Fig; 3.*; u.r. *Pl;6*

67d. Veins in Syenitic Rock 1829
Etching on wove paper; 22.0 × 13.5 (plate)
Inscribed in plate u.c. *Fig; 4.*; c. *Fig; 5.*; l.c. *Fig; 6.*; u.r. *Pl; 7*; in upper and lower figs. *Syenite*

68. Plan of the New Settlements on the River Etchemin 1829
Etching and engraving on wove paper; 23.0 × 33.5 (plate)
Scale: 2½ miles to 1 inch
Inscribed in plate u.l. *PLAN / of the / New Settlements / ON THE RIVER ETCHEMIN. / and the / proposed roads thence to the / R.ᵛ S.ᵗ JOHN. / J. Smillie Jun. sc. Quebec.*

This map is bound with the 1829 *Journals of the House of Assembly of Lower Canada*. It refers to the *Reports of the Special Committee...Relating to Roads and Other Internal Communications...*, 17 December 1828 to 10 March 1829, and especially to the Fourth Report, 11 February 1829, regarding lands on Lake Etchemin. The map was also issued separately in the 1829 *Rapports du comité spécial sur les chemins et autres communications intérieures*.

REFERENCES: Lower Canada, House of Assembly 1829a, 1829c; PAC 1976, vol. 2, p. 309 (B/310, H3/310).

69. Picture of Quebec 1829
Rev. George Bourne, *Picture of Quebec* (D. & J. Smillie, Quebec, 1829), 139 pp.; seven plates and title page vignette drawn and etched by James Smillie, folding plan of Quebec drawn by J. Hamel, surveyor, and printed by P. Desobry's Lithography, New York; 13.0 × 8.9 (each sheet).

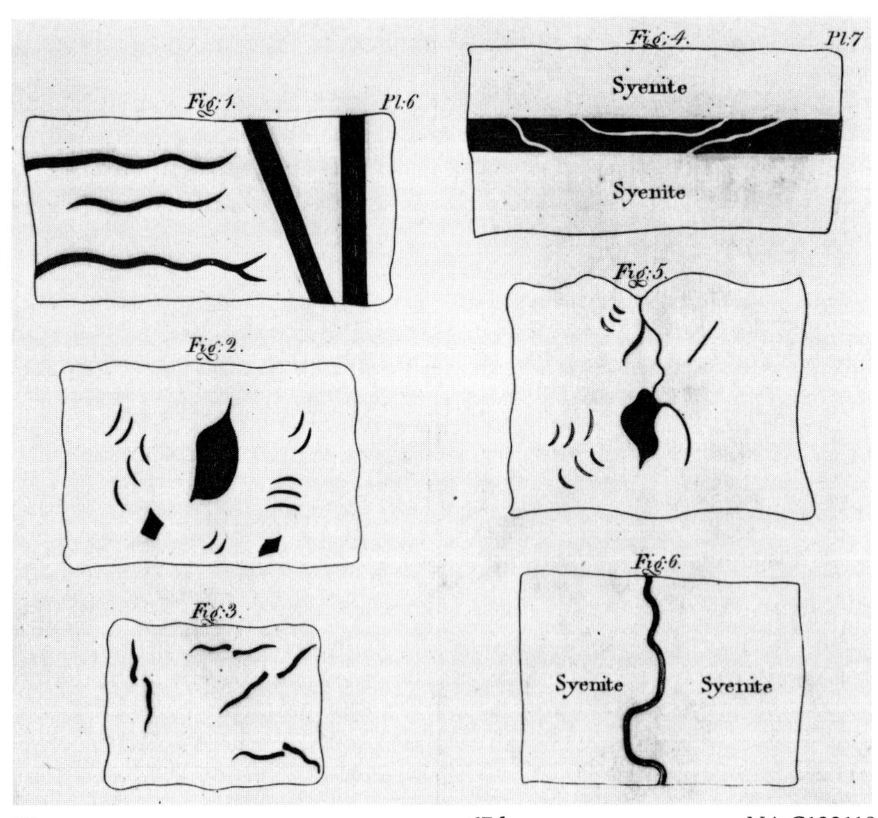

67c 67d NA C122118

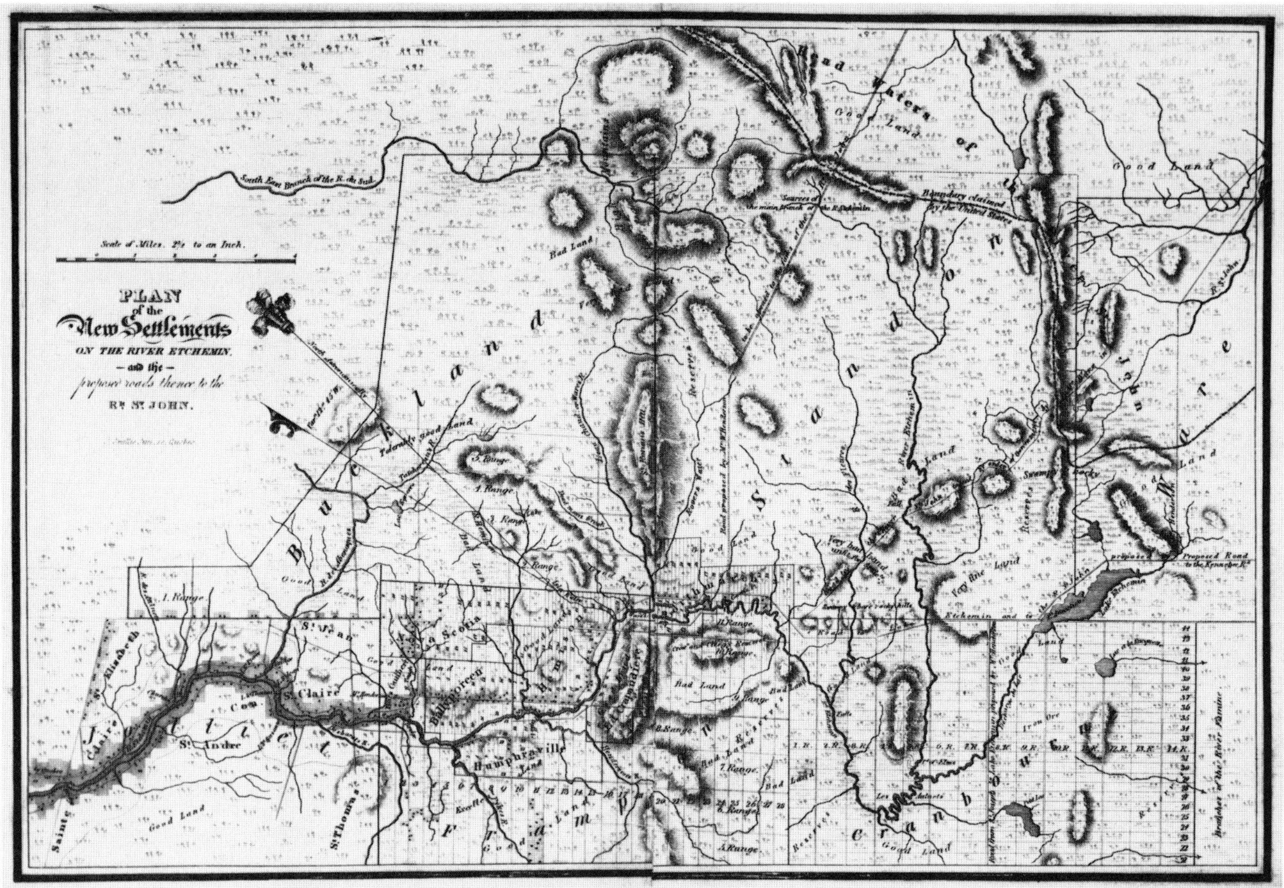

68 NA-CAA 1108

According to his memoirs and papers in the Scrapbook, James Smillie drew and etched this series of guidebook illustrations in Quebec during the early months of 1829 and had them printed in New York City that spring. His records of expenses show that the cover was engraved on wood and that the map was lithographed in New York. The text was printed by Robert Armour of Montreal. Quebec booksellers P. & W. Ruthven paid Bourne and Smillie for 1229 copies of the book, or most of the first edition of 1500. The Ruthven firm also bought the original plates from Bourne for $100, and acquired 500 copies of "impressions in covers" (presumably the etchings, without text), and they published the 1831 edition of *Picture of Quebec*.

Despite a sellout to 1500 subscribers at $1.00 per book, Smillie says that he made little profit after expenses. According to the account sheets that survive, Smillie and his brother David realized a profit of $398.38, for approximately six months' work (Appendices G–K).

With the exception of the *Quebec Driving Club* after William Wallace, Smillie affirms that all the views are his own original work. The view of the New Exchange building, listed with the plates but not included among the etchings, appears as a vignette on the lithographed plan of Quebec.

On 9 July 1829 an advertisement appeared in Quebec newspapers announcing that the guidebook was ready for delivery. On 11 July 1829 the editor of the *Quebec Mercury* noted that

> A very neat little volume has just been published. . . . The graphic part is neatly executed, and reflects great credit on Mr. Smillie. This publication has been got up with great care, and at considerable expense, and will, we hope, meet with such encouragement as may remunerate the publisher;—it is the first work of the kind which has been published in Canada.

Picture of Quebec was a success and went into several editions. It was subsequently published in New York in 1830 by George Melksham Bourne's Depository of Arts and in Quebec in 1831 by P. & W. Ruthven. By 1844 W. Cowan & Son of Quebec had purchased the Smillie plates from Ruthven and reissued seven of them in *The Quebec Guide* (without the title page and omitting the view of Castle St. Lewis from another plate, because by then the building had burned). All of these publishers were Smillie's friends.

REFERENCES: Scrapbook, nos. 80–92; Pilgrimage, p. 27; *La Gazette de Quebec*, 9, 13 July 1829; *Quebec Mercury*, 9, 11 July 1829; *Star and Commercial Advertiser*, 17 July 1830; Staton and Tremaine 1934, no. 1537; Lande 1965, no. 1599.

69a. Picture of Quebec (cover) 1829
Wood engraving on buff wove paper; 13.0 × 8.9 (sheet)
Inscribed u.c., on block, *PICTURE OF QUEBEC.*; l.c. *QUEBEC: / D. & J. SMILLIE, / 1829.*

This wrapper cover, with its vignette of trees, rocks, and waterfall, is found on some copies of the publication, mounted on the outside cover. It was engraved by Alexander Anderson of New York (1775–1870), and printed there, at a cost of three pounds five shillings to James Smillie, as noted in his accounts (Appendices I–J). In subsequent editions, decorative borders and the publisher's name are changed.

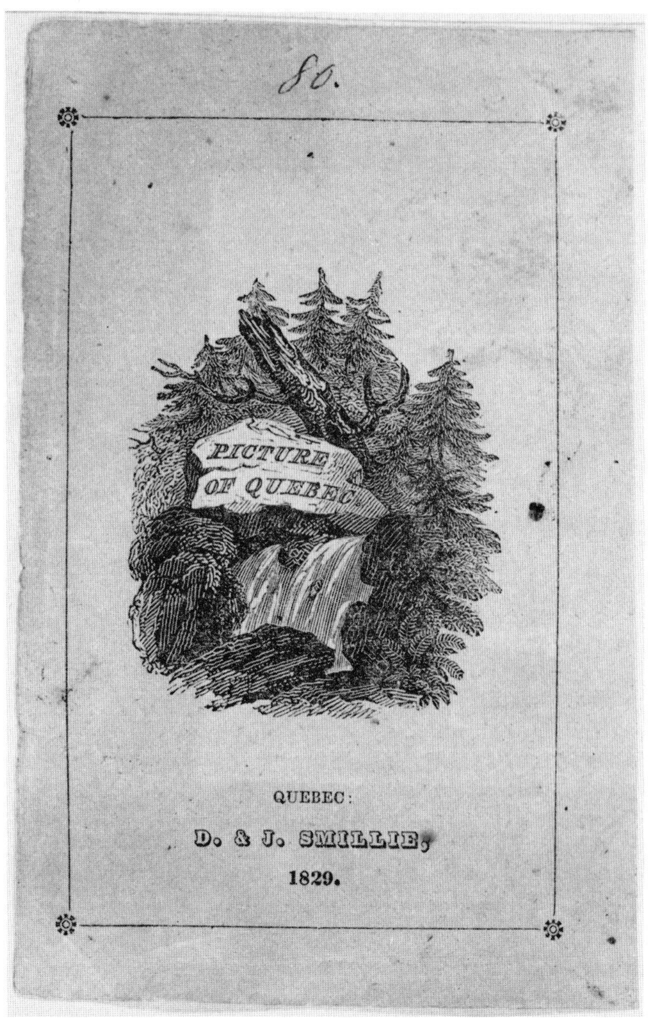

69a

REFERENCES: Scrapbook, no. 80; Pilgrimage, p. 27; Anderson scrapbook vol. 10, p. 97, NYPL; Jane Pomeroy, The Burntcoat Press, communication to authors, concerning projected bibliography of Alexander Anderson's engravings.

69b. Picture of Quebec (title page) 1829
Etching on wove paper; 10.1 × 6.1 (image)
Inscribed in plate u.c. *PICTURE OF QUEBEC.*; l.c. *Drawn & Eng.^{d} by J. Smillie J.^{r} / VITA DIGNA SEMPER PERPETUA. / QUEBEC. MDCCCXIX.*

James Smillie comments, in a manuscript note attached to the Scrapbook, "No. 81. We sold 1500 copies at $1 each. Published by subscription. 1829." See also Cat. No. 69c.

REFERENCES: Scrapbook, no. 81; Pilgrimage, p. 27.

69c. The Picture of Quebec (variant title page) 1829
Etching on laid paper; 12.5 × 7.9 (sheet)
Inscribed in plate u.c. *THE / PICTURE OF QUEBEC; / With Engravings.*; l.c. *Drawn & Engraved by James Smillie Junr / VITA DIGNA SEMPER PERPETUA. / QUEBEC; / 1829.*

This larger and more elegant version of the title page composition was not used in the final publication. It illustrates the same view of the monument to Wolfe and Montcalm as Cat. No. 69b, but here the vignette adds three figures to the foreground and omits the sentry and sentry boxes.

REFERENCES: Scrapbook, no. 82; Pilgrimage, p. 27.

69d. General View of Quebec 1829
Etching on wove paper; 5.4 × 9.2 (image)
Inscribed in plate l.c. *Drawn & Engraved by James Smillie Junr~ / QUEBEC.*

This plate faces the title page and is the most ambitious view in the publication. James Smillie singled it out when describing *Picture of Quebec* in "A Pilgrimage."

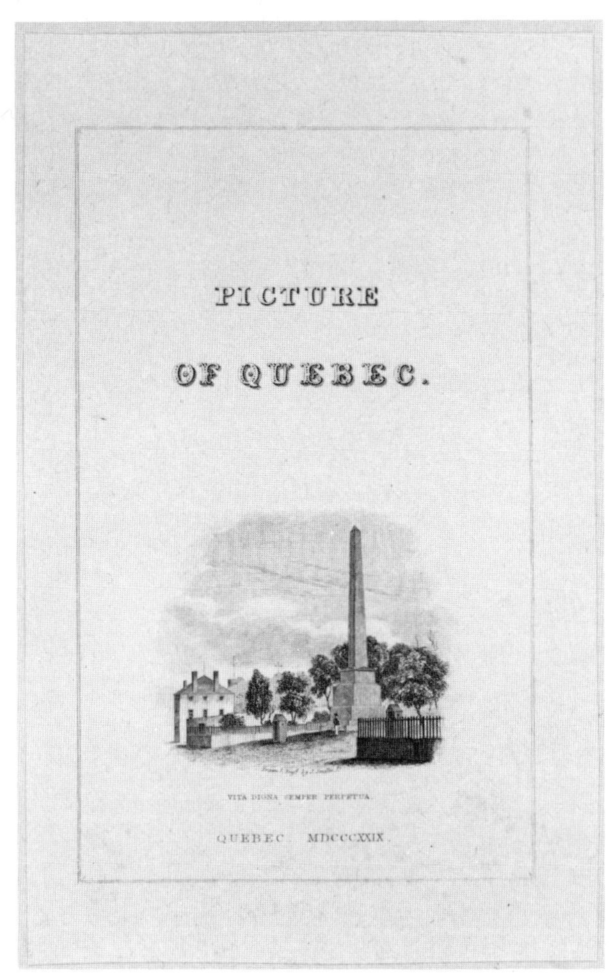
PICTURE
OF QUEBEC.
VITA DIGNA SEMPER PERPETUA
QUEBEC MDCCCXXIX.

69b

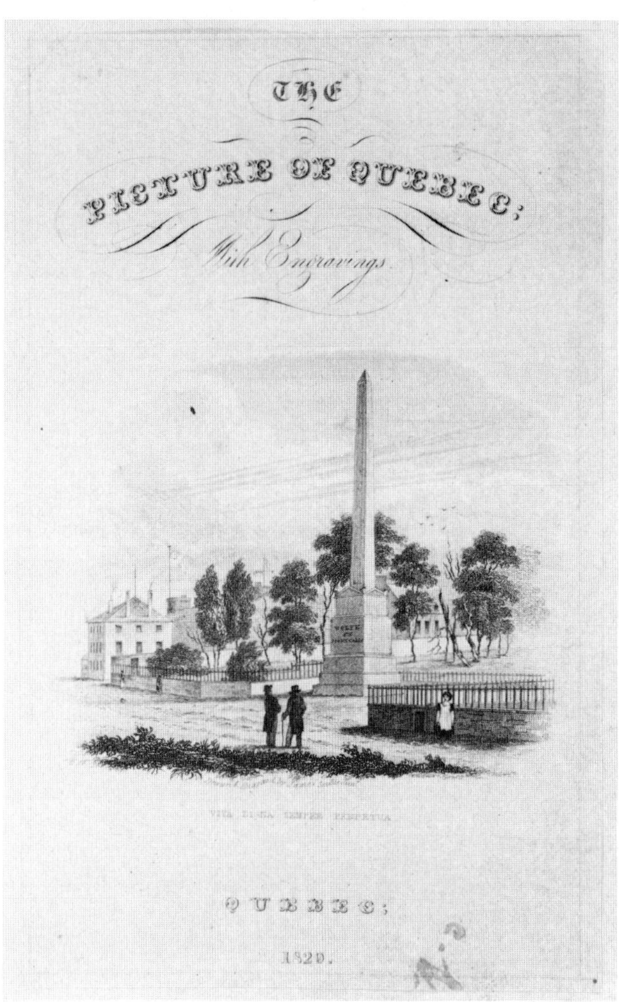
THE
PICTURE OF QUEBEC;
With Engravings
VITA DIGNA SEMPER PERPETUA
QUEBEC;
1829.

69c

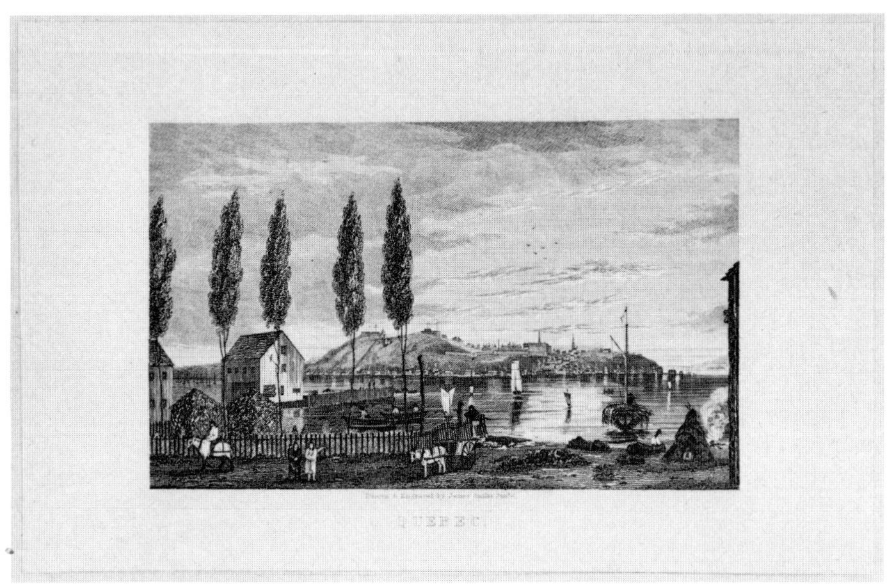
QUEBEC.

69d

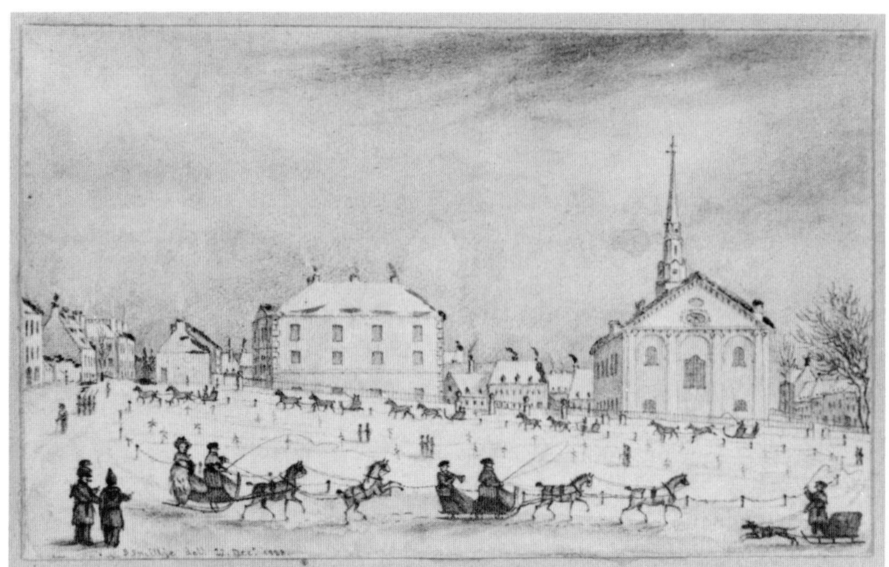

69e

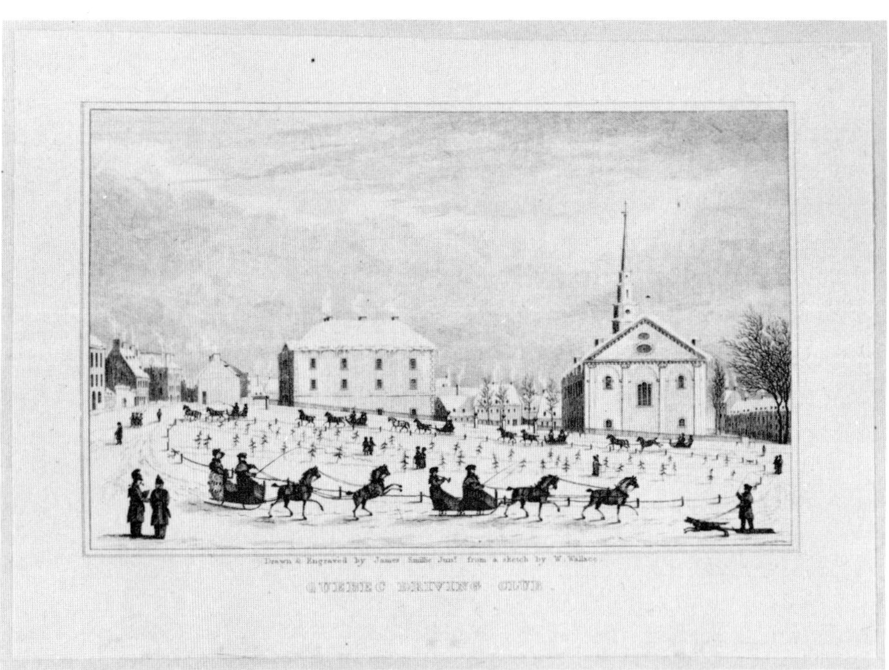
Drawn & Engraved by James Smillie Junr. from a sketch by W. Wallace
QUEBEC DRIVING CLUB.

69f

One wonders whether the plate derived from the general view of Quebec that Smillie was supposed to etch for John Crawford Young (1788–c. 1859) in 1828 (see Young's letter, Cat. No. 65).

REFERENCES: Scrapbook, no. 83; Pilgrimage, p. 27.

69e. Quebec Driving Club 1829
Graphite, heightened with white, on wove paper; 5.7 × 9.5
Inscribed l.l. *J Smillie del! 22. Dec! 1828.*

This is either James Smillie's preparatory drawing for the etching (Cat. No. 69f), or a later version of the same subject. The composition is the same as the etching's, but the figure on the lower right drives a dog sleigh, like the one in Cat. No. 32, rather than a sledge.

REFERENCES: Scrapbook, no. 84.

69f. Quebec Driving Club 1829
Etching on wove paper; 5.9 × 9.5 (image)
Inscribed in plate l.c. *Drawn & Engraved by James Smillie Jun! from a sketch by W. Wallace. / QUEBEC DRIVING CLUB.*

This composition is a variant based on James Smillie's 1826 etching after a watercolour by Ensign William Wallace (see Cat. No. 32).

REFERENCES: Scrapbook, no. 85; Pilgrimage, p. 19.

69g. Episcopal and Presbyterian Churches 1829
Etching on wove paper (two views on one plate); 4.1 × 6.0 (each image)
Inscribed in plate c. *EPISCOPAL CHURCH.*; l.c. *PRESBYTERIAN CHURCH. / Drawn & Engraved by James Smillie Jun!*

REFERENCES: Scrapbook, no. 88; Pilgrimage, p. 27.

69h. Roman Catholic Church and Parliament House 1829
Etching on wove paper (two views on one plate); 4.1 × 6.0 (each image)
Inscribed in plate c. *ROMAN CATHOLIC CHURCH.*; l.c. *PARLIAMENT HOUSE. / Drawn & Engraved by James Smillie Jun!* ~; on broadside posted on building at right of church *JAMES SMILLIE / 1829*.

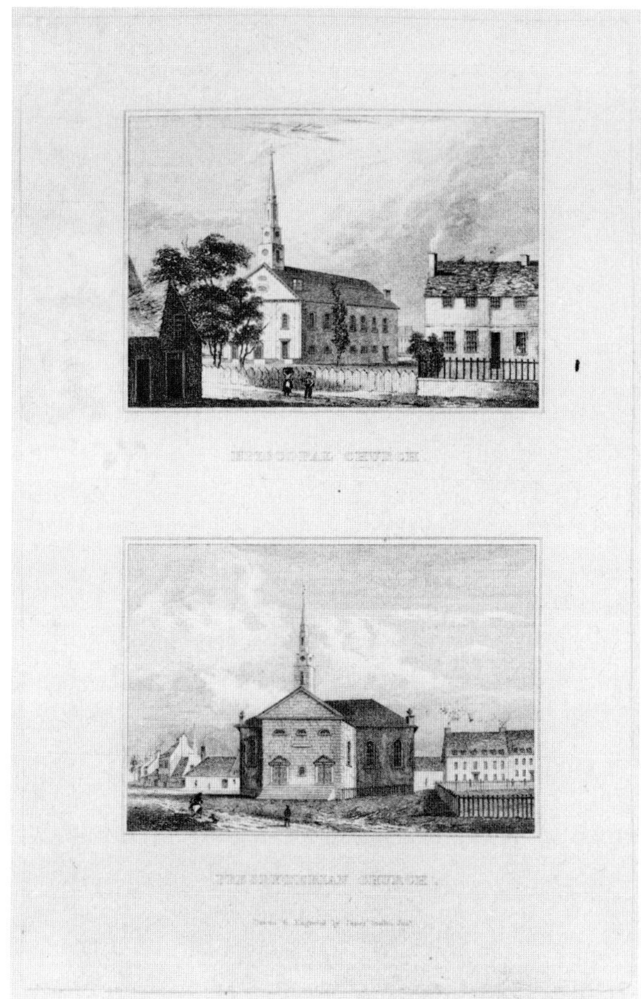

69g

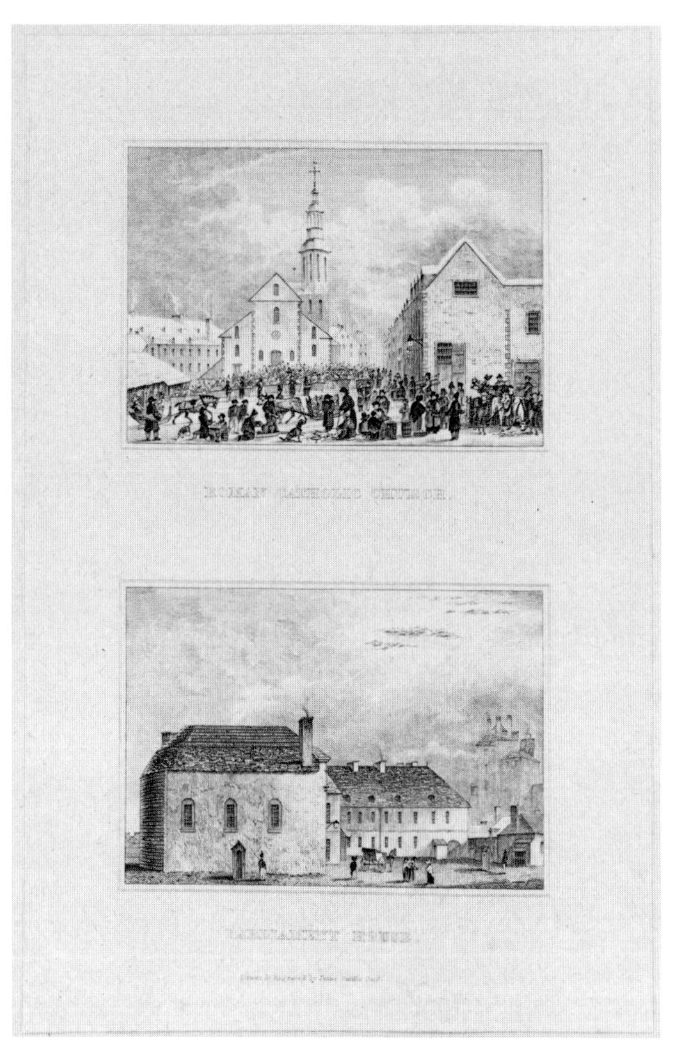

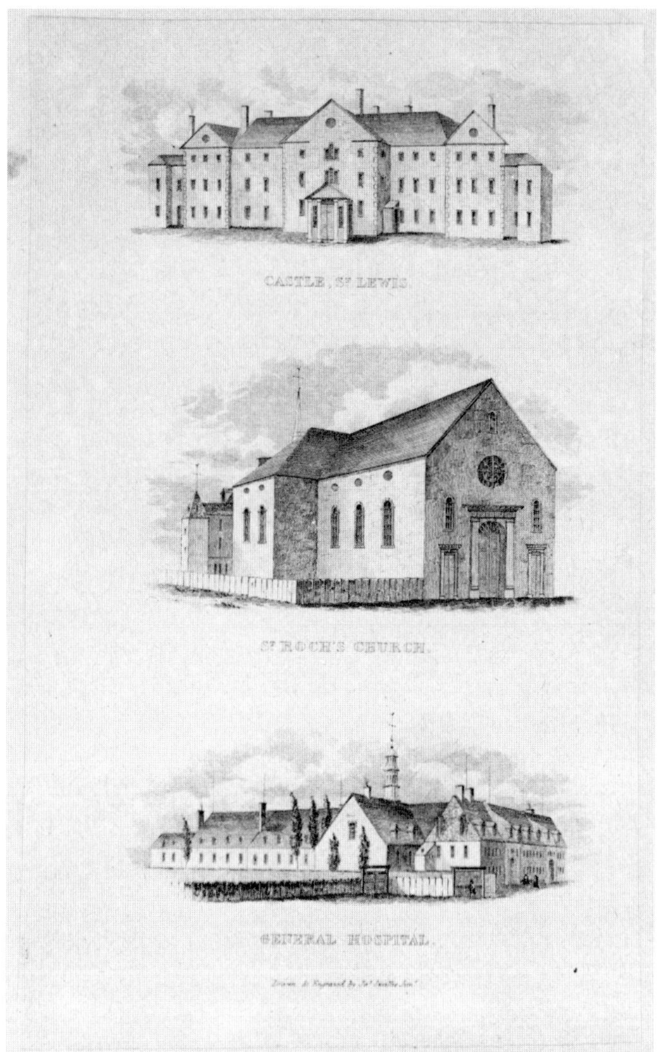

69i

The view of the Roman Catholic church is similar in composition to the vignette on the Dorion trade card (Cat. No. 26).

REFERENCES: Scrapbook, no. 89; Pilgrimage, p. 27.

69i. Castle St. Lewis, St. Roch's Church, General Hospital 1829
Etching on wove paper (three vignettes on one plate); 2.4 × 6.0, 3.6 × 6.1, 2.5 × 6.2 (images, top to bottom)
Inscribed in plate u.c. *CASTLE, St LEWIS.*; c. *St ROCH'S CHURCH.*; l.c. *GENERAL HOSPITAL.* / *Drawn & Engraved by Jas Smillie Junr*

REFERENCES: Scrapbook, no. 90; Pilgrimage, p. 27.

69j. Chapel of the Holy Trinity, and Episcopal Church, Point Levi 1829
Etching on wove paper (two vignettes on one plate); 5.1 × 5.2, 3.7 × 5.5 (images, top to bottom)
Inscribed in plate c. *CHAPEL OF THE HOLY TRINITY.*; l.c. *EPISCOPAL CHURCH.* / *Point Levi.* / *Jas Smillie Junr Sculpsit.*

REFERENCES: Scrapbook, no. 91; Pilgrimage, p. 27.

69k. St. John's Chapel, Court House, and Methodist Chapel 1829
Etching on wove paper (three vignettes on one plate); 3.6 × 5.2, 3.0 × 5.8, 3.7 × 5.3 (images, top to bottom)
Inscribed in plate u.c. *St JOHN'S CHAPEL.*; c. *COURT*

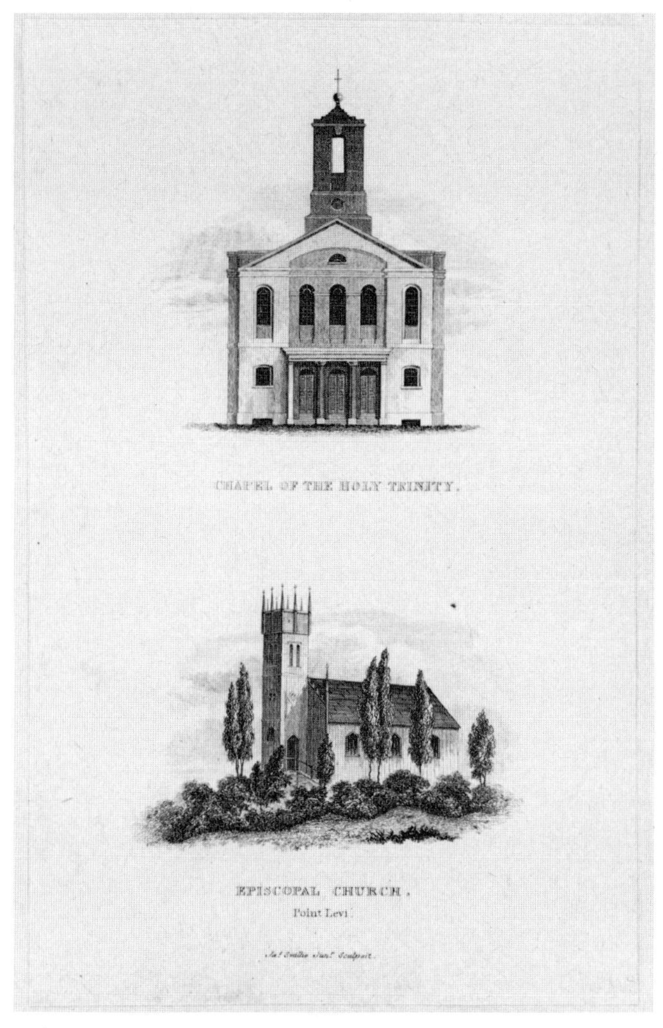

69j

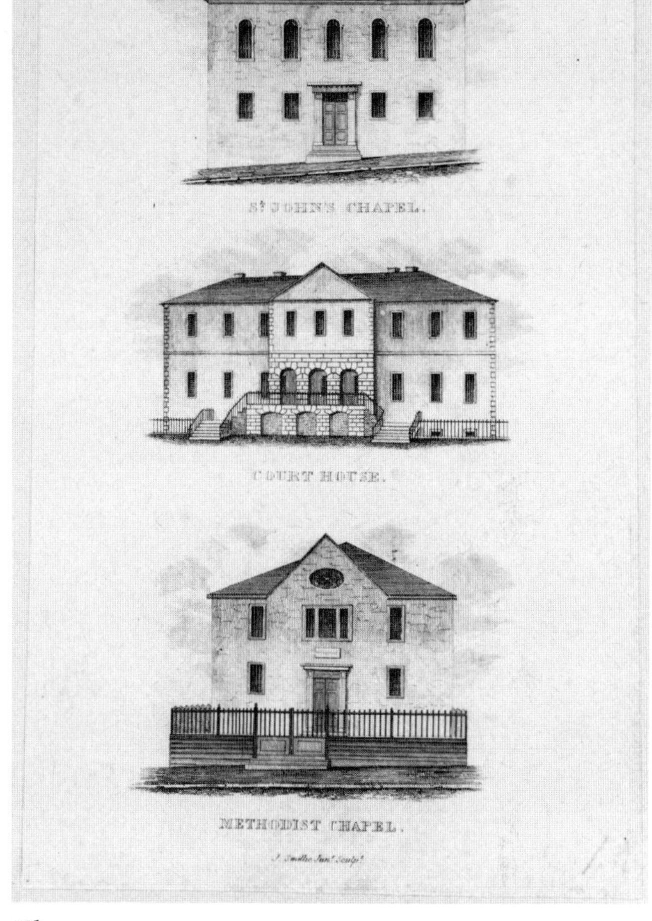

69k

HOUSE.; l.c. *METHODIST CHAPEL. / J. Smillie Junr Sculpt*

REFERENCES: Scrapbook, no. 92; Pilgrimage, p. 27.

70. École Élémentaire 1830
Brown wash over graphite on wove paper; 10.1 × 15.3

See Cat. No. 71 for James Smillie's etching of this subject.

REFERENCES: Scrapbook, no. 78.

71. École Élémentaire 1830
Etching on card or chine collée; 9.1 × 14.5 (image), 12.0 × 20.5 (sheet)

Inscribed in plate l.c. *Drawn & Engraved by J. Smillie / Ecole Elémentaire Françoise de Monre Perrault, Protonotaire a Quebec, 1830.*

This illustration shows one the newest buildings in Quebec at that time, a non-denominational school founded by Joseph-François Perrault (1753–1844) in 1829 for the free education of some three hundred children from the Saint-Louis suburbs.

The French title suggests that this plate may have been commissioned by the school. James Smillie's wash sketch (Cat. No. 70) is not as detailed as his etching.

REFERENCES: Scrapbook, no. 78; Supplementary Scrapbook, no. 13; Noppen, Paulette, and Tremblay 1979, p. 350.

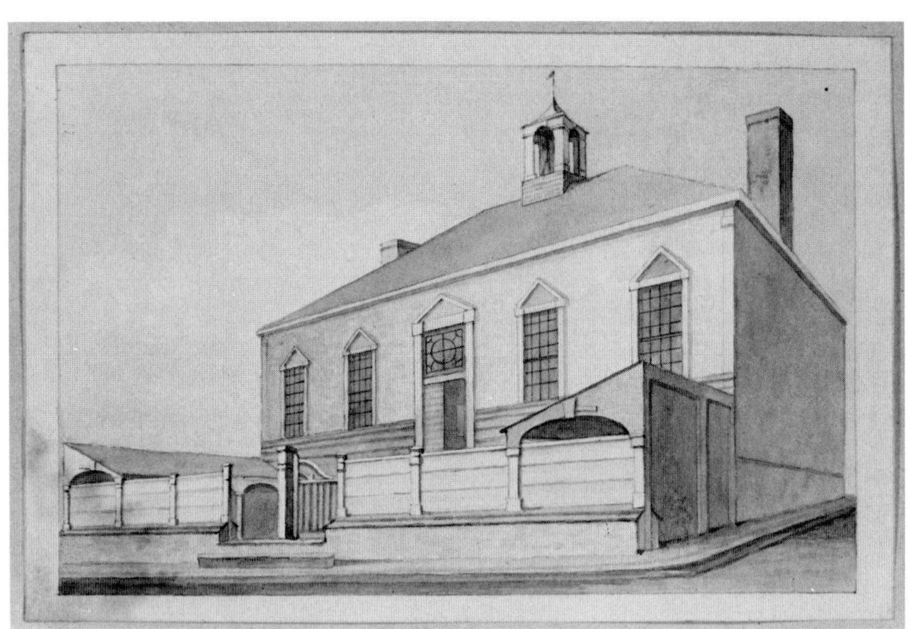

70

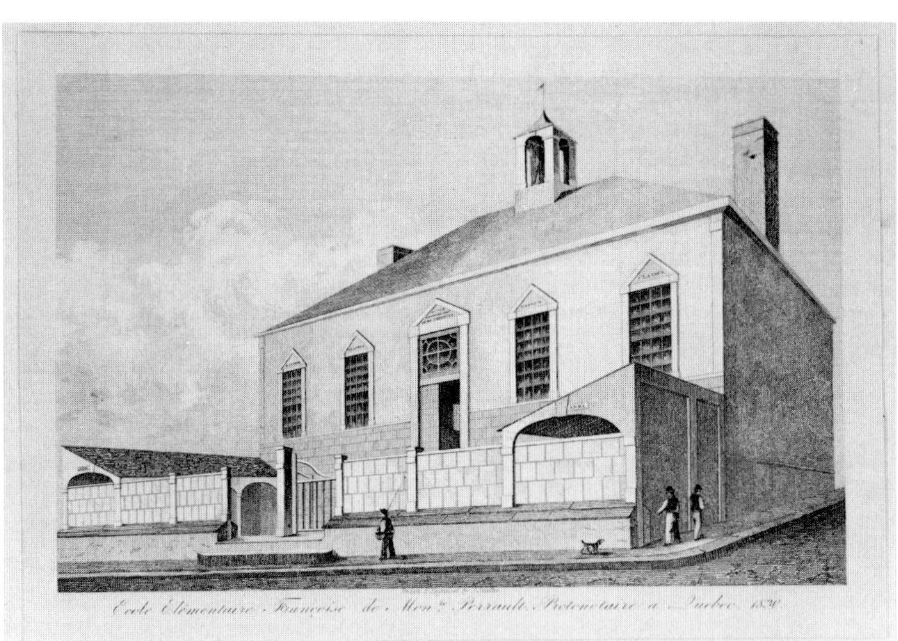
Ecole Élémentaire Françoise de Monsr. Perrault Protonotaire a Quebec 1830

71

72

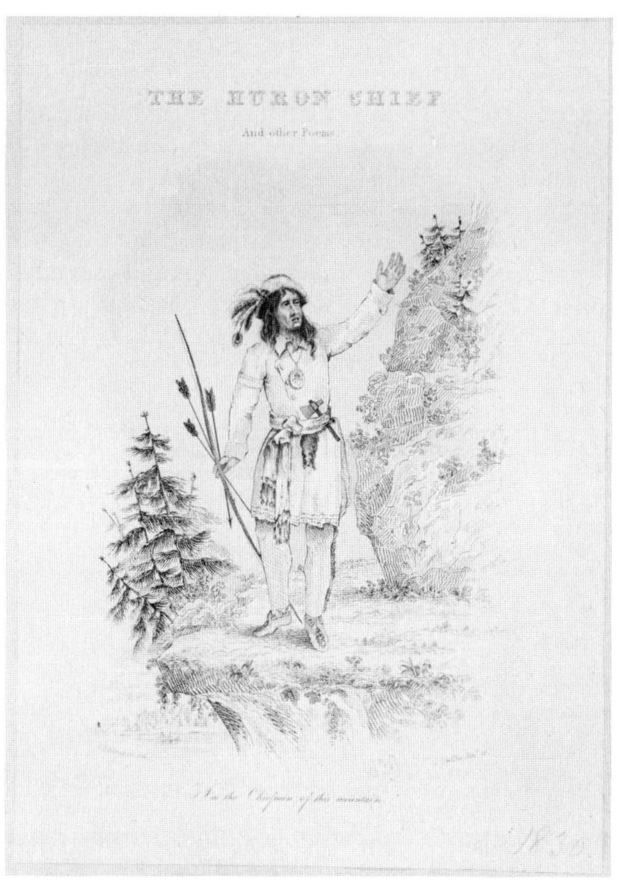

73

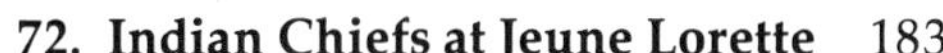

72. Indian Chiefs at Jeune Lorette 1830
Watercolour over graphite on wove paper; 17.8 × 14.9
Inscribed in pencil l.l. *Quebec April 1830*; l.r. *J Smillie*

James Smillie's manuscript note attached to the Scrapbook reads as follows:

No. 59. Three Indian Chiefs of Indian Lorette nine miles from Quebec. Copied from a coloured lithograph. The one sitting was Dr. Kauska. He prescribed for father in roots and herbs. The patient thought he was benefitted but it was only temporary. 1826.

Smillie copied the lithograph *Three Chiefs of the Huron Indians Residing at La Jeune Lorette Near Quebec, in Their Costume*, after a painting by Edward Chatfield (1802–1839). The lithograph was printed by C. Hullmandel and published by J. Dickinson, London, in 1825. Stanislaus Coska (Kostka), Aharathaha, was second chief of the council at Jeune Lorette.

REFERENCES: Scrapbook, no. 59.

73. The Huron Chief 1830
Etching on wove paper or chine collée; 19.2 × 11.2 (sheet)
Inscribed in plate u.c. *THE HURON CHIEF / And other Poems.*; l.c. *"I'm the Chieftain of this Mountain." / (page 22)*, l.l. *S. H. Gimber del.*, l.r. *J. Smillie Jun: sc.*
State I: Lacks inscription "(page 22)" (illustrated)
State II: Inscription "(page 22)" added

In a note attached to the Scrapbook, James Smillie identifies this print, "No. 94. The first plate I engraved after coming to New York with a view to settle, but became homesick and returned to Quebec after three or four months."

Smillie's commission was for a frontispiece illustration for a volume of poetry by Adam Kidd of Quebec (c. 1802–1831). On his second visit to New York City in 1829 Smillie met a young artist-engraver, Stephen Henry Gimber (c. 1806–1862), who drew the composition for him. The book *The Huron Chief* was printed in 1830 at the office of the *Herald and New Gazette* in Montreal. In most bound copies examined, Smillie's name has been almost effaced from the plate.

Kidd and Smillie were probably on friendly terms, and each was portrayed in watercolour by Edward Heaton in the mid-1820s (see Cat. No. 40). Kidd, who was a native of Northern Ireland, frequently contributed poems to Quebec newspapers under the *nom de plume* of "Slievegallin." He reviewed Smillie's work in 1830 for a Montreal newspaper. *The Huron Chief* was Kidd's major poetical work. In the preface he wrote that he had received much encouragement in the Canadas, and that fifteen hundred copies of this book had already been subscribed. He died at Quebec on 6 July 1831, aged 29 years (Appendix L.13).

REFERENCES: Scrapbook, no. 94; Supplementary Scrapbook, no. 15 (imp. on chine collée); Pilgrimage, p. 28; *Vindicator* 25 January 1830; *Quebec Mercury*, 7 July 1831.

74. New Roman Catholic Church, Montreal
c. 1830
Etching on heavy wove paper; 43.8 × 54.9 (plate)
Inscribed in plate l.c. *Drawn by John Okill. / NEW ROMAN CATHOLIC CHURCH, MONTREAL. / CONSECRATED JULY 1829.*; l.r. *Calculated to hold upwards of 10,000 persons.*
State I: Lacks inscription "Calculated. . . ." (illustrated)
State II: Inscription "Calculated. . . ." added

In his autobiography James Smillie dated his work on this etching to 1825, but contemporary newspaper accounts suggest 1830 as the date of execution. It was not until July 1829 that John Leigh Okill (fl. 1824–1830) exhibited his drawing of the church in Montreal and announced his intention of publishing a print. In April 1830 Smillie was reported as still working on the plate (see Cat. No. 66). The etching may have been unfinished when Smillie left for New York sometime between late May and late July 1830 (Appendix L.10), which would account for the very spare image, and for the omission of Smillie's name in the inscriptions. It should also be noted that the church was consecrated on 13 June 1829, rather than in July, as inscribed in the plate.

Okill, an architect and drawing master, was the son of John Okill of Philadelphia and a first cousin of the Reverend George Okill Stuart, archdeacon of York and rector of Kingston. In 1824/1825 John Leigh Okill was working in Kingston. From March through May of 1828 he advertised drawing classes in Quebec, and in 1829 he was listed at a Montreal address.

One impression of this print is watermarked "J WHATMAN / TURKEY MILL / 182—" (McG.RBD.LR, no. 27). A watercolour of this subject by Okill is dated 1829 (ASQ, Album 159G, p. 27, tiroir 112 [ancienne cote]).

REFERENCES: Pilgrimage, p. 20; Allodi 1980, no. 27; *Star and Commercial Advertiser*, 26 March–21 May 1828, 22 July 1829, 24 April, 17 July 1830; John Leigh Okill to Major George Hillier, 15 November 1824, Civil Secretary's Correspondence (arch. mat.); *Kingston Chronicle*, 17 December 1824, 31 December 1824–4 June 1825; Mr. Stephen A. Otto, Toronto, communication.

75. Catholic Church, Montreal post-1830?
Brown wash, pen and brown ink on wove paper; 8.1 × 11.2
Inscribed in pencil u.r. *Catholic Cathedral / Montreal 1828.*

James Smillie may not have had an impression of his etching of this subject (Cat. No. 74) when compiling his Scrapbook; whatever the reason, he filled the space with this wash sketch. The sketch is remarkably faithful to the printed subject; only the foreground figures are changed.

REFERENCES: Scrapbook, no. 52.

76. Plan for Moving Boats over Rapids c. 1830
Etching on wove paper; 12.1 × 23.6 (sheet)
Inscribed in plate l.r. of vignette *Smillie sc. Quebec.*; typeset on verso *A few remarks on internal improvements in the Canadas.*

This etching illustrates James George's 1835 pamphlet *A Few Remarks on Internal Improvements in the Canadas*. Facing the illustration is a "Description of the Annexed Plate."

> It represents a part of the Rapids called les Cedres in Lower Canada; at the head of a very bad pass, where a towing steam Boat would be stopped by the rapidity of the current, there is placed a chain fixed to a rock or anchor, the other end of which is at the foot of the Rapid, where the steam towing vessel finds it attached to a small Buoy, this taken on board gives the end of the chain, which when attached to a capstern, attached to the Engine, upon the principle of Captain Boswell's Patent, is worked by the steam power and delivers itself off without riding, and with the Buoy thrown over the stern, when the next Boat in succession, will find and use it in the like manner.

James George (c. 1791–1841) was a Quebec merchant specializing in the import, export, and forwarding of goods. He was one of the instigators of the St. Lawrence

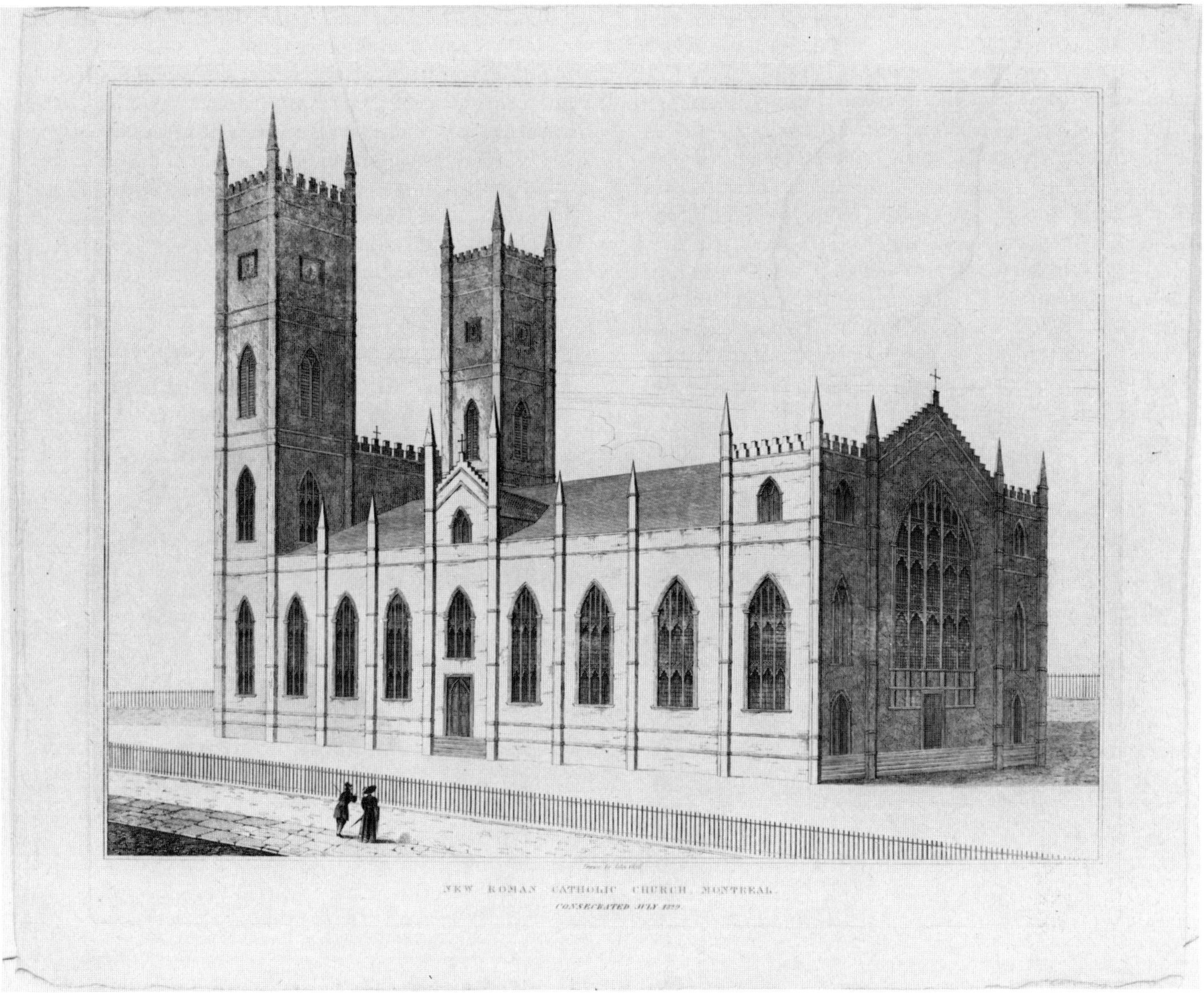

NEW ROMAN CATHOLIC CHURCH, MONTREAL.

CONSECRATED JULY 1829.

74

ROM 968.147.12

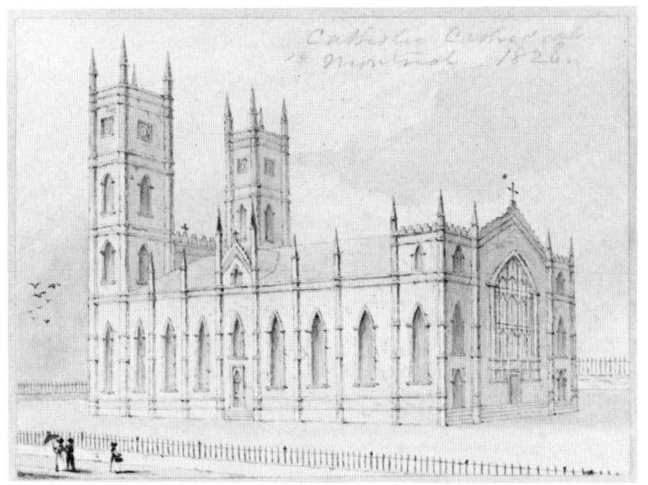

75

Association, founded in Quebec in 1824 to raise funds and seek methods to improve navigation of rapids on the St. Lawrence River between Lachine and Prescott. During a ten-year period he made numerous suggestions in letters to the press, publications, scale models, and drawings, on subjects including wooden railroads, bridges, ice ponts, and tide docks.

A naive drawing by James George, dated in pencil 1824, illustrates a plan to move ships over portages by rail (NA 1958-192). A prospectus of the St. Lawrence Association, dated 10 December 1824 and published in *La Gazette de Québec* on 27 January 1825, was headed with a vignette engraving of the same size and composition as the central view in the James Smillie etching; the earlier print has less detail and is simpler in style. The engraver of the 1824 illustration may have been Smillie. The vignettes in his 1825 *Notes of Exchange* are similar in subject matter (Cat. No. 17). His etching that accompanied the 1835 pamphlet is certainly based on the 1824 vignette; the former may have been etched before he left Quebec in 1830 and printed at a later date. One impression is watermarked "[Prince of Wales crest] / HB / 1832" (NA Library).

George addressed the Quebec Literary and Historical Society in 1834 on his proposal for moving boats over rapids. In 1835 he put his suggestions to the test by sailing his own barge as far as Toronto. George is said to have had the curious habit of conversing in rhyme.

REFERENCES: George 1835; Gagnon 1895, nos. 1493, 2500; *La Gazette de Québec*, 27 January 1825; Quebec Mercury, 10 February 1827, 3 January 1829; Scadding 1873, pp. 573–574.

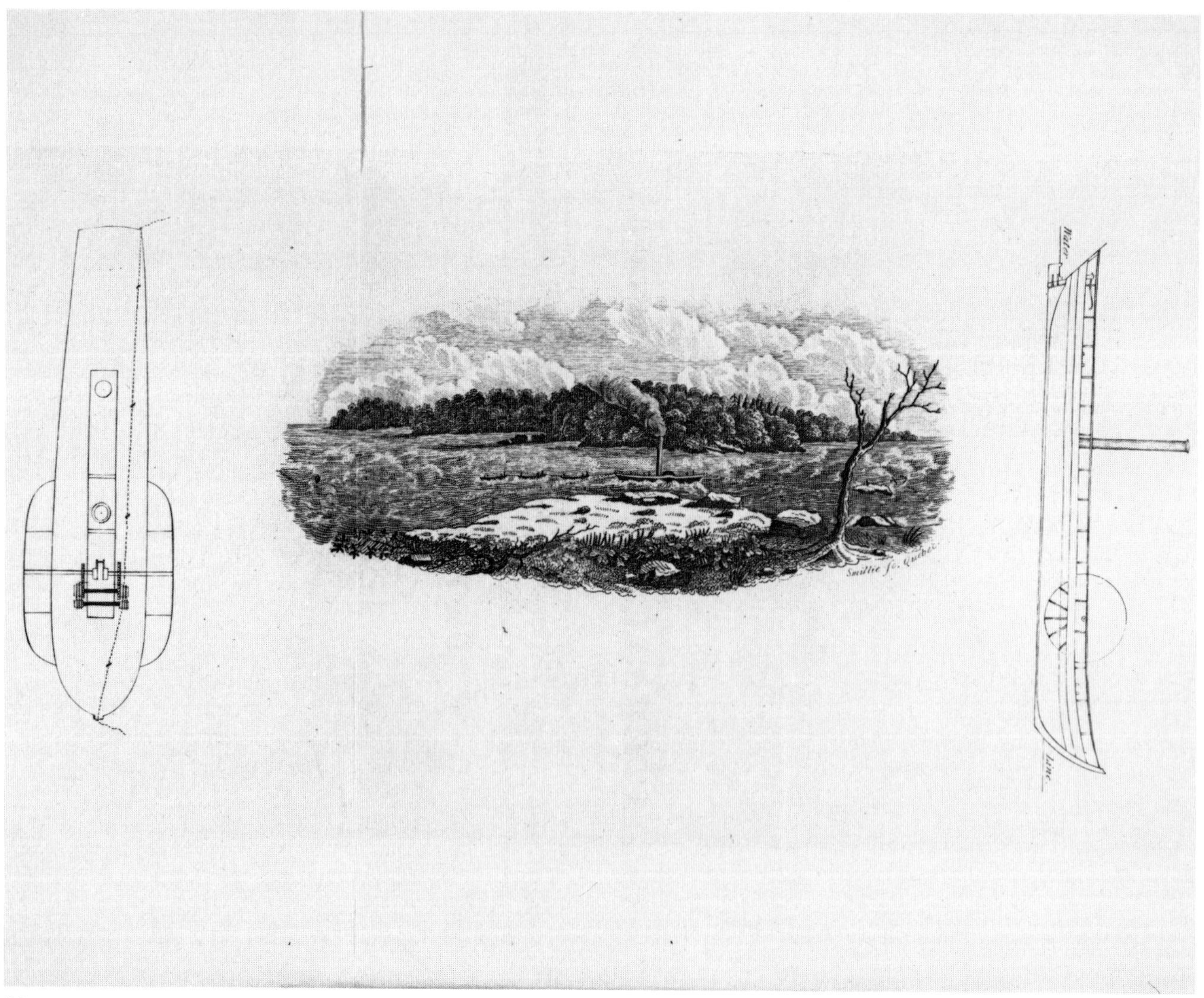

76 NA C122249

Appendices

Appendices A through K are documents from James Smillie's scrapbook, "In Memoriam." Items that were pasted into the album either have a scrapbook number or are noted as facing a numbered item. Those recorded as "Scrapbook, not numbered" are loosely inserted between the scrapbook's leaves.

Appendix L contains selected excerpts from letters that Smillie received from various correspondents during the years 1827 to 1839. The original letters belong to the Smillie Family Collection. These excerpts have been transcribed as written, with some additional punctuation for clarity.

Appendix A: Indenture of Apprenticeship
Scrapbook no. 1

James Smillie attached the following note to this document in the Scrapbook: "Scrapbook No. 1 My Indenture with Mr. Ja[s] Johnston Silver Engraver, Edinburgh, in 1819."

Indenture betwixt James Johnston and James Smillie For 7 years from 22[d] October 1819

It is contracted and agreed betwixt the parties following viz. James Johnston Engraver in Edinburgh on the one part and James Smellie son of David Smellie Jeweller in Potterrow of Edinburgh, with the special advice and Consent of Richard Haxton also Jeweller Potterrow, as his Cautioner in this indenture for his due performance of the obligations thereby incumbent on him as aftermentioned on the other part: That is to say the said James Smellie hereby becomes bound Apprentice and Servant to the said James Johnston in his business of an Engraver, and that for the term of Seven years from and after the twenty second day of October last, during which space the said James Smellie and his said Cautioner hereby Bind and Oblige themselves conjunctly and severally that he shall faithfully and honestly serve and obey the said James Johnston by day or by night, every lawful day of the week, excepting when in sickness, and not absent himself from his service without leave first obtained from his said Master, and for each day so absent shall be obliged to serve two days after the expiration of this Indenture, such absent days to be ascertained by the said James Johnston's signed accompt thereof and attested by his Oath if required, in full of all other proof; As also the said James Smellie obliges himself not to frequent immoral or idle company, play at unlawful games or be accessary to any riot or tumult in the City or Suburbs of Edinburgh, and that he shall not know of any damage intended to be done to the property of his said Master without timeously revealing the same to him and endeavouring to prevent it himself to the utmost of his power. For which causes and on the other part the said James Johnston hereby Binds and Obliges himself not only to teach and instruct the said James Smellie in his said art of Engraving in all the Branches thereof which he himself carries on, and that in so far as he is capable or the said apprentice is willing to learn or able to understand, but also to make payment to him of the following sum weekly towards his Maintenance and Clothing during his apprenticeship, namely, two shillings during the third year, two shillings and six pence in the fourth and three shillings during the fifth, sixth and seventh years. And lastly the said parties Bind and Oblige themselves to fulfil their respective parts of the premises to each other under the penalty of Five pounds Sterling to be paid by the party failing to the party performing or willing to implement their part thereof besides performance. And they consent to the registration hereof in the books of Council and Session or other competent record, that Letters of Horning on six days charge and all other execution necessary may be directed hereon in form as effeirs; and thereto Constitute [blank] Their procurators. In witness these presents, consisting of this and the two preceding pages, written on stamped paper by James Lothian Clerk to William Lothian Writer in Edinburgh, are subscribed by the said parties at Edinburgh the twenty seventh day of November One thousand eight hundred and nineteen years before these Witnesses Alexander Gibson also apprentice to the said James Johnston and the said William Lothian, by whom the place and date of signing with the names of designations of the Witnesses are added—

[signed]	Alexander Gibson	Witness	James Johnston
	William Lothian	Witness	James Smillie
			Richard Haxton

[postscript] Edin 29 August 1820 In consequence of the death of Mr. Johnston this Indenture is discharged & given up by me as his widow & Executrix—at the same time I hereby certify that the apprentice during the period of his Indenture conducted himself to the perfect satisfaction of Mr. Johnston & myself.
Jain Johnston

Appendix B: Impression of Snuffbox Lid
Scrapbook no. 17

In the Scrapbook, James Smillie identified an impression of an engraved snuffbox lid made by David Smillie, Sr., as follows: "No. 17. Engraved on the top of a silver snuff box (made by father). This impression I took with the burnisher." The impression of the engraved lid measured approximately 5.3 cm × 7.6 cm; it was removed from the Scrapbook by James David Smillie in April 1902 with the intention of presenting it to the New York Public Library. The impression has not been located.

Appendix C: Trade Cards by Edward Bennet
Scrapbook nos. 22–26

James Smillie kept trade cards by Edward Bennet (act. Quebec 1821–1828)[1] in his Scrapbook, to which he appended this note:

> Nos. 22, 23, 24, 25, 26, are specimens of the work of the only man I had to compete with. Father tried to prevail on him (Mr. Bennet an Englishman) to take me as an apprentice but did not succeed.

The following five cards are Scrapbook nos. 22 to 26.
Scrapbook no. 22: *Dr to Robert Scott, Confectioner & Pastry Cook. / E Bennet Sct*, etching, 6.7 × 18.5 (sheet).
Scrapbook no. 23: *C. STRICKLAND, Neptune Inn & Coffee House, Mountain Street, Quebec. / E. Bennet, Sct*, etching, 11.3 × 7.6 (sheet).
Scrapbook no. 24: *THE NEW EXCHANGE HOTEL BY ROBERT SCOTT St. Paul's Street. QUEBEC. / E Bennet*, etching, 11.2 × 7.4 (sheet).
Scrapbook no. 25: *JAs SAUNDERS & Co Glass, China, Earthen Ware & general Warehouse No 5 Buade Street Upper Town QUEBEC / E. Bennet Sct. Quebec*, etching, 8.9 × 6.1 (sheet).
Scrapbook no. 26: *JAs BIRCH Cooper and Culler of Staves Quebec. / E. Bennet*, etching, 5.6 × 7.8 (sheet).

Bennet advertised in 1821 as an engraver of crests, coats of arms, and cyphers "in the first London style."[2] In 1822 he gave his profession as an "Engraver and Copper-plate printer" and announced his publication of an

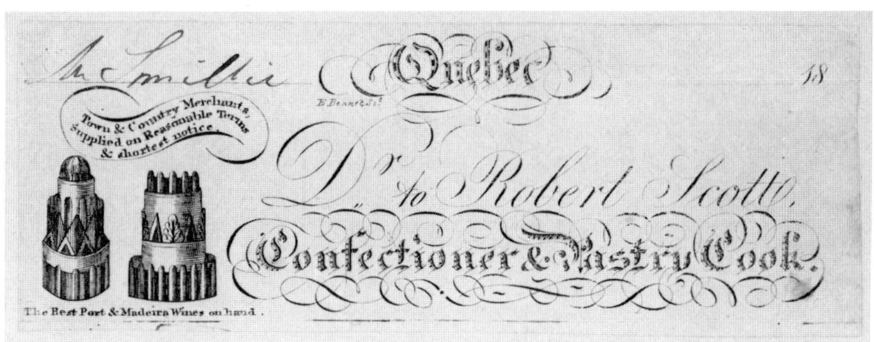

Scrapbook no. 22

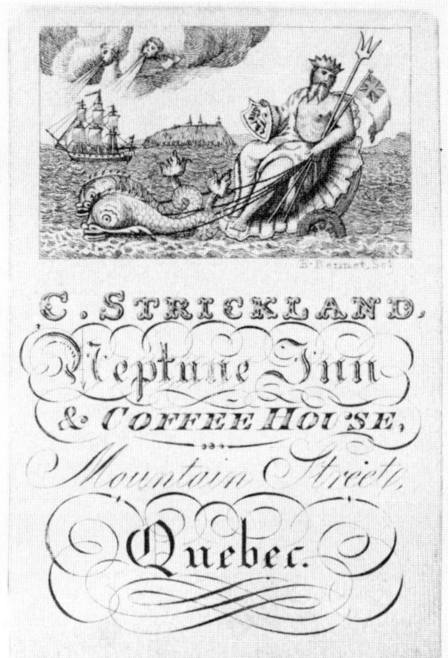

Scrapbook no. 23

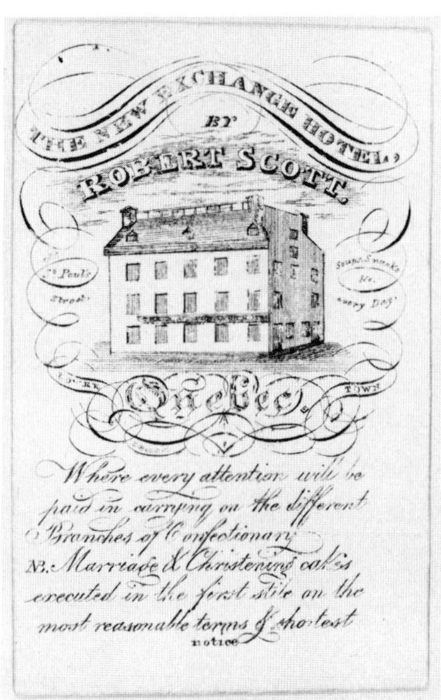

Scrapbook no. 24

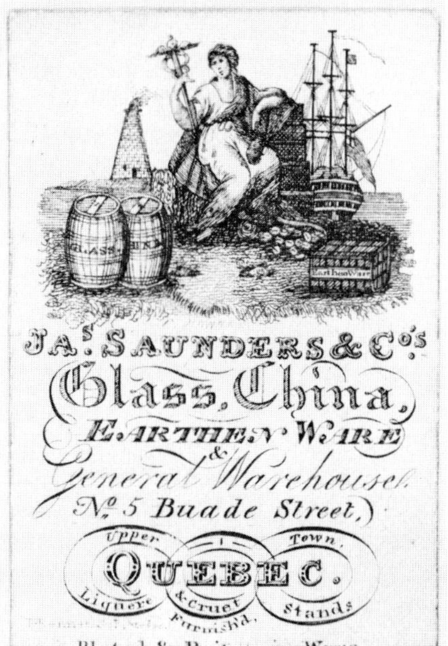

Scrapbook no. 25

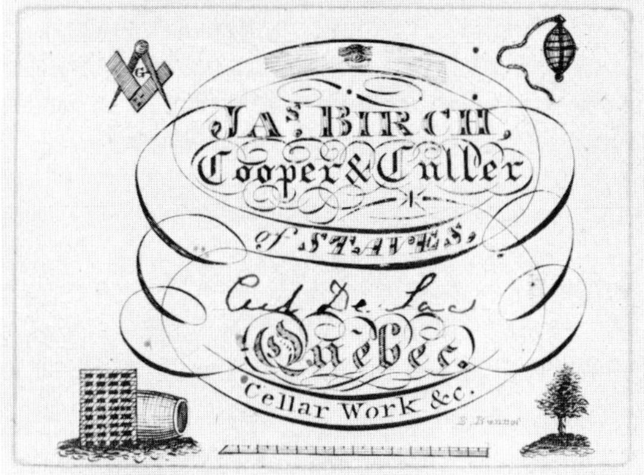

Scrapbook no. 26

engraving depicting "The Signals of the repeating Telegraph upon Cape Diamond."[3] In the same year he engraved a plan of Quebec City after the survey by John Adams; however, because of distortions in scale, this plan was later engraved in London and reissued.[4] He also etched a plan of lots to be sold near Citadel Hill, Montreal, for the Royal Engineers' Office, Quebec, in 1822.[5] His trade card for John Graddon, Linen & Woollen Draper, illustrated Quebec's Upper Town Market and cathedral (NA C102267). In 1828 his diagramatic engraving of a keyboard was bound with the *Elementary Treatise on Music* by T. F. Molt (1828).

Appendix D: Etchings by James Pattison Cockburn Scrapbook, facing no. 59

James Smillie inscribed these two prints in pencil "Etched by Col. Cockburn, Royal Artillery." The etching of the château is almost identical to a lithograph after Cockburn, plate 8 in *Views of the Valley of Aosta*, drawn on stone by T. M. Baynes, printed by C. Hullmandel, and published by D. Walther, London, in 1822.

Appendix E: Invoice of James & John Johnstone, Edinburgh Scrapbook, not numbered

Mr. Jas Smillie

134 High Street
Edinburgh
First Entry above the
TRON CHURCH.

To James & John Johnstone
Engravers
and
Copper Plate Printers

1828						
Feb	28	2 lb 3 oz Copper	4/6		9	9
Mar	13	1 proof Policy—Quebec	4to back			3
	25	1 Do Ship Vic: of Lon:	4to—			3
	"	1 Do Policy Quebec	4to Ind			4
	27	12 Do Do	folio 6 Do		4	6
April	8	1 Do Portrait	8vo 1—			3
	14	1 Do Do	8vo 1—			3
	"	2 Do Do & Ship	4to 1—			7
May	1	2 Do	4to 1—			7
	6	2 Do Ship & Etching	8vo 2—			6
	9	3 Do 2 Do 1 Do	8vo 2—			8½
	"	balance *fm* purchase Hoyrood &c				6
		750 Vicinity of London	@3/	1	2	6
		18 Portraits plain				6
		18 Do India	2d		3	
		8 qa 5 oh Bestplate Demy, *English*	3/9	1	10	9
				£3	15	2½
		Dis[t]			4	2½
June 4th 1828		Referred to in our Stamp Receipts of this date James & John Johnstone		3	11	—

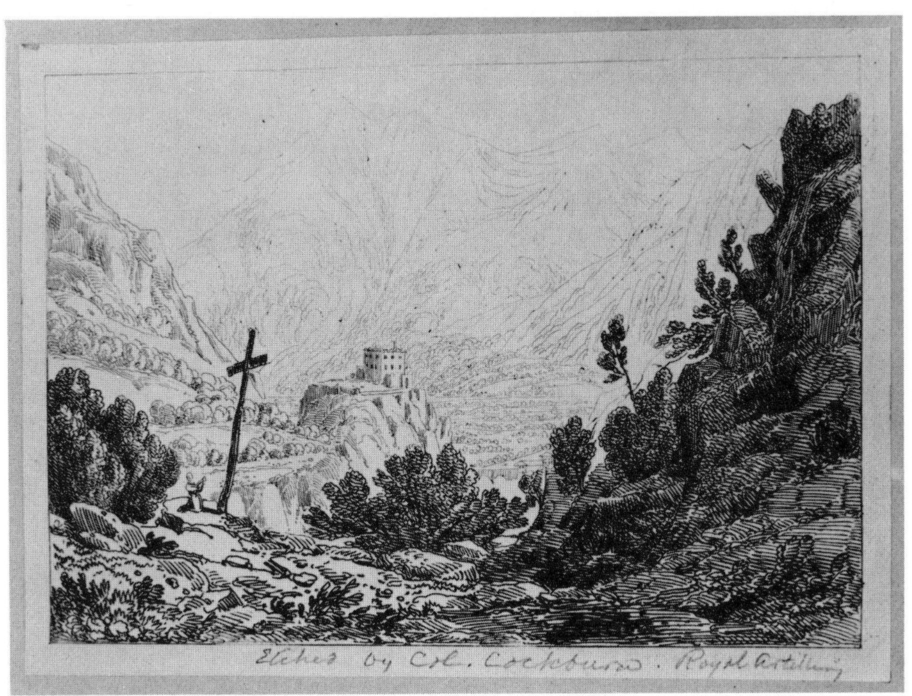

James Pattison Cockburn, *Château of the Counts of Verrex*, etching on wove paper, 11.0 × 16.0 (image).

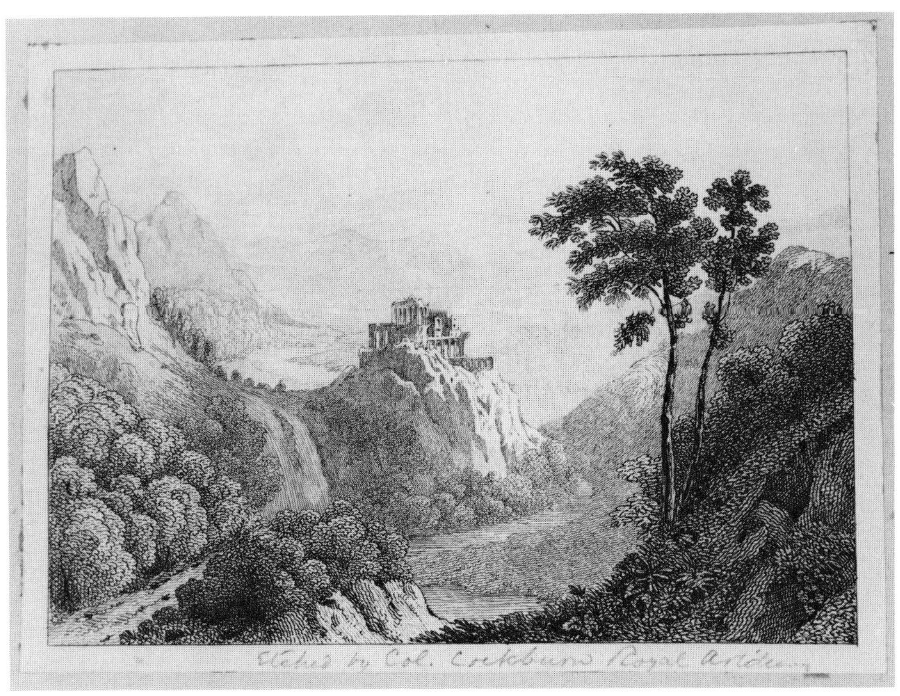

James Pattison Cockburn, *Swiss Landscape*, etching on wove paper, 11.1 × 15.9 (image).

Appendix F: Jonathan Wurtele, Quebec, to James Smillie, Quebec, 26 February 1829 Scrapbook no. 76

Sir

I have the honor to acquaint you that on this day you were elected an ordinary member of the Society for the encouragement of Arts and Sciences in Canada[1]

I am
Sir
Your obdt Serv[t]
Jonathan Wurtele
Secry

Mr James Smillie Jr

Appendix G: Contract for *Picture of Quebec* Scrapbook, not numbered

Whereas George Bourne and James Smillie Junior both of the city of Quebec, have agreed to publish a book, to be called, the "Picture of Quebec"—Now be it known, that the following conditions constitute the said agreement between the said parties—
I. The said George Bourne doth covenant to furnish the literary matters—and the said James Smillie Junior doth agree to finish the Maps and engravings, according to the Prospectus.
II. The said George Bourne and James Smillie Junior do also mutually covenant that after the Printer, the Lithographer, the Agent for striking off the engravings, and the Binder, with every other incidental expence shall have been discharged, in full—the overplus whether in money or books shall be equally divided between them the Authors and Proprietors of the said Picture of Quebec.
III. The said George Bourne and James Smillie Junior do further agree—that in case of any more editions of the said "Picture of Quebec"—the same contract shall be in force—and each of the said parties doth bind himself to make any subsequent improvements and additions in his peculiar department, which may increase the sale—upon the same terms. After all the actual expenditures of this publication are defrayed; an equal division of the surplus money and books shall be made between the said contracting parties.

In Testimony whereof—the said George Bourne and James Smillie Junior have hereunto affixed their hands and seals, at Quebec, this [blank] day of January, in the year one thousand, eight hundred and twenty nine.
[signed] George Bourne
JSmillie J[r]

Signed, sealed and delivered in the presence of
John Bean
James Smillie

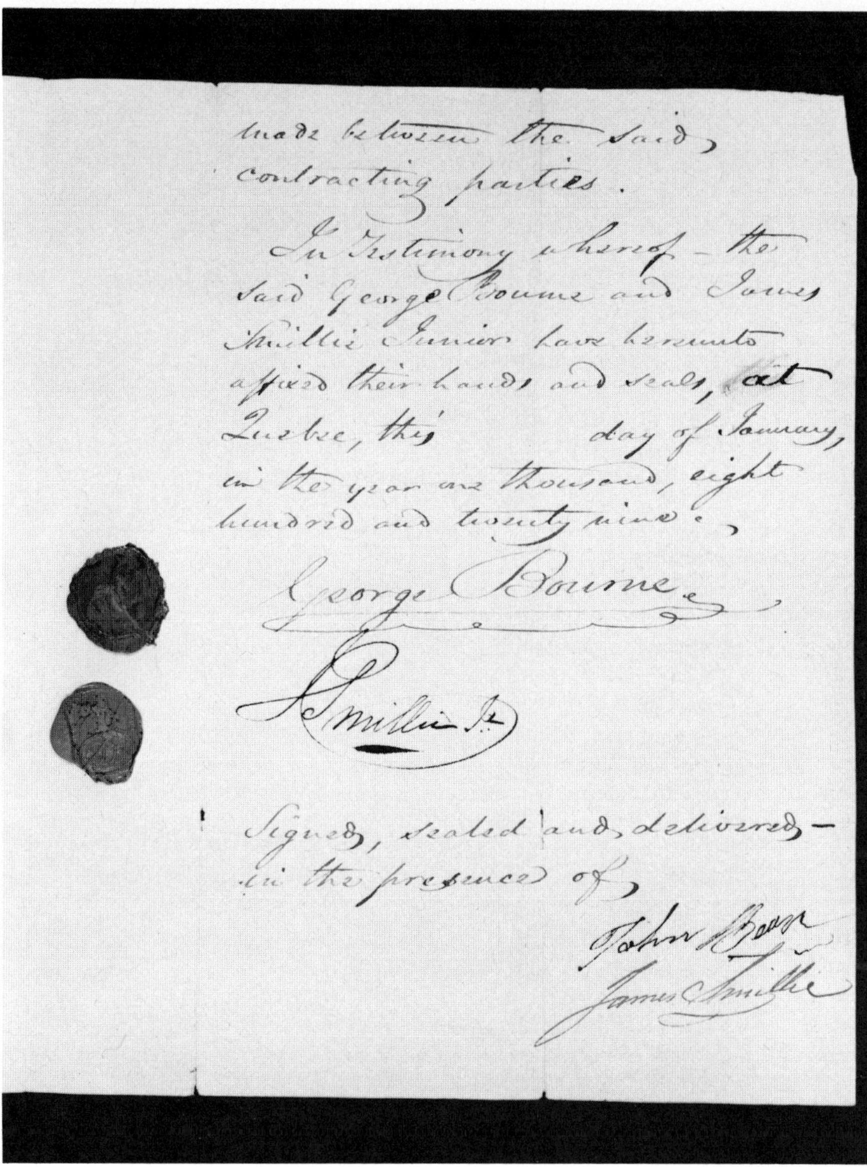

made between the said contracting parties.

In Testimony whereof – the said George Bourne and James Smillie Junior have hereunto affixed their hands and seals, at Quebec, this day of January, in the year one thousand, eight hundred and twenty nine.

George Bourne

J. Smillie Jr.

Signed, sealed and delivered – in the presence of,

John Bean

James Smillie

Page from the contract between George Bourne and James Smillie.

Appendix H: Lieutenant Colonel George Couper to James Smillie, Quebec, 6 December 1828 Scrapbook no. 79

Lt. Col. Couper[1] has pleasure of informing Mr. Smillie that His Excellency has been pleased to permit him to dedicate the Picture of Quebec to His Excellency.[2]

Appendix I: Travel Expenses for *Picture of Quebec* Scrapbook, not numbered

The trip to which this list of expenses refers was made for the printing of the plates for *Picture of Quebec* (Cat. No. 69).

Information in square brackets was added from another partial account sheet leafed into the Scrapbook, which bears Appendix J on the verso.

[1829]
Expenses to New York.

		£	s	d
8th May	Lady of the Lake [Steamboat] (to Montreal) [with 3 vols. Picture of Quebec]	£ 1	5	"
10th	Breakfast in Montreal		1	6
	Carriage of Portmanteau			6
	Supper, Bed & Breakfast		5	"
11.	[Edmund Henry] Steam Boat to Laprairie		1	3
	Dinner at Laprairie		1	6
	Stage to St. Johns		7	6
12.	Tea, Bed, Breakfast & Dinner [Watson's Hotel, St. Johns]		7	6
	Carriage of Portmanteau		4	
	Steam Boat Franklin to Whitehall	1	5	"
13th	Breakfast in Whitehall		2	
	Stage to Albany	"	15	"
	Refreshments on the road		3	
	Supper and Bed in Albany		5	
14th	Carriage of Portmanteau		1	
	Steam Boat N: America to New York		15	
	Carriage of Portmanteau to the Western Hotel		1	
		£ 5	17	1

Expenses in N: York.

		£	s	d
(15th) to 20th May	for Board in the Western Hotel	£ 1	13	9
[21st]	Shoe Black & carriage of Port: to Broad Street		3	
June 9	for Board to Miller / 3 Weeks and 1 day	3	18	9
	Carriage of Portmanteau & Box to Steam Boat Dewitt Clinton		2	
		£ 5	17	6

Expenses to Quebec

		£	s	d
11th June	Steam Boat Dewitt Clinton to Albany	£	15	
	Freight of Box		2	6
12th June	Steam Boat to Troy & freight of Box		1	6
	Carriage of do.		1	
	Stage to Whitehall		15	
	Freight of Box		10	
	Breakfast		1	6
	Dinner & refreshments on the road		4	3
13th	Bed, Breakfast & Dinner in Whitehall		5	6
	Steam Boat Franklin to St. Johns	1	5	
	Freight of Box		2	6
14th	Breakfast & Dinner, St. Johns		4	9
	Stage to Laprairie		7	6
	Steam Boat to Montreal		1	3
	Freight of Box			7½
15th	Bed, Breakfast, Dinner & Tea in Montreal		10	
	Steam Boat Hercules to Quebec	1		
	Freight of Box		2	6
	Carriage of do.		1	
		£ 6	12	4½
	Total, of the Trip	£17	11	11½

Work done in New York.

		£	s	d
Map on Stone		£ 8	15	—
Printing of do.		10	—	—
paper for do.		9	7	6
	Total of Map	£28	2	6
Wood cut		£ 1	—	—
Printing of do.		1	10	—
paper for do.			15	
	Total for covers	£ 3	5	—

[verso]

		£	s	d
	Printing of Plates			
by Mr., G & I Neale—				
pr Acct. recd. for printing		£ 8	2	6
pr Acct. recd. from Mr Smith (for printing)		£ 2	5	″
pr Acct. recd. from Mr Miller (for printing)		£ 9	1	10½
Paper for copper plates		£ 5	11	3
	packing box	£ ″	7	6
	Total, Work & Trip	£74	7	7½

Appendix J: Printing Expenses for *Picture of Quebec*
Scrapbook, not numbered

"Work done in N.Y."	
Miller[1]—work & Board	$ 52 ... 12
Smith[2]	9
Anderson[3]	4
Neale[4]	32 ... 50
Gratton	6
Desobry[5]	75
Paper—covers—	3
do—copper Plates	22 ... 25
do—Maps	37 ... 50
	$241 ... 37
Hx Curcy[6]	£60 — 6 — 10

Appendix K: Summary of Expenses and Revenues for *Picture of Quebec*
Scrapbook, not numbered

D & J Smillie received from P & W Ruthven[1] 594 copies of the Picture of Quebec @ 8/—	$594.00
	195.62
leaves in D.& J. Ss hands	$398.38
D. & J. Smillie paid:	
Expenses from Quebec to New York	$22.42
Expenses in N.Y.	22.50
do from N.Y. to Quebec	26.47
paid P. & W. R:	67.00
do Custom house, St John's	5.23
to Mr Cary,[2] prospectus's	6.00
to 4 large lables @ 8/—	4.00
to Mr Hamel,[3] plan of Quebec	24.00
Brothers time collecting Subscribers	18.00
	$195.62
Mr Bourne received from P. & W. Ruthven 635 copies of the Picture of Quebec @ 8/—	$635.00
500 copies impressions in covers, @ 2/—	125.00
By Note from P. & W. R:	63.00
Recd from P. & W. R: for plates of Picture of Quebec	100.00
	$923.00
	387.12½
leaves in Mr B's hands	$535.87½

Mr. Bourne paid	
Mr Armour[4] of Montreal for printing Book	$100.00
Copper plate printing, paper, wood cut, printing &c	227.12½
	$387.12½

Errors excepted

Appendix L: Excerpted Letters to James Smillie, 1827–1839

1. David Smillie, Jr., Quebec, to James Smillie, London (redirected to Edinburgh), 31 October 1827

It is with feelings of the most lively greif that I write you at this time. You may remember about 2 days before you left this our poor Father was taken worse which was on a Friday, those violent fits of shivering continued with interruptions until the second Friday after when it pleased God to take him to himself. After You went away he did not speak a Dozen times to any one, in fact he was insensible for 2 or 3 Days before his Death. . . .

Dear James I hope you found every thing to your mind on your arrival in London. I sincerely hope you will make the best use of your time and talent. . . .Mr. Leggo[1] will be done with the plate in a few days and I shall send it by the Otawa. . . .

2. David Smillie, Jr., Quebec, to James Smillie, London (redirected to Edinburgh), 14 November 1827

. . .I intend to write you by Captn. McDougal[2] who is going to London. . .he has been very kind to us, he sent a Barrel of Sugar of 2 Cwt. the other day, we have laid in 112 lbs. of Oatmeal also. We have almost as much money out as will pay the next quarter rent so I think we will weather the winter pretty snugly. . . .

Dr. Blanchet[3] has ordered Leggo[4] to print 100 more maps so that it will be about a week yet before I can send you the plate. Be sure you send out gravers to Willy [William Cumming Smillie] as early as possible and if you can spare money to purchase a few odds and ends out of the Jewellers rubbish drawers it will serve me very much but do not scrimp yourself for me. . . .

3. J. W. Brent,[5] Quebec, to James Smillie, London (redirected to Edinburgh), 17 December 1827

I take the opportunity of writing by Mr Musson.[6] . . .I requested him to take charge of the seal & to pay the expense of engraving. You will therefore, if you please, give it to him by the by if on receipt of this letter, it should not be done, be kind enough to have JWB instead as I told you, of J.B. I think I told you to have it done in old English. . . .

4. David Smillie, Jr., Quebec, to James Smillie, London (redirected to Edinburgh), 17 December 1827

. . .I wrote you by Miss Heritage who went in the Kingfisher but I suppose you have heard ere this of her loss together with the *Ottawa* which last it is supposed will be a total loss. The Kingfisher I believe will be got off in the Spring. It is said to have been a grand sight to see them. Coll. Ramsay and Mr. Antrobus[7] went down to endeavor to render them some assistance which however was impossible as the Ottawa was fast on the ice and the K— fully worse as she was drifting about at the mercy of the wind and ice in the middle of the river. However she got in shore on a good muddy bottom and the Ottawa was secured likewise but afterwards dragged her anchor and drifted 5 leagues farther down, where she struck on the rocks and it is thought will be a *total wreck*.

I will now give you a word or two on Politics, although you know I am no great politician. In the first place then you must know the Majority of the House of Assembly chose *Papineau*[8] for their Speaker again. The Governor very properly refused this choice. They persisted in it and the consequence was that the Governor prorouged the Parliament until the *3d of January 1828*. There is a report in circulation here that Lord Dalhousie is going home and to be succeeded by the Duke of Gordon.[9] If that is the case the Canadians will find the difference to their cost, for it seems he is a second Sir James Craig[10] and will stand no nonsense. I must now give you some Domestic news. We are all well at present and going on much in the same way as when you left. I got the plate from Leggo[11] and sent it by Miss Heritage but of course got it back when she was wrecked and will send it either with this or Mr. Symes[12] and I hope you will exert yourself when you get it as you know the charge I have now and which is shortly to be increased as I intend to get Married on my Natal Day....

My Uncle [James Smillie, Sr.] has been ill for some time past and so has *she* but he is better now. Jas. Bennet is a Father but not a Husband, a Girl who was servant in the House is with Child to him. He has not been at work for this fortnight past.[13]...Captn. Young[14] has been enquiring very kindly for you and desired me to let him know as soon as we heard from you. I think he has your welfare at heart. I must beg of you not to forget the *gravers* for Willy [William Cumming Smillie] as he is very ill supplied at present, and if you can without running yourself short get a few odds and ends for me you would oblige me much. I have sent a letter inclosed in this for my *Uncle William.*[15] I have left it open so that you may write him a few lines in it and if you would write to my Uncles James & George at Hamilton I would thank you. The address is Townhead, Hamilton near Glasgow.

Mr H[urst][16] has taken sick again at engraving. I think he is a lazy fellow. You are much wanted here again, your loss is much felt. Bennet gets worse if possible and Hurst is too lazy to improve....

I must beg of you not to forget the transparancy[17] for Captn. Young....

5. John McDougal,[18] London, to James Smillie, Edinburgh, 20 December 1827

I felt sadly disapointed on my arrival here at not having the pleasure of seeing you....

David [Smillie, Jr.] I believe wrote you...& sent the Inclosed by me. Be sure and write me on the receipt of this and let me know how you are situated at present...I hear that Lord Dalhousie is comming home and that Sir Francis Burton[19] is to take his place. Will that make any difference in your future prospects? Let me know....

6. John McDougal,[20] London, to James Smillie, Edinburgh, 4 January 1828

...I would have wrote sooner but Mr. Thirlwale has been puting me of from day to day, before I could get money from him. However I have got it at last and I hope it may be of service to you.[21]...

I was to have brought the plate home that you Engraved in Quebec but Mr. Leggo[22] it seems had got an order to take of some more impressions so that I Could not Get it [in] time Enough....

Dear James keep your heart up you will do well yet. I wish to God I had a few hundreds—but never mind we all will have some by and by.

...The number of the note is 16452 when you send an answer I shall send the other half.

7. John McDougal,[23] London, to James Smillie, Edinburgh, 10 January 1828

I received your letter last night and am happy to hear that your prospects Brighten a little more. I have inclosed the other half of the note in this letter. You Can paste the two halves together & get it Changed at the Bank there....

When you are Comming to Quebec Capt. Lowrie of the Rebecca or Capt. W. Cole of the Ariadne or any of the Quebec traders will give you a passage without paying untill you arrive in Quebec. Should it Be with a stranger that you Come I will hold myself responsible for the money to be paid directly on your arrival....

8. David Smillie, Jr., Quebec, to James Smillie, Edinburgh, 20 March 1828

...Give my most hearty and sincere thanks to Mr. Drysdale[24] for his kindness to you. He and I were great friends at one time but I never thought he would have had occasion to show his friendship in such a manner when you had relations in the place. My Dear James you have just received a very flattering Compliment from the Society for the *Encouragement* of *Arts* and *Sciences* in *Canada*. Coll. Bouchette[25] called on me a few days since and requested me to send a specimen of your Engrg. to them. I accordingly did, accompanied with the following note

> Sir
>
> My Brother has directed me to lay before the Society for the encouragement of Arts and Sciences in Canada a Specimen of his Engraving viz. the Accompanying Map which in consequence I respectfuly present to the Society in his name.
>
> I am Very Respectfully
> Sir your Most Obt.
> Humbl. Servt.
> (signed) David Smillie
> for my Brother James Smillie.
>
> To/R.S.M. Bouchette Esqr
> Asst. Secy to the Society.

The enclosed extract from the *Quebec Star* will show what has been the result.[26]...We are doing pretty well and will be able to keep things square till the fall and as you say I am sure we may make a good thing of it....There has been lots of work for you and every probability of more this Summer. It is true that Lord Dalhousie is to leave this. He is appointed Governor General of India. As to a war being likely to take place, tis all Fudge. There is no more probability of it than when you left so you may make yourself easy of that score....I wish you would before you come out call at some of the Jewellers shops and get some of their old rubbish which will be of great use to me here, that is if you can afford it without hurting yourself. Also a few white stones....My Mother intended to have gone home this summer but as you are coming out she has dropt the idea. Bring all the newest fashions in Printing, Engraving &c., you can, it will take well. I wish you would ask my Aunt for my Fathers Portrait.[27] If she will not part with it you can take a copy from it as we should like to have it....My Uncle [James Smillie, Sr.] is not going home as he said....Endeavor to find out whether Millar[28] has been heard of since we came out and if his Wife is in Edinburgh....

9. David Chisholme,[29] Three Rivers, to James Smillie, Quebec, 30 January 1830

The enclosed is a production of mine which was published in the Quebec Official Gazette of the 1st of March 1827.[30]...Should you be of opinion, that I have succeeded in conveying a conception of what the genius of Canada ought to be, perhaps, at your leisure you might be tempted to send him down to posterity in a more desirable and tangible form. You will observe, however, that two plates would be necessary—one to represent the genius and his attendants on land, and the other on water. Yet I doubt whether the country contains sufficient encouragement for such an undertaking; and for my own part, I have too little worldly gear and too little vanity to bear the expense of it, though I should ever be ready to contribute my mite to this, or *any other subject* you may be induced to undertake. The subject of the enclosed, might be a good frontispiece to views of this Country that you may publish, with such alterations and modifications as your own better taste and judgement might suggest....I thank you for your Con[vent Gate].[31] It is a most beautiful production and does you more credit than I can convey in words. Please let me know the price of it, and I shall be happy to send it to you. Any word of my office Seal?...

10. Christopher S. Bourne,[32] Quebec, to James Smillie, Quebec, 20 May 1830

The following is an extract from a letter recd. from my Bro. George[33] this morning—"What is Smillie doing? What a simpleton the Chap was for going away. Shew him Gimber's[34] little design, and give him one of the Proofs *for me*. They are put in the Catalogues. Tell him if he was here now, he might have perhaps 50 to 100 of those to do in the Course of time. He might be kept busy on them for probably more than a year, as

I intend to do a whole series in New York &c. of about that size. Gimber has engaged to do a lot of them, tell him, for $15. rather larger than that & better. *If he has nothing to do, I feel assured he would be employed here, even if he did not agree to do them.* Tell him his Convent Gate has been universally admired, that *I know of at least a doz. Copies that* have been *sent to Europe*. Tell him I think he was the greatest Ass in the world for going away."

The above was *very hastily* written by George, but you can see from what he has said, that he feels interested for you. . .although he expresses himself rather harshly. . . . At any rate from what he says, I am confident if you could not do better in Quebec that he would readily give you employ. You can think of it. I would be very sorry to be the cause of your leaving Canada against the wish of your family, but I say it in case you should not do so well here as you expected, so that at least if you did return to N.Y. you might do it with hopes of meeting with employ.

11. David Smillie, Jr., Quebec, to James Smillie, New York, 25 October 1830

. . .I am extremely happy to hear that the Family got safe to their destination and the more so that they are so highly pleased with the place. . . .There have been wonderful changes here since they left, our new Governor, Lord Aylmer[35] and Lady arrived here on the 16th and on the 20th he took the oaths on which occasion our new Bells were rung. . . .I am highly pleased with Weirs[36] conduct. Such a man is one in ten thousand. It is extremely rare to meet with such disinterested friendship and I need not tell you to cultivate it. Independant of his good qualities as a man, his merits as an artist mark him as a man whose esteem you should endeavour to gain, the benefits will be mutual.

You ought by no means let old Bourne[37] slip with the Picture of Quebec. He ought at all events pay you for the plates and you will be to blame if you do not enforce it. I was quite astonished to learn by Willies [William Cumming Smillie's] letter that Walker said there was a balance in his favor. Bourne has not got Guillbault's money yet. Leggo[38] threatens to make me accountable for his note, he is a great scoundrel Leggo. Coll. Cockburn[39] sent for his plates a few days ago as he could not let them go on your terms—selfish again—. . .I think we are going to have a gay winter here. Lord Aylmer seems to be a dasher. I have had orders for 22 Crests already and there is every appearance of a stir in that way. I am happy to say that George [Smillie] is behaving himself very well. My Uncle [James Smillie, Sr.] has not been in town since they left. He is expected tomorrow. . . .I wish you would send me Impressions of the plates you have done. Jackson[40] is enquiring almost every day about his plate. I have not heard yet from that man at Laprairie to whom you wrote about the trunk. I shall request Mr. Lyman to enquire about it as he goes on. I believe Mr. Daly's[41] plates were in it. . . .I wish you would send down my seal by the first safe hand. I do not want it Engraved. $7 is too much to pay. . . .Cunningham is publishing Scraps of a Literary Lounger by Willis.[42]. . .

12. J. W. Brent,[43] Quebec, to James Smillie, New York, 22 March 1831

. . .I am rather disappointed in not receiving the Plate but trust that you will send it when practicable,. . .I have been busying myself with a trifle for the Bazaar. Its taken from an Engraving likeness of Queen Elizabeth of England. . . .I don't know whether you saw a Painting of the King in the Society's rooms—by Audy[44] I believe. Poor stuff and such a fist as he gives our King, as well as made of him out of all proportion & as shapeless as any thing resembling a hand could well be. . . .

13. J. H. Willis,[45] Quebec, to James Smillie, New York, 23 April 1831

Accompanying is a Copy of my Book,[46] which accept from me, as a token of a friendship which I regret only in its not commencing at an earlier date. You will find in it your favorite song. The book is full of typographical blunders; but with all its faults it had a ready sale,—and I got a *decent* sum for the Copy-right. So I have no reason to complain. . . .I expect to be in N. York in the *fall*, to publish a New Work there; and you must drop copper and graver for *one day* for me. . . .

. . .Scrape me a line by George [Smillie] on his return,—and oblige me by sending me a list of the *names* and *address* of 3 or 4 of your most respectable publishing booksellers, Chaps eligible for *my trade*, when I get on the Spot.

Hawley[47] has published again. And *Kidd*,[48] I am told, is making rapid strides to Kingdom come; as he is very sick somewhere in Upper Canada.

Doctor Waller[49] is going to N. York to Study *Painting*, and quits the pestle and mortar for the varnish brush. . . .

I have your beautiful pencilling *"the farewell"* in full preservation. I was looking at it but a little time ago. . . . If among the stray lumber of your portfolio, you have a very beautiful female head, send it me by George if you can spare it, as I am going to study the delineation of womanly beauty. . . .

14. H. Cowan,[50] Quebec, to James Smillie, New York, 6 August 1832

. . . in these portentious Times of Cholera it is prudent as well pleasant to keep up brisk correspondence. . . . you surely might write in a few words once a month *at least*, as we (Neilson/Cowan) keep a running a/c with the Post Office. . . .

And now my dr. friend I must say a few words relative to the direful scourge which has visited this Continent. You are I suppose generally acquainted with the dreadful ravages it committed on its arrival here. Words are inadequate to convey a just idea of the disease as it existed here for the first 3 weeks after its appearance among us. The Panic prevailed and took such hold of mens Souls, that every consideration gave way to that of self preservation. Thousands betook themselves to flight. Too sanguine of escaping the destroyer, they only carried with them the tainted atmosphere of the City, to infect the families of their friends in the country. Our family remained at their post and did not quit the City. I attended the office regularly and endeavoured to repress a fear which at times almost unmanned me while passing the dead & dying. It is indeed dreadful to contemplate the first days of this desolating scourge and I feel my heart swell with gratitude that myself and my family have all been spared in passing this ordeal of eminent danger. Numbers have been carried of in our neighbourhood and in a house opposite to ours nearly a whole family was cut of in twenty four hours. The regulation of our Board of Health required the cholera bodies to be interred 2 hours after death, and when I saw the corpses of this family borne to the grave, how often and forcibly did the words recur to me that *"In the midst of Life we are in death"*.

The disease has latterly mitigated considerably, and God grant that our City and yours may assume its wonted health. New York has suffered little compared with Quebec & Montreal. The disease does not seem to bear the same malignancy as it did here. The ratio of deaths here has been about 1 in 12!! *which is full 6 times greater than N.Y.* While in London the ratio was 1 in *2800*!!!

. . . amuse yourself in sketching and hope you will not fail to do me something in oil as you promise. I am much pleased with the prints you sent me. "Hoboken" is beautiful and worthy of your graver. Every succeeding picture bears improving traits and you are fast fulfilling the prediction that you have heard me repeatly make with others, that you are intended to reach the pinnacle of your profession. I have been taking lessons of Woodley[51] in drawing and have finished several pencillings.

15. David Chisholme,[52] Three Rivers, to James Smillie, New York, 9 March 1833

Alloo me to introduce to ye'r knowlege and acquaintance ane clever cheel like ye'rsel, Maister H. F. Meyer,[53] a son of the gret Meyer's of Lonan, an' in every respect a brither artist of thene ane. Be kind, gin he please, to the callant, for he is a good fello'. . . . He gangs to Noo-York a perfect stranger. . . .

16. David Smillie, Jr., 64 Notre Dame St., Montreal, to James Smillie, Kingston, New York, 31 May 1837

. . . I shall not say anything about our journey. . . I shall only say that things are not quite so bad here as in N. York and that is all we can say. . . . We got ready to work a week ago but as yet have had only a few trifling jobs. What time will bring forth I do not know but things look rather "queerish or so" at this present writing. The Banks having suspended payments in specie has affected the domestic business very much. . . . Mr. Bourne[54] left this for N. York last friday. He intends staying about eight days. I wish dear Jamie you would write me a long letter and have it sent by him. He will be at Hinshelwoods.[55] I wrote Willie [William Cumming Smillie] by him, he will probably go to Philadelphia, let me know how your business is likely to be affected. You are lucky to be in the country. . . . The weather here is still very cool. We have burned nearly a corde of maple since we have been here, provisions are as high as in N. York with the exception of eggs and bread. If things do not go on brisker than they are likely to do now we must move. I should dread to be here a winter without settled prospects. . . . I have seen young Veit, Charlies brother. His wife shewed me a gold medal which was presented to her Father (Sergt. Major Raston) by the noncommissioned officers of the 70th Regt. It is engraved by you. I remember it was thought a splendid specimen of the art when it was done. It made me laugh when it was shewn to me. . . .

17. George Smillie, Montreal, to James Smillie, New York, 17 June 1837

. . . Mrs. Drysdale[56] wrote David last week. They were burned out last March. Bartie's[57] house is sold at last, for seven hundred and fifty pounds; he is still the occupant. . . . The Canadas are filled with soldiery, among the rest are two regiments of horse dragoons, fine looking men. . . .

18. David Smillie, Jr., Montreal, to James Smillie, Kingston, New York, 1 July 1837

Your affectionate letter by Mr. Bourne[58] was duly received. . . . We are still in the "status quo" as regards to business. We can just manage to get as much as is necessary for the loaves and fishes but as to keeping up the stock or wearables, that is out of the question. We have a great deal of trouble here with the currency, the place has been completely flooded with base coppers, you may think they could scarcely be worse than they were when you were here but you have no idea what miserable trash has been passing, coppers weighing 4 dwts, you may think what like they are. The shopkeepers had a meeting last saturday night when they came to the determiniation to take them at two for one. We had $^{2}/_{6}$ in copper then, and were rather astonished on monday morning to find that we were worth only $^{1}/_{3}$. They have since refused to take any but old english coppers or American cents, the consequence is that we see scarcely anything but little shin plasters which it is unsafe to take, as they are mostly all issued by grocers, tavern keepers, and such like. I do not see what the end of all this will be, but things are in a very deranged state at present. There is to be a great meeting on constitutionalists on monday. I believe we are on the eve of a great change here. The Canadians seem to be very indignant at Lord Russell's resolutions in the Imperial parliament. Some of their head men use most treasonable language and openly recommend smuggling in preference to using any article that has paid a tax to Britain. I am sorry to say that our business prospects appear about the same as when I last wrote you. . . .

19. George Smillie, Montreal, to James Smillie, Kingston, New York, 28 August 1837

. . . You express some anxiety to know how our business is. Dear James. It is as bad as it can be so that we have the Consolation of knowing that it cant be worse. You know the old fashioned style of things in Ann St. Quebec as well as I do, Just so they are here. Disgusting. I am willing to be a shoemaker but not a Cobbler. . . . We have just returned from Quebec. . . . Poor Bartie[59] is to be sold out in september, he was very kind to us. He wants you to write him immediately and let him know whether you would assist him in procuring a farm somewhere near you. I wish you would write him on the subject as he may think I have omitted telling you. . . .

I have had a sale of my furniture. They sold well, some of the things for three times what they cost me so that I lost nothing on that score. My sofa I sold for £ 7/10. I have kept some of my things to serve us untill we leave, which I think will be about the end of september. . . I may as well Close with this request that you will answer this as soon as possible, and that you will write my Uncle likewise and tell him whether you can assist him in the way he says. . . .

20. William Cumming Smillie, Montreal, to James Smillie, New York, 23 June 1839

. . .I leave this tomorrow morning for the Upper Province. I will stay likely two days in Kingston, I will then go on to Toronto and from that I shall go to Hamilton from which place I expect a great deal of entertainment in the way of jaunting. I will go from that place to the falls with some of the Ruthvens and likely return. I wish to see something of the Indians of the Upper Province. . .I shall be in New York. . .on the 6th July. . . .I wish you would cause to be put up in a box, One Thousand Sheets of my Bk. paper[60] cut into half size and direct as I shall afterwards herein insert, and also 1/4 oz. gold foil for dentists from Mr. Ball of any no. he may think best. . . .

[postscript by Adolphus Bourne]
direct Box, A. Bourne, Montreal, Care J. C. Pierce, St. Johns. P. S. Please write me when the Box leaves N. York and send it by Troy Tow Boat here. A. Bourne.

Notes

Introduction

1. See Dusseault-Letocha 1975.
2. Advertisement, QD 1822, appendix, p. 135. James Smillie, Sr., makes mention of having worked in "the finest shops of Edinburgh and London many years."
3. *Daily Mercury*, 27 July 1819.
4. From 1819 to 1831 James Smillie, Sr., is listed at either 16 or 24 Mountain Street (*Daily Mercury*, 27 July 1819; QD 1822, 1826; *Quebec Mercury*, 12 April 1823; *La Gazette de Québec*, 9 July 1829; *Star and Commercial Advertiser*, 19 May 1831). The building was in effect a double house with the numbers 16 and 24. Both halves included an apartment and a shop, one of which James Smillie, Sr., advertised for rent in the *Quebec Mercury* from 12 April to 20 June 1823. He advertised both sides for rent on 8 October 1825, also in the *Quebec Mercury*.

   In 1822 he had some construction work done on his house (Richardson et al. 1984, pp. 400–401, 501–502).
5. James Smillie, Sr., was a contributor to the Quebec Fire Society (*La Gazette de Québec*, 16 April 1821) and the Quebec Immigrant Society (*Quebec Mercury*, 28 October 1823). He was also an active member of the Wesleyan Missionary Society, collecting donations from the public (*Quebec Mercury*, 9 October 1824). His honesty is attested to in an advertisement he placed about a gold seal brought into his shop by a dubious owner (*Quebec Mercury*, 10 August 1823).
6. It is known James Smillie, Sr., had one daughter, who by February 1841 was married to Thomas Drysdale, possibly the same jeweller and watchmaker whom James Smillie, Jr., knew in Edinburgh in 1828. See "Fire and Melancholy Loss of Life," *Quebec Mercury*, 4 February 1841; funeral announcement, *Quebec Mercury*, 6 February 1841; "Distressing Fire at Quebec," *La Gazette de Québec*, 5 February 1841.
7. Marriage bond between David Smillie and Mary Wood, witnessed by James Smillie, Sr., Quebec City, 26 December 1827 (Lower Canada Marriage Bonds [arch. mat.]).
8. James Smillie, Sr., placed the following advertisement in the *Montreal Herald* on 17 November 1821. It is quoted in its entirety to demonstrate not only Smillie's business contacts with Montreal but also to describe the type of merchandise Smillie sold.

   > NOTICE JAMES SMILLIE JEWELLER & LAPIDARY OF QUEBEC
   >
   > BEGS leave most respectfully to inform the Ladies and Gentlemen of Montreal, that, having been repeatedly requested, by some of them whom he has had the honour to serve in his line, to visit this City.
   >
   > He intends to exhibit (in a Room belonging to Dr. Loedle, No. 31, Place D'Armes,) a small, but select, collection of rare and valuable articles, comprising Gaspe Pebble Necklaces, &c. in complete sets; Cape-Diamond Rings in complete set of incomparably fine Oriental Blood Stones from Ceylon, Cameo, Moco, and Lapis-Lazuli Broaches; Cameo and Emerald Rings, and Riband-Onyx ditto, from the Ferro Isles; with other articles which he forbears to enumerate. The greater part of these articles having been manufactured by himself, and the remainder under his immediate inspection, J.S. will warrant them to be equal, in point of workmanship, to the finest productions of London or Edinburgh.

   Further evidence of his Montreal clientele is shown in seven receipted invoices from James Smillie, Sr., to Jacques Viger, dated from 1822 to 1833; they are for jewellery and for gilding a snuffbox (ASQ, Fonds Verreau 39, no. 155).
9. Langdon 1960, p. 90; 1966, p. 129.
10. Lord Chamberlain's and Lord Steward's Departments Papers (arch. mat.). See Cat. No. 23.

11. *Quebec Mercury*, 31 October 1829. James Smillie, Sr., had briefly contemplated returning to Scotland during the winter of 1827/1828 (Appendix L.8).
12. *Star and Commercial Advertiser*, 19 May 1830.
13. *Quebec Mercury*, advertisement, 24 May–4 October 1831.
14. *La Gazette de Québec*, 5 March 1841; "Inquest at Marine Hospital," *Quebec Mercury*, 6 March 1841. See also Introduction, n. 6.
15. Biographical dates are recorded in the Smillie family bible (Smillie Family Collection).
16. The eight children were Margaret (1802–1871), David (1804–1865), James (1807–1885), Eliza (1809–1824), George (1811–1881), William Cumming (1813–1908), Mary Ann (1817–1870), and Jessie (1819–1913). A ninth child listed in the family bible, Catherine Haxton Smillie (1822–1823), was probably the daughter of Margaret Smillie and James Salker Millar.
17. Nevertheless, in 1822 David Smillie, Sr., contributed to the building fund of St. Andrews Presbyterian Church (Price 1981, appendix 3, D, p. 83).
18. Biographical fragment in William Cumming Smillie Papers (arch. mat.).
19. D. Smillie & Sons must have moved to 10 Ste. Anne Street in early 1826. This new address is listed in the city directory for that year (QD 1826), whereas the shop on Garden Street is shown in the print of the Tandem Sleigh Club (Cat. No. 32). For full description of shop addresses, see Pilgrimage, n. 14.
20. *Quebec Mercury*, 12 August 1828. The advertisement ran until mid-November.
21. Langdon 1966, p. 129, cites a letter that David Smillie, Jr., wrote to John Clark of Clarksville, Napanee, Ontario, in which he quotes a price of five pounds for a medal to be engraved with an inscription of Clark's choosing. (The authors have not been able to locate this letter.)
22. *La Gazette de Québec*, 9 July 1829.
23. *Star and Commercial Advertiser*, 21 April, 19 May 1830.
24. *La Gazette de Québec*, 4 October 1831.
25. Fox 1985, p. 22.
26. *Montreal Gazette*, 3 September 1839.
27. The only Canadian subject matter published by William Cumming Smillie during his early career is an 1835 map of Quebec. The map was printed in five states and his name disappears from the map in the second state published in 1840 (Dahl et al. 1975, pp. 212, 261–262). Information on the states of the map was kindly supplied by Edward Dahl.
28. William Cumming Smillie Papers (arch. mat.); Bond 1984, pp. 160–161; Boggs 1945, pp. 109–112; Smedley 1958, pp. 771–780. The last publication is a good source for information on the third generation of North American Smillies.
29. Ruddel 1987, pp. 253, 256.
30. Although there are no definitive statistics to state categorically that many of these new settlers to Quebec came from the urban artisan class of Great Britain, it is an assumption that can be put forward. The artisan class remained remarkably stable at approximately seven per cent of the population between 1805 and 1831, while the population jumped by nearly three hundred per cent. Given that this was a time of unprecedented emigration from the British Isles, the additional increase in the artisan class must have been of British stock (Hardy and Ruddel 1977, p. 189).
31. For a detailed study on the history of the Citadel construction and its effects on Quebec, see Charbonneau, Desloges, and Lafrance 1982.
32. Ruddell 1981, pp. 367–374.
33. Many references appear regarding Dalhousie's encouragement of artists in his letters and journals. See Dalhousie Papers (arch. mat.); Whitelaw 1978–1982.

    Dalhousie's propensity for rewarding talented amateur artists with attractive appointments may have been well known. Lieutenant Henry Pooley of the Royal Engineers found quick success when he brought himself to Dalhousie's attention by presenting the governor in chief with a collection of watercoloured views of the ports and harbours he surveyed in the Maritimes. Pooley's reward was an appointment as engineer on the construction of the Rideau Canal as well as his temporary appointment to Dalhousie's staff in Quebec. See Conolly 1898, no. 551. Pooley to

Dalhousie, 20 April 1821; Dalhousie to Sir James Kempt, 16 June 1821; Pooley to Dalhousie, 8 May 1824; Pooley to Dalhousie, 10 May 1824; Dalhousie Papers (arch. mat.).

Pooley's maps and watercolours may be found in the William Inglis Morse Collection, Dalhousie University Library, Halifax; the NA; and the NGC.

34. John Elliott Woolford watercolours from the Dalhousie collection are now in the NSM, the NA, the NGC, and the ROM. An important collection of Woolford's work is also in the MTL.

William Roebuck watercolours are in the collections of the NA, the ROM, and the AEAC. They are similar to the drawings of Coteau-du-lac and the lower St. Lawrence in Woolford's 1819 album. Between 1818 and 1824 Roebuck was living in this area. The works attributed to him are after Woolford, his brother John Arthur Roebuck (1802–1879), and Joseph Bouchette (1774–1841). Roebuck's stepfather was Lord Dalhousie's private secretary, and many works by John and William Roebuck were once in Dalhousie's collection.

For further information on William Roebuck, see Cooke 1983, pp. 169–171. For information on John Roebuck, see Marleau 1983, pp. 5–7.

Charles Ramus Forrest's watercolours after Woolford sketches are to be found in the collections of the NGC and the ROM. For a biography on Forrest, see Cooke 1983, pp. 81–85. The Forrest birth date was provided by the artist's descendants.

35. There were two Andrew Browns (father and son) in Quebec, who could qualify as the artist. Brown, Sr., was colonel of the Seventy-ninth Regiment of Foot and present in Quebec from 1825 to 1828. His son was a lieutenant in the same regiment and was present in Quebec from 1827 to 1828. For further information, see Cooke 1983, pp. 31–32.
36. Illustrated in Sotheby & Co. (Canada) 1968, lot 70.
37. Thomas George Marlay (1809–1837). Marlay arrived in Quebec in 1830 and served in the Royal Artillery under James Pattison Cockburn. A large group of Marlay's drawings are in the collection of the AGH. See Oko 1984, p. 43.
38. The connection of John Crawford Young, James Pattison Cockburn, and John Elliott Woolford with both James Smillie and Lord Dalhousie is well documented in Smillie's autobiography. See Pilgrimage, nn. 23, 24 for biographical information on Young and Cockburn. The connection of William Wallace with both the engraver and Dalhousie must have been through the presentation of the Wallace/Smillie print *The Quebec Driving Club* to Dalhousie. Three impressions of that print remained in the Dalhousie collection until 1931 (Sotheby and Co. [London] 1931, lot 74.)
39. In the Scrapbook James Smillie included the following letter, noted as no. 45, from Lord Dalhousie at Sorel to Smillie at Quebec, dated 20 August 1827.

> Mr. Smillie
>
> I spoke to Captain Young as arranged & plan for you on arrival in London but have gone down to Gaspe & may not be back before 20th Sept. after that I will give you letters which may be useful, but I can't before that.
>
> Yours
> Dalhousie

40. *Star and Commercial Advertiser*, 15 July 1829.
41. *Quebec Mercury*, 12 August 1828.
42. A pencil drawing of Ste. Foy Church, traditionally attributed to James Smillie, is more probably by James Pattison Cockburn (MQ A56.346D). The drawing is inscribed "Ste. Foy Church near Quebec / 19th June 1829 J.S—." The date has also been interpreted as reading "1825" (Morriset 1959, no. 213). The style of drawing is closer to Cockburn's, and the handwriting—including the nines that look like fives—resembles that of his inscriptions. Moreover, a watercolour by Cockburn of the same subject in a private collection bears the identical date (Cameron and Trudel 1978, p. 152, pl. 139).
43. *La Gazette de Québec*, 9 September 1790.

44. *Quebec Mercury*, 30 May 1829.
45. *Quebec Mercury*, 12, 18, 20, 23, 25 August 1831. The sale was evidently successful, and on 5 September 1831 R. W. Kelly, auctioneer, was advertising in the *Quebec Mercury* the sale of another group of prints sent to him by George M. Bourne.
46. Lacroix 1984, pp. 155–184; Béland and Lachapelle 1982; Martin 1980. It was not uncommon to find such engravings in the houses of the merchants and legislative councillors of Quebec (Bervin 1983, pp. 45–62, table 2).
47. The Scrapbook, consisting of 116 leaves measuring 32.1 cm × 28.6 cm each, is half-bound with red leather and cloth covered boards, 33.0 cm × 28.6 cm. The title, "In Memoriam," in gold tooling on red leather, is affixed to the front cover. The prints and drawings are glued to the leaves, as are Smillie's manuscript notes on separate strips of ruled paper. A few documents and prints are loosely inserted between leaves.
48. In 1901 James David Smillie donated a large number of his father's prints to the NYPL. Frank Weitenkampf, keeper of prints, was given a free hand in the selection, and he made careful lists of the desired works. He chose two Canadian works for the library's collection (Cat. Nos. 6, 53). Because of their large size, these prints had never been mounted in the Scrapbook. Therefore, despite James David Smillie's notations, the NYPL's selection and acquisition cannot explain the absence of two works (Cat. No. 3, Appendix B), which were removed from the pages of the Scrapbook.

    See entries for 9–12, 14, 17–19, 20–21 May 1901, Diaries of James David Smillie (arch. mat.), roll 2853; receipt from Frank Weitenkampf, 20 May 1901, James David Smillie Papers (arch. mat.); NYPL Print Room accession log.
49. Although this is the first time that "A Pilgrimage" has been published as written, the manuscript has been used as the basis for several biographies on the engraver. The most notable is the four-part article on James Smillie by Thomas F. Morris (1944–1945). This biography is a paraphrase of "A Pilgrimage," written without the assistance of the accompanying document, the scrapbook "In Memoriam."

Pilgrimage

1. Guthrie, Guthrie, and Guthrie 1874–1875. Reverend Thomas Guthrie (1803–1873) was a Scottish preacher and philanthropist (*DNB*).
2. Sir George MacKenzie (1780–1848), mineralogist, led an expedition to the Faeroe Islands in 1812 as a follow up to an 1810 expedition to Iceland (*DNB*). Thomas Allan (1777–1833), banker and mineralogist, accompanied MacKenzie to the Faeroe Islands (*DNB*). It is possible that the later trip David Smillie, Sr., made to Norway may have been for Thomas Allan, who was a noted collector of mineral samples from northern regions, particularly Greenland.
3. Margaret Smillie (1802–1871), daughter of David Smillie, Sr., and Elizabeth Cumming. She married James Salker Millar in 1820 and Robert Hinshelwood (1812–post-1875) in 1834.
4. No information about the silver engraver James Johnston has been found. For indenture, see Appendix A.
5. Edward Mitchell (act. 1805–1821), an engraver in Edinburgh, known chiefly for portrait engravings (Bushnell 1929, p. 266; Guy 1916, pp. 85, 97). In 1805 he engraved a series of views of Scotland, including four after John Elliott Woolford (*Edinburgh Scene* 1951, pp. 159, 259; see also Cat. No. 4).
6. "Port of Quebec: Arrive 6 [June] Brig Neptune, Bell, sailed 19th April from Leith to order, ballast, 59 settlers" (*Daily Mercury*, 8 June 1821).
7. James Salker Millar does not appear to have served in the Royal Marines before his marriage to Margaret Smillie. On 8 July 1821 he advertised in the *Daily Mercury* as a writing master giving lessons at 19 Mountain Street, that is, across the street from James Smillie, Sr. He described himself as an expert, from long practice received under his father, late writing master in Edinburgh. On 20 July 1821 he submitted a new advertisement to the *Daily Mercury*, for classes to begin 23 July. On 31 July the

editorial section of the *Daily Mercury* noted that Mr. Millar would remain in the city all winter, and would expect no payment from unsatisfied pupils. No report has been found in Quebec newspapers regarding the bigamy lawsuit brought against him.

8. The voyage from Leith to Quebec must have been unusually difficult. Twenty-five of the passengers from both the steerage and cabin class took out an advertisement in the *Daily Mercury*, 12 June 1821, to thank Captain W. Bell for his "gentlemanlike conduct and kind treatment." Needless to say, the family of David Smillie, Sr., did not participate in this public acknowledgement.
9. *The New York Tribune* obituary (6 December 1885) for James Smillie describes his early life in Quebec as an engraver, stating that "In those days and in that place so little was known of art that one can hardly understand the difficulties that had to be met. For his plates he had to get copper sheathing from the ship yard, which he planished and prepared himself." This information no doubt came from the family.
10. The time of the falling out may have occurred in 1822, when David Smillie, Sr., took a shop at 8 Garden Street (QD 1822).
11. The Tandem Club was a social gathering of prominent members of Quebec society, most of them connected with the garrison, who met for sleigh outings during the long winter months. Lord and Lady Dalhousie were patrons of the club.
12. The house of James Smillie, Sr., burned on 4 February 1841.
13. An album of Lady Dalhousie's drawings is in the collection of the NSM.
14. James Smillie may be mistaken about the date of this move. From the examination of various sources, it appears that by 1822 David Smillie, Sr., had moved the business to 8 Garden Street (QD 1822), where the family remained until at least April 1826 (Cat. No. 32). In that same year, the family moved to 10 Ste. Anne Street (QD 1826) and remained there through the summer of 1828 (advertisements, *Quebec Mercury*, 15 July, 12 August 1828). In July 1829 D. & J. Smillie advertised from a St. Stanislas Street address (*La Gazette de Québec*, 9 July 1829).
15. Mrs. Otte began advertising her laundry business on 8 July 1821 when she received her mangle (a machine for pressing laundry by passing it between heated rollers) from London. At this time she was established in St. John suburb, opposite the English burial ground, and her advertisements ran through late January 1822. On 2 June 1827 a laundress with a mangle, Mrs. A. E. Collins—either Mrs. Otte remarried or her successor—advertised her business on St. John Street. By 17 June 1828 Mrs. Collins had moved to Ste. Anne Street "at Mr. Smillie's, Gold Smith &c." (advertisements, *Daily Mercury/Quebec Mercury*, 8 July 1821–15 July 1828).

    James Smillie probably received the press from Mrs. Otte before March 1823 (his first dated print), rather than in 1824.
16. William Gale (act. 1809–1838). In 1819 Gale emigrated from Scotland, where he had been a private teacher for ten years. He was able to boast of testimonials from the Reverend Dr. Chalmers and Professors Jardine, Walker, and Young from the University of Glasgow. His system of teaching was the Bell or Madras System "as formulated by Dr. Bell's Schools in England."

    Gale and his wife opened their English Commercial Academy for girls and boys at 4 Hope Street in 1819. In May 1823 the school expanded, becoming the French and English Academy at 14 Rampart Street in the Montcalm House. A few boarders were planned for at this time. As the Gales' school flourished, the curriculum expanded. In May 1825 the Gales moved their school to St. Augustine, 12 miles from Quebec. They now advertised themselves as a "Boarding School for Young Ladies & Gentlemen." Here they prospered for many years.

    The biographical information comes from the many advertisements Gale placed (*Daily Mercury/Quebec Mercury*, 1820–1838; QD 1822).
17. "DIED On Saturday Morning, 5th inst. aged 16 years, Eliza, second daughter of Mr. David Smillie, of the City" (*Quebec Mercury*, 8 June 1824).
18. No documentation has been found regarding a change in address in 1824. See Pigrilmage, n. 14.
19. No examples of James Smillie's work as a silversmith have been located.
20. The dating is incorrect here. In 1824 James Smillie etched a map of St. Gabriel (Cat.

No. 12). The map of the Saint John River Valley was published in 1827 (Cat. No. 54). On 6 March 1828, at its annual meeting, the Society for the Encouragement of Arts and Sciences in Canada awarded him its first-prize medal for the Saint John map. In 1829 he was made a member of the society. See *Star and Commercial Advertiser*, 19 March 1828; Appendices F, L.8).

21. This commission may have been initiated through Marie-Louise McLoughlin (1780–1846), who, as Mère de Saint-Henri, was superior of the Ursulines of Quebec from 20 April 1818 to 27 April 1824.
22. This reference is to a newspaper clipping about the fire.
23. John Crawford Young (1788–c. 1859). Born in Scotland, Young joined the Ninety-first Regiment of Foot in 1804, eventually rising to the rank of captain. In 1817 he transferred to the Seventy-ninth Regiment of Foot (Queen's Own Cameron Highlanders), which was posted to Quebec in October 1825. He served on the staff of the Earl of Dalhousie as acting aide-de-camp from October 1826 to June 1827. In 1828 his regiment was transferred to Montreal. He then served at Île-aux-Noix, Kingston, and York. Receiving a leave of absence from his regiment, Young returned to Edinburgh in 1835.

    Young produced many watercolours of Canadian scenery and costumes, some of which he presented to Dalhousie in May 1827. This collection is now in the NGC and includes Young's designs for his best-known artistic production, the monument to Wolfe and Montcalm, which was erected in the Jardin des Gouverneurs in 1827/1828. Young's watercolours can also be found in the collections of the ROM, the NA, and the McC. For further information on Young, see Cooke 1983.
24. James Pattison Cockburn (1779–1847). Cockburn was one of the best and most prolific of the military artists to have served in Canada. He entered the Royal Military Academy at Woolwich in 1793 where he studied under Paul Sandby (1725–1809), who was Woolwich's drawing master at the time. As an officer in the Royal Artillery, Cockburn served twice in Quebec: from November 1822 to June 1823 and, as commander of the Royal Artillery in Canada, from August 1826 to August 1832. Before coming to Canada, Cockburn had already had a number of his watercolours printed in etching, aquatint, and lithography. His earliest publication was in 1807, and he regularly used the finest printers and publishers London had to offer. For further information on Cockburn and for the text of *Quebec and Its Environs*, see Bell and Cooke 1978.

    The close association between John Crawford Young and Cockburn went beyond a mutual desire to co-publish a set of their watercolours. Both officers sat on the committee to choose the design for the monument to Wolfe and Montcalm. They also exhibited together at the Ladies Bazaar on 7 April 1828 (review, *Quebec Mercury*, 8 April 1828).

    Lord Dalhousie seems to have taken delight in this association. After returning from a brief visit to the Ottawa River in 1827 with Young in his entourage, Dalhousie wrote: "Capt. Young has made a large selection of drawings which he will certainly tempt Colonel Cockburn to visit the Ottawa. . . ." Eight days later he remarked: "[Colonel Cockburn] is gone on to the Ottawa, truly as I expected stirred up by the sketches which Young has shewn him" (Whitelaw 1982, vol. 3, p. 109, entries for 11, 19 August 1827). The Young drawings of the Ottawa River are in the collection of the NGC. The Cockburns are in the collections of the ROM and the NA.
25. See Introduction, n. 39.
26. Arthur Aikin (1784–1854), mineralogist, author, editor, and resident secretary of the Society of Arts for many years. He is described as a man of quiet, retiring habits (Baillie and Sleveking 1984).
27. "'Port of Quebec' In the transport Heydon sailed this day for Portsmouth,. . .Dr. Forbes and a number of invalids belonging to regiments serving in the Canadas" (*Quebec Mercury*, 16 October 1827).
28. John Landseer (1763–1852).
29. Sir Edwin Landseer (1802–1873).
30. Thomas Landseer (1795–1880).

31. Emma Landseer (n.d.).
32. Charles Landseer (1799–1879).
33. No engraver by the name of Warrener has been found. The person Smillie is referring to may possibly be Alfred William Warren, a reproductive engraver in London during the first half of the 19th century.
34. George Cruickshank (1792–1878).
35. George B. Gale was an actor and stage manager recruited in England by William Blanchard, owner of Quebec's Royal Circus. Gale arrived in Quebec in September 1825 and did well during his first season. After a poor performance of *Richard III*, however, actors from the Theatre Royal in Montreal came to take over the roles. Gale apparently returned to Montreal with Frederick Brown and the Theatre Royal troup, for his wife Sophia Frances died there in May 1826. By August, Gale was back in Quebec, receiving good reviews for his performances. His return to England in November 1826 was delayed because of a shipwreck; he left Canada in late May 1827, after giving a concert at La Fontaine's Tavern to raise money for his passage home. He returned to Quebec and the Royal Circus about 1830, with a new actress-wife. In July 1831 he opened his own theatre in Quebec, the Theatre Royal, Haymarket, which featured Frederick Brown in its opening production. Gale left Quebec not long after this date. This biographical note was compiled from numerous advertisements and reviews in the *Quebec Mercury* (1825–1831).

    The George Gale (1797?–1850) mentioned in the *DNB* may be the same person. This man was acting in New York in 1831, returned to England with a tribe of Indians whom he exhibited at the Victoria Theatre, and ended his days as a balloonist. He was last seen alive clinging to the tackle of his balloon over Bordeaux.
36. "Aunt Haxton," sister of James and David Smillie, Sr., was married to Richard Haxton, jeweller of 11 Sellars Court, Potter Row, Edinburgh. Richard Haxton witnessed the apprenticeship indenture of James Smillie, Jr., in 1819 (Appendix A).
37. "'Died' Last Night, Mr. David Smillie, Silversmith of this city" (*Quebec Mercury*, 27 October 1827). See Appendix L.1.
38. The only Andrew Wilson noted in several biographical dictionaries is the well-known Scottish landscape painter (1780–1848), who was also an engraver specializing in portraits and bookplates. A letter from Mr. Wilson of 13 Hill Place, Edinburgh, to James Smillie, dated 1 January 1828, is included in the Scrapbook as no. 60. According to the letter, Smillie is to pay ten pounds for six months' instruction in engraving and is expected to furnish his own tools, copper plates, etc.
39. "'Port of Quebec' Arrived Aug. 10—Margaret, Smith, 19th June from Leith, to Lawrie & Spence, coals" (*Star and Commercial Advertiser*, 13 August 1828).
40. George Bourne (1780–1845). Born and trained in England as a Presbyterian minister, Bourne came to Virginia and Maryland after his ordination. While in these Southern states, he was so revolted by slavery, that he became one of the first abolitionists, publishing a tract in 1814 in favour of immediate emancipation. Bitterly persecuted and condemned for heresy by his own church, Bourne left for Pennsylvania and then New York State. He finally emigrated to Quebec, taking up the ministry of St. John's Chapel in February 1825. Shortly afterwards, in May, he was elected secretary of the Quebec Bible Society. While in Quebec he became a strong opponent of Catholicism. In 1829 he was "Librarian & Keeper of the Cabinet" of the Literary and Historical Society of Quebec. Bourne returned to New York City in 1830, but without a church. During 1831 and 1832 he joined the more liberal Dutch Reformed Church. For the remainder of his career he was a prominent and active abolitionist. See *Quebec Mercury*, 28 February, 31 May 1825; *Star and Commercial Advertiser*, 24 June 1829; *DAB*.
41. William Augustus Leggo (act. Quebec 1825–1855) printed several of James Smillie's plates in Quebec (see Cat. No. 22). The only other person to whom Smillie might be referring is Edward Bennet (act. Quebec 1821–1828), who listed his profession as "Engraver and Copper-plate printer" (Appendix C).
42. George Melksham Bourne was a news agent in New York in 1827; he operated the Depository of Arts, Engravings and Fancy Store at 359 Broadway, New York, from

1828 to 1832. He was the son of the Reverend George Bourne. See Peters 1931, p. 101.

43. Possibly Robert Miller, engraver, printer, and lithographer, listed in New York City directories from 1830 to 1843 (Groce and Wallace 1957).
44. Stephen Henry Gimber (c. 1806–1862). Gimber was an engraver and portrait and miniature painter. Born in England, he moved to New York City about 1829, where he worked in association with Archibald L. Dick. In 1842 Gimber moved to Philadelphia. He was an associate member of the National Academy of Design. See Groce and Wallace 1957.
45. Robert Walter Weir (1803–1889). Weir was born in New York City and was one of the first Americans to study painting in Italy, which he did from 1824 to 1826. From 1834 to 1876 he taught drawing at the United States Military Academy, West Point, on the Hudson River and played a significant role in the Hudson River School movement.
46. Asher Brown Durand (1796–1886). Durand began his career as an engraver, although he is best known for his work as a painter. He was one of the principal artists of the Hudson River School and president of the National Academy of Design from 1845 to 1861. It is difficult to know precisely why Durand would need James Smillie's participation on this project, unless he was pressed for time. Durand, in fact, engraved all the prints in this series, except for the folio cover, which was done by Smillie. Smillie also commenced work on the print *Fort Putnam*, but it was finished by Durand (Stauffer 1907, vol. 2, nos. 672, 676).
47. Scrapbook no. 102 is a proof engraving by Stephen Henry Gimber, after C. Burton, inscribed "BROADWAY, NEAR FRANKLIN ST. NEW YORK." The view includes Bourne's store at 359 Broadway.
48. "We regret to learn that the ingenious young artist DAVID [mistakenly for James] SMILLIE finds it necessary to leave Quebec for want of encouragement, and to proceed to New York" (*Star and Commercial Advertiser*, 17 July 1830).

Appendices

Appendix C

1. QD 1822; Harper 1970.
2. *Daily Mercury*, 20 April 1821.
3. *Quebec Mercury*, 2 August 1822.
4. Dahl et al. 1975, no. 83, pp. 123–125.
5. J. S. McCord Family Papers (arch. mat.).

Appendix F

1. The society joined with the Quebec Literary and Historical Society later in 1829.

Appendix H

1. Lieutenant Colonel George Couper, aide-de-camp first to Lord Dalhousie and then Sir James Kempt.
2. *Picture of Quebec* was dedicated to Sir James Kempt (1764–1854), at that time administrator of the government of Canada. Smillie's name, however, did not appear on the dedication page beside that of George Bourne.

Appendix J

1. Robert Miller, engraver, printer, and lithographer, listed in New York City directories from 1830 to 1843.
2. Possibly Peter C. Smith & Joseph B. Smith (act. New York City 1824–1828), printers and booksellers.
3. Alexander Anderson (1775–1870), wood engraver, miniaturist, and physician. Anderson was the first known engraver on wood in the United States. See Cat. No. 69a.

4. Charles Neale (act. New York City 1843–1851), engraver, and/or John Neale (act. New York City 1844), printer and engraver.
5. Prosper Desobry (act. New York City 1824–1844), lithographer.
6. Halifax currency, which rated the dollar at five shillings. In Appendix K, Smillie uses the New York exchange rate of eight shillings to the dollar, a rating common in Lower Canada at that time.

Appendix K

1. P. & W. Ruthven, booksellers and publishers in Quebec, were selling agents for the first edition of the *Picture of Quebec*, and the publishers of the second edition. The family were also friends of the Smillies.
2. Thomas Cary & Co., booksellers and publishers, were founded by Thomas Cary (1751–1823) and continued in family ownership. Cary also founded the *Daily Mercury* in 1805.
3. Joseph Hamel (act. 1829–1866), Quebec surveyor.
4. Robert Armour (1781–1857), businessman and publisher. He was King's printer for the Montreal district from 1827 to 1832, bought the Montreal Gazette in 1827, and founded other publishing firms with his sons.

Appendix L

1. The printer William Augustus Leggo. See Cat. No. 22.
2. John McDougal, ship captain and good friend of the Smillie family. He was also an unsuccessful suitor for Margaret Smillie.
3. Dr. François Blanchet (1776–1830). In 1827 he was chairman of the committee of the Legislative Assembly reporting on the opening of roads for the colonization of the Province of Lower Canada. See Cat. No. 52.
4. See Appendix L, n. 1.
5. J. W. Brent, a member of the Literary and Historical Society of Quebec in 1831. See Appendix L.12.
6. J. Musson, apothecary and chemist at 3 Buade Street, Quebec, in 1826.
7. John Ramsay (1775–1842), colonel in chief of the Seventy-ninth Highlanders and military secretary to Lord Dalhousie from 1826 to 1828, and Edmund William Romer Antrobus (1795–1852), army officer and overseer of highways for the district of Quebec.
8. Louis-Joseph Papineau (1786–1871).
9. No Gordon came to Canada as governor. The person referred to is either Alexander, fourth Duke of Gordon (1743–1827), or his son George, fifth Duke of Gordon (1770–1836).
10. Sir James Henry Craig (1748–1812), governor in chief of British North America from 1807 to 1811 and virulent opponent of the Parti canadien.
11. See Appendix L, n. 1.
12. George Symes (act. 1793-d. 1833), prominent Quebec merchant, or one of his sons (Gagnon 1913, nos. 4342–4345).
13. James Bennet, mentioned again in this letter, was evidently employed as an engraver in the Smillie shop.
14. Captain John Crawford Young. See Introduction, pp. 5, 8, 9; Cat. Nos. 64–65; Pilgrimage, n. 23.
15. "Uncle William" may be the same person depicted in Cat. No. 61.
16. Mr. Hurst was not listed in the QD. Presumably he was employed in the Smillie shop.
17. Possibly a proof engraving on transparent paper.
18. See Appendix L, n. 2.
19. Sir Francis N. Burton (1766–1832), lieutenant governor of Lower Canada from 1808 to 1832, although he left the country in 1825. He undermined Dalhousie's policies and had hoped to succeed him.
20. See Appendix L, n. 2.
21. See Pilgrimage, p. 25.
22. See Appendix L, n. 1.

23. See Appendix L, n. 2.
24. Thomas Drysdale. See Cat. No. 62.
25. Robert Shore Milnes Bouchette (1796–1842), fourth son of Surveyor General Joseph Bouchette (1774–1841).
26. *Star and Commercial Advertiser*, 19 March 1828; see also Appendix F.
27. *David Smillie, Sr.*, oil on canvas, 24.5 × 19.5 (Introduction, p. 3), now in the Smillie Family Collection.
28. James Salker Millar. See Pilgrimage, pp. 15, 16; n. 7.
29. David Chisholme (1796–1842), journalist and author, at this date postmaster for Trois Rivières. See Pilgrimage, p. 30.
30. The enclosed was a poem entitled "The Genius of Canada," which James Smillie kept in his Scrapbook.
31. An etching after Robert W. Weir. See Pilgrimage, pp. 28–29.
32–33. Christopher S. Bourne (act. Quebec 1830–1831), and his brother George Melksham Bourne (act. New York City 1827–1835), sons of the Reverend George Bourne (1780–1845), author of *Picture of Quebec*. George M. Bourne operated a print shop in New York and in 1831 published a fine set of views of the city, engraved by James Smillie, Stephen Henry Gimber, and others. See Pilgrimage, p. 30, n. 47.
34. Stephen Henry Gimber (c. 1806–1862). See Pilgrimage, n. 44.
35. Matthew Whitworth-Aylmer, fifth Baron Aylmer (1775–1850), governor in chief of Canada from 1831 to 1835.
36. Robert W. Weir. See Pilgrimage, p. 28, n. 45.
37. Reverend George Bourne. See Pilgrimage, p. 27, n. 40.
38. See Appendix L, n. 1.
39. James Pattison Cockburn. See Introduction, pp. 5, 8, 9; Pilgrimage p. 20, n. 24.
40. Probably Nicholas Jackson, barber, at 18 St. Peter Street, Quebec (QD 1826), who later advertised himself as "Emperor of the North" at 20 St. John Street (*Quebec Mercury*, 15 July 1828).
41. Possibly Sir Dominick Daly (1798–1868), at that date provincial secretary for Lower Canada.
42. John Howard Willis (act. 1830–1841), *Scraps and Sketches; Or, the Album of a Literary Lounger* (Montreal: H. H. Cunningham, 1831).
43. See Appendix L, n. 5.
44. The portrait of George IV exhibited at the Literary and Historical Society of Quebec was a copy after the painting by Sir Thomas Lawrence (1769–1830), by Mr. Wheatley, a drapery painter in the Lawrence studio (*Quebec Mercury*, 4 August 1829). In 1830 Jean-Baptiste Roy-Audy (1778–c. 1848) completed his version of the Wheatley oil, and it was purchased by the members of the Legislative Council for placement in the Château Saint-Louis. It has since disappeared and was probably burned in the fire that destroyed the château in 1834 (*La Gazette de Québec*, 15 January, 18 March 1830; *Quebec Mercury*, 20 March 1830). Another copy of the Wheatley-Lawrence portrait of George IV was painted by Joseph Légaré (1795–1855) in late 1829 (*Quebec Mercury*, 7 November 1829).
45. John Howard Willis (act. 1830–1841), author and artist (Gagnon 1895, nos. 3220, 4399).
46. See Appendix L, n. 42.
47. William Fitz Hawley (1804–1855), poet.
48. Adam Kidd, poet. See Cat. No. 73.
49. Dr. Waller has not been identified; at the end of this letter, Willis sketched a head and entitled the drawing "Sam Waller of Canada."
50. H. Cowan was a son or relative of William Cowan of the printing and publishing firm of Neilson & Cowan, which commissioned the firm of D. Smillie & Sons to print and engrave two hundred cards and to engrave letters on a box (Invoice, ASQ, Polygraphie 36, no. 23A). In 1844 the Cowans, as W. Cowan & Son, reissued James Smillie's etchings for *Picture of Quebec* in *The Quebec Guide*, which had an additional four illustrations by "H. Cowan." See Cat. No. 69.

51. Mr. Woodley (act. Quebec 1830–1834), miniature painter and drawing teacher (Harper 1970).
52. Chisholme (see Appendix L, n. 29) has playfully chosen to write to his countryman in the Scottish dialect of their native land.
53. Hoppner Francis Meyer (1811–post-1861), son of London engraver Henry Meyer (c. 1782–1847), active as a painter of small watercolour portraits, and also as an engraver and lithographer. He visited Quebec in 1832, and went to New York in 1833. He returned to Canada in 1841 and lived in Toronto until c. 1861.
54. Probably the Montreal printer Adolphus Bourne (1795–1886); it is not known whether he was related to the New York Bournes (Allodi 1980, nos. 28–33; *DCB*).
55. Engraver Robert Hinshelwood (1812–post-1875), who married Margaret Smillie in 1834.
56. Mrs. Thomas Drysdale, daughter of James Smillie, Sr. (Cat. No. 62).
57. From the context of Appendix L.19, it seems that "Bartie" was a familiar name for James Smillie, Sr. He continued to live in the Mountain Street house, but according to his death notice in 1841, he no longer owned the property.
58. See Appendix L, n. 54.
59. See Appendix L, n. 57.
60. The "Bank paper" was evidently intended for Montreal printer Adolphus Bourne (see Appendix L, n. 54). The gold foil may have been destined for George Smillie's dentistry work.

Selected Bibliography

Archival Material

Canada Company Papers. *Accounting Records*, C-2, vol. 1, 1824–1849; *General Letterbook*, 1824–1831, A-6-1, vol. 1; *Commissioners' Reports, London*, 30 March, 23 June 1831, A-4-4, Ms. 564, roll 7. Archives of Ontario, Toronto.

Civil Secretary's Correspondence. Upper Canada Sundries, 1824. RG5, A1, 36447–36448. National Archives of Canada, Ottawa.

Dalhousie Papers. Scottish Records Office, Edinburgh. Microfilm MG24, A12. National Archives of Canada, Ottawa.

Lord Chamberlain's and Lord Steward's Departments Papers, 1824. LC. 3.69(62) (Household Index). Public Record Office, London, England.

Lower Canada Marriage Bonds. RG4, B28, vol. 34, 808. National Archives of Canada, Ottawa.

J. S. McCord Family Papers. McCord Museum, Montreal.

Smillie Family Papers, Smillie Family Collection.

James David Smillie Diaries, 1868–1910. Microfilm roll 2850, 2853. Archives of American Art, Smithsonian Institution, Washington, D.C.

________ Papers. Microfilm roll 1710. Archives of American Art, Smithsonian Institution, Washington, D.C.

William Cumming Smillie Papers. Memoranda and Agreements. MG29, A33. National Archives of Canada, Ottawa.

City Directories

MD 1842–1844
Robert W. S. Mackay. *The Montreal Directory*. Montreal: Lovell & Gibson; Robert W. S. Mackay, 1842–1844.

MD 1844–1854
Robert W. S. Mackay. *The Montreal Directory*. Montreal: Robert W. S. Mackay, 1844–1854.

MD 1855–1863
Mackay's Montreal Directory. Montreal: Mrs. R. W. Stuart Mackay, 1855–1863.

MD 1863–1868
MacKay's Montreal Directory. Montreal: John Lovell, 1863–1868.

MD 1868–1871
Montreal Directory. Montreal: John Lovell, 1868–1871.

QD 1822
Thomas Henri Gleason. *The Quebec Directory for 1822*. Quebec: Neilson and Cowan, 1822.

QD 1826
John Smith. *The Quebec Directory, or Strangers' Guide in the City, for 1826*. Quebec: T. Cary & Co., 1826.

QD 1844
Alfred Hawkins. *The Quebec Directory and Strangers' Guide to the City and Environs, 1844–45*. Quebec: W. Cowan & Son, 1844.

QD 1848
Robert W. S. Mackay. *Mackay's Quebec Directory for 1848–49*. Quebec: Robert W. S. Mackay, 1848.

QD 1850
Robert W. S. Mackay. *Mackay's Quebec Directory, Corrected to July 1850*. Quebec: Robert W. S. Mackay, 1850.

QD 1855
S. McLaughlin. *McLaughlin's Quebec Directory in Three Parts*. Quebec: Bureau and Marcotte, 1855.

Newspapers

Acadian Recorder (Halifax) 1819.
Kingston Chronicle, 1824–1825.
Montreal Gazette, 1839.
Montreal Herald, 1821.
Vindicator (Montreal), 1830.
New York Tribune, 1885.
Le Canadien (Quebec), 1819–1830.
La Gazette de Québec, 1819–1841.
The Daily Mercury/The Quebec Mercury, 1819–1821/1822–1841.
Star and Commercial Advertiser (Quebec), 1828–1830.
Upper Canada Gazette (York), 1823.

Other Publications

Allodi 1980
Allodi, Mary. *Printmaking in Canada: The Earliest Views and Portraits*. Toronto: Royal Ontario Museum, 1980.

Army Lists
Great Britain, War Office. *A List of the Officers of the Army and of the Royal Marine Forces....* London: William Clowes, 1755–1969.

Arnold 1822
The Case of George Arnold Plaintiff. vs. John Boyle and Others, Defendants. Argued and Determined in the Court of King's Bench, for the District of Quebec, in the Term of April 1822. Quebec: Printed by Neilson and Cowan, n.d.

Arnold 1823a
In Appeal, George Arnold, Appellant, and John Boyle and Others, Respondents. Quebec, 1823, pp. 1–3.

Arnold 1823b
Report at Large of a Trial before a Special Jury in the Case of L. T. M'Pherson, Esqr., Plaintiff vs. George Arnold, Defendant [Reported by W. S. Simpson]. Quebec, 1823, pp. 24–27.

Baillie and Sleveking 1984
Baillie, Loreen; and Sleveking, Paul; eds. *British Biographical Archives*. Munich, New York, London, Paris: K. G. Saur, 1984 (microfiche edition).

Béland and Lachapelle 1982
Béland, Mario; and Lachapelle, François. "Répertoire des gravures conservées au monastère des Ursulines de Québec." Typescript. Quebec, 1982.

Bell and Cooke 1978
Bell, Michael; and Cooke, W. Martha E. *The Last "Lion": Rambles in Quebec with James Pattison Cockburn*. Kingston: Agnes Etherington Art Centre, Queen's University, 1978.

Bervin 1983
Bervin, George. "Environnement matériel et activités économiques des conseillers éxécutifs et législatifs à Québec, 1810–1830." *Material History Bulletin* 17 (Spring 1983): 45–62.

La Bibliothèque canadienne
La Bibliothèque canadienne [Quebec: M. Bibaud] 3, no. 1 (juin 1826): 35; 7, no. 3 (août 1828): 118–119.

Blue Book 1867
[Government of Canada.] *Blue Book: Or Statement of the Public Service of Canada for*

the Year 1866. Ottawa: Hunter, Rose & Company, 1867.

Boggs 1945

Boggs, Winthrop S. *The Postage Stamps and Postal History of Canada*. Kalamazoo, Mich.: Chambers Publishing Co., 1945.

Bond 1984

Bond, Courtney C. J. *Where Rivers Meet: An Illustrated History of Ottawa*. Woodland Hills, Calif.: Windsor Publications, 1984.

Bouchette 1815

Bouchette, Joseph. *A Topographical Description of the Province of Lower Canada*. London: W. Faden, 1815.

Bourne 1829

Bourne, Rev. George. *Picture of Quebec*. Quebec: D. & J. Smillie, 1829.

British Museum 1959–1966

Trustees of the British Museum. *British Museum General Catalogue of Printed Books*. London: British Museum, 1959–1966.

Bushnell 1929

Bushnell, George H. "A Dictionary of Scottish Engravers of the Eighteenth Century." *The Print Collector's Quarterly* 16, no. 3 (July 1929): 251–277.

Calderisi 1981

Calderisi, Maria. *Music Publishing in the Canadas, 1800–1867*. Ottawa: National Library of Canada, 1981.

Cameron and Trudel 1978

Cameron, Christina; and Trudel, Jean. *The Drawings of James Patterson Cockburn: A Visit through Quebec's Past*. Agincourt, Ont.: Gage Publishing, 1978.

Cauchon 1971

Cauchon, Michel. *Jean-Baptiste Roy-Audy, 1770–c. 1848*. Quebec: Ministère des affaires culturelles, 1971.

Charbonneau, Desloges, and Lafrance 1982

Charbonneau, André; Desloges, Yvon; and Lafrance, Marc. *Quebec, the Fortified City: From the 17th to the 19th Century*. Ottawa: Parks Canada, 1982.

Cockburn 1831

[Cockburn, James Pattison.] *Quebec and Its Environs: Being a Picturesque Guide to the Stranger*. Quebec: Thomas Cary & Co., 1831.

Conolly 1898

Conolly, T. W. J., comp. *Roll of the Corps of Royal Engineers from 1660 to 1898*. Chatham, England: Royal Engineers Institute, 1898.

Cooke 1983

Cooke, W. Martha E. *W. H. Coverdale Collection of Canadiana: Paintings, Watercolours, and Drawings*. Ottawa: Public Archives of Canada, 1983.

DAB

Dictionary of American Biography. Edited by Alan Johnson. New York: Charles Scribner's Sons, 1929.

Dahl, Espesset, Lafrance, and Ruddell 1975

Dahl, Edward H.; Espesset, Hélène; Lafrance, Marc; and Ruddell, Thiery. *La Ville de Québec, 1800–1850: Un inventaire des cartes et plans*. National Museum of Man Mercury Series, History Division Paper No. 13. Ottawa: National Museums of Canada, 1975.

DCB

Dictionary of Canadian Biography. Toronto: University of Toronto Press; Quebec: Les Presses de l'Université Laval, 1966–

DNB

Dictionary of National Biography. Edited by Sidney Lee. London: Smith Elder & Co., 1892.

Dusseault-Letocha 1975

Dusseault-Letocha, Louise. "Les Origines de l'art de l'estampe au Québec." Master's thesis, Université de Montréal, 1975.

Edinburgh Scene

The Edinburgh Scene: Catalogue of Prints and Drawings in the Edinburgh Room, Central

Public Library. Edinburgh: Public Libraries Committee, 1951.
Encyclopaedia Britannica. Toronto: Encyclopaedia Britannica of Canada, 1941.
Encyclopedia Canadiana. Ottawa: Grolier, 1958.

Firmin-Didot 1977
Firmin-Didot, Ambroise. *Les Graveurs de portraits en France*. Vol. 2. Nieuwkoop, Neth.: B. de Graaf, 1977.

Fox 1985
Fox, Ross. *Presentation Pieces and Trophies from the Henry Birks Collection of Canadian Silver*. Ottawa: National Gallery of Canada, 1985.

Gagnon 1895
Gagnon, Philéas. *Essai de bibliographie canadienne*. Quebec: Private publication, 1895.

Gagnon 1896
Gagnon, Philéas. "Gravures canadiens." *Bulletin de recherches historiques* 2 (July 1896): 108–109.

Gagnon 1913
Gagnon, Philéas. *Essai de bibliographie canadienne*. Vol. 2. Montreal: Cité de Montréal, 1913.

George 1835
George, James. *A Few Remarks on Internal Improvements in the Canadas*. Quebec: Private publication, 20 March 1835.

Godenrath 1938
Godenrath, Percy F. *Three Centuries of Canadian History in Picture and Story, 1630–1930: Catalogue of the Walter H. Millen Collection of Canadiana*. Toronto: Kiwanis Club of West Toronto, 1938.

Groce and Wallace 1957
Groce, George C.; and Wallace, David H. *The New York Historical Society's Dictionary of American Artists: 1564–1860*. New Haven, Conn.: Yale University Press, 1957.

Guthrie, Guthrie, and Guthrie 1874–1875
Guthrie, Thomas; Guthrie, Rev. David K.; and Guthrie, Charles J. *Autobiography of Thomas Guthrie, D.D., and Memoir by His Sons, Rev. David K. Guthrie and Charles J. Guthrie, M.A*. New York: R. Carter & Brothers, 1874–1875.

Guy 1916
Guy, John C., ed. *Book of the Old Edinburgh Club*. Vol. 9. Edinburgh, 1916.

Hall 1931
Hall, Lillian Arvilla. *Catalogue of Dramatic Portraits in the Theatre Collection of the Harvard College Library*. Cambridge, Mass.: Harvard University Press, 1931.

Hardy and Ruddel 1977
Hardy, Jean-Pierre; and Ruddel, David-Thierry. *Les Apprentis artisans à Québec 1660–1815*. Montreal: Les Presses de l'Université du Québec, 1977.

Harper 1970
Harper, J. Russell. *Early Painters and Engravers in Canada*. Toronto: University of Toronto Press, 1970.

Hillebranal 1933
Hillebranal, Harold Newcome. *Edmund Kean*. New York: Columbia University Press, 1933.

Kidd 1830
Kidd, Adam. *The Huron Chief*. Montreal: Herald and New Gazette, 1830.

Klein 1972
Klein, A. Owen. "Theatre Royal, Montreal, 1825–44." PhD. thesis, Department of Theatre and Drama, Indiana University, 1972.

Lacelle 1979
Lacelle, Claudette. *The British Garrison in Quebec City as Described in Newspapers from 1764–1840*. History and Archaeology No. 23. Ottawa: National and Historic Sites and Parks Branch, Parks Canada, Indian and Northern Affairs Canada, 1979.

Lacroix 1984
Lacroix, Laurier. "Les Estampes des Ursulines de Québec." In *Le Grand Héritage: L'Église catholique et les arts au Québec*. Quebec: Musée du Québec, 1984, pp.

155–184.
Lande 1965
Lande, Lawrence. *The Lawrence Lande Collection of Canadiana in the Redpath Library of McGill University*. Montreal: McGill University Press, 1965.
Lande 1971
Lande, Lawrence. *Rare and Unusual Canadiana*. Supplement to *The Lawrence Lande Collection of Canadiana in the Redpath Library of McGill University*, by Lawrence Lande. Montreal: McGill University Press, 1971.
Langdon 1960
Langdon, John Emerson. *Canadian Silversmiths and Their Marks 1667–1867*. Lunenburg, Vt.: The Stinehour Press, 1960.
Langdon 1966
Langdon, John Emerson. *Canadian Silversmiths 1700–1900*. Toronto: The Stinehour Press, 1966.
Langdon 1976
Langdon, John E. *Clock and Watchmakers and Allied Workers in Canada 1700 to 1900*. Toronto: Anson-Cartwright Editions, 1976.
Literary and Historical Society
Transactions of the Literary and Historical Society of Quebec. Quebec: Literary and Historical Society, 1829.
Lower Canada, House of Assembly 1824
Lower Canada, House of Assembly. *Eighth Report of the Committee of the House of Assembly on That Part of the Speech of His Excellency the Governor in Chief Which Relates to the Settlement of the Crown Lands, with the Evidence Taken before the Committee*. Quebec: Neilson & Cowan, 1824.
Lower Canada, House of Assembly 1827a
Lower Canada, House of Assembly. *Journals of the House of Assembly of Lower Canada*. Vol. 36, Appendix A-M. Quebec: Neilson & Cowan, 1827.
Lower Canada, House of Assembly 1827b
Lower Canada, House of Assembly. *Rapport d'un comité de la Chambre d'Assemblée sur l'opportunité d'ouvrir des chemins de colonisation dans la Province de Québec, ayant siège pendant l'année 1827*. Quebec: 1827.
Lower Canada, House of Assembly 1829a
Lower Canada, House of Assembly. *Journals of the House of Assembly of Lower Canada*. Vol. 38, Appendix A-Z. Quebec: Neilson & Cowan, 1829.
Lower Canada, House of Assembly 1829b
Lower Canada, House of Assembly. *Rapport des commissaires pour explorer le Saguenay*. Quebec: 1829.
Lower Canada, House of Assembly 1829c
Lower Canada, House of Assembly. *Rapports du comité spécial sur les chemins et autres communications intérieures*. Quebec: Neilson & Cowan, 1829.
MacDonald 1986
MacDonald, Sheldon. "An Old Stager Revived." *The Occasional* [Nova Scotia Museum, Halifax] 10, no. 2 (1986): 22–26.
Marleau 1983
Marleau, Martha. "The Roebuck Album: 'Sketches in the Canadas.'" *The Archivist* [Ottawa: Public Archives of Canada] 10, no. 6 (November/December 1983): 5–7.
Martin 1980
Martin, Denis. "Les Collections de gravures du Séminaire du Québec: Histoire et destins culturels." Master's thesis, Université Laval, Quebec, 1980.
Millman 1959
Millman, Thomas Reagh. *A History of the Parish of New London, Prince Edward Island*. Toronto: Private publication, 1959.
Molt 1828
Molt, T. F. *Elementary Treatise on Music*. Quebec, 1828.
Morisset 1959
[Morisset, Gérard.] *The Arts in French Canada*. Vancouver: Vancouver Art Gallery, 1959.

Morris 1944–1945
Morris, Thomas F. "James Smillie." *The Essay Proof Journal* 1, no. 2 (April 1944): 67–74; no. 3 (July 1944): 133–141; no. 4 (October 1944): 199–207; 2, no. 1 (January 1945): 19–24.
Noppen, Paulette, and Tremblay 1979
Noppen, Luc; Paulette, Claude; and Tremblay, Michel. *Québec, Trois siècles d'architecture*. Quebec: Éditions Libre Expression, 1979.
O'Donoghue 1914
O'Donoghue, Freeman. *Catalogue of Engraved British Portraits*. 6 vols. London: British Museum, 1914.
Oko 1984
Oko, Andrew J. *Canada in the Nineteenth Century: The Bert and Barbara Stitt Collection*. Hamilton: Art Gallery of Hamilton, 1984.
PAC 1976
Public Archives of Canada. *Catalogue of the National Map Collection, Public Archives of Canada*. 16 vols. Boston: G. K. Hall, 1976.
Penfold 1974
Penfold, P. A., ed. *Maps and Plans in the Public Record Office*. London, 1974.
Peters 1931
Peters, Harry T. *America on Stone*. New York: Doubleday, 1931.
Porter 1977
Porter, John R. "Un projet de musée national à Québec à l'époque du peintre Joseph Légaré (1833–1853)." *Revue d'histoire de l'amérique française* 31, no. 1 (juin 1977): 75–82.
Porter 1978
Porter, John R. *The Work of Joseph Légaré 1795–1855*. Ottawa: National Gallery of Canada, 1978.
Prescott 1919
Prescott, Winward, ed. *A List of Canadian Bookplates, with a Review of the History of Ex Libris in the Dominion*. Boston and Toronto: Society of Bookplate Bibliophiles, 1919.
Price 1981
Price, Lynda. *Introduction to the Social History of Scots in Quebec (1780–1840)*. National Museum of Man Mercury Series, History Division Paper No. 31. Ottawa: National Museums of Canada, 1981.
Procter 1824
Procter, Bryan Waller. *Effigies Poeticae*. London: J. Carpenter & Son, 1824.
Quebec Almanac
Almanach de Québec/The Quebec Almanac and British American Royal Kalendar. Quebec: William Brown, 1821–1823, 1824–1828.
Ray 1976
Ray, Gordon N. *The Illustrator and the Book in England from 1790 to 1914*. New York: Pierpont Morgan Library, 1976.
Richardson et al. 1984
Richardson, A. J. H.; Bastien, Geneviève; Dubé, Doris; and Lacombe, Marthe. *Quebec City: Architects, Artisans and Builders*. Ottawa: National Museum of Man and Parks Canada, 1984.
Ruddel 1987
Ruddel, David T. *Quebec City 1765–1832: The Evolution of a Colonial Town*. Ottawa: Canadian Museum of Civilization, 1987.
Ruddell 1981
Ruddell, David T. "Quebec City, 1765–1831: The Evolution of a Colonial Town." PhD. thesis, Université Laval, Quebec, 1981.
Sayer and Bennett
Sayer and Bennett's Catalogue of Prints for 1775. Reprint. London: Holland Press, 1970.
Scadding 1873
Scadding, Henry. *Toronto of Old: Collections and Recollections*. Toronto: A. Steven-

son, 1873.
Schweizer 1986–1987
Schweizer, Paul D. "'So Exquisite a Transcript': James Smillie's Engravings after Cole's 'Voyage of Life.'" *Imprint* 11, no. 2 (Autumn 1986): 2–13; 12, no. 1 (Spring 1987): 13–24.
Smedley 1958
Smedley, Glen B. "The Smillie Family: American Engravers and Painters." *The Numismatist*, July 1958: 771–780.
Sotheby and Co. (Canada) 1968
Sotheby and Co. (Canada). *Catalogue of Watercolours, Prints and Maps from the Collection of Canadiana Formed by the Late Robert W. Reford of Montreal*. Catalogue of an auction held 27–29 May 1968. Toronto: Sotheby and Co. (Canada), 1968.
Sotheby and Co. (London) 1931
Sotheby and Co. (London). *Catalogue of...an Important Series of Drawings of North American Scenery, Collected by George, 9th Earl of Dalhousie, G.C.B., Governor of Canada, 1819–28, and Sold (with a Few Printed Books) by Order of His Great-granddaughter, Mrs. Broun Lindsay, of Colstoun, Haddington....* Catalogue of an auction held 23 June 1931. London: Sotheby and Co., 1931.
Staton and Tremaine 1934
Staton, Frances M.; and Tremaine, Marie. *A Bibliography of Canadiana*. Toronto: The Public Library, 1934.
Stauffer 1907
Stauffer, David McNeely. *American Engravers upon Copper and Steel*. 2 vols. 1907, reprint. New York: Burt Franklin, n.d.
Stokes 1915–1928
Stokes, Isaac Newton Phelps. *The Iconography of Manhattan Island, 1498–1909*. New York: R. H. Dodd, 1915–1928.
Stokes 1932–1933
Stokes, Isaac Newton Phelps. *American Historical Prints. Early Views of American Cities, etc*. New York: New York Public Library, 1932–1933.
Tatham 1984
Tatham, David. "David Claypoole Johnston's Theatrical Portraits." *In American Portrait Prints: Proceedings of the Tenth Annual American Print Conference*, edited by Wendy Wick Reaves. Charlottesville, Va.: National Portrait Gallery, Smithsonian Institution; University of Virginia Press, 1984, pp. 162–193.
Upper Canada, House of Assembly 1818–1821
Upper Canada, House of Assembly. *The Journals of the Legislative Assembly of Upper Canada for 1818–1821*, First Session, Eighth Parliament. Ontario Department of Printed Records and Archives, Report no. 10. Toronto: L. K. Cameron, 1913.
Upper Canada, House of Assembly 1821–1822
Upper Canada, House of Assembly. *The Journals of the Legislative Assembly of Upper Canada for 1821–1822*, Second Session, Eighth Parliament. Ontario Department of Printed Records and Archives, Report no. 11. Toronto: L. K. Cameron, 1914.
Les Ursulines
Les Ursulines de Québec, depuis leur établissement jusqu'à nos jours. 4 vols. Quebec: 1864–1866.
Whitelaw 1978–1982
Whitelaw, Marjory, ed. *The Dalhousie Journals*. Vols. 1–3. Ottawa: Oberon Press, 1978–1982.
Whitthoft 1987
Whitthoft, Brucia. "James Smillie's Engraving after Albert Bierstadt's 'The Rocky Mountains.'" *The American Art Journal* 19, no. 2 (1987): 40–51.
Yung and Pettman 1981
Yung, K. K.; and Pettman, Mary. *National Portrait Gallery, Complete Illustrated Catalogue 1856–1979*. New York: St. Martin's Press, 1981.

Concordance

Single Sheet Prints	Cat. No.	Scrapbook No.	Other Collections Examined
Chaudière Falls near Quebec	3	16 (missing)	
Dalhousie Castle from the N.W.	4	3	
Dalhousie Castle from the S.W.	5	4	
Crucifixion of Our Saviour and the Two Thieves	6		NA, NYPL
Mr. Ramage as Bob Logic	15	5	
Prisoner in Confinement	16		
The Virgin and Infant Saviour	18		
Fort Chambly	19	9	
Isaac Watts	24	15	
The Quebec Driving Club	32		AGGV, NA, ROM
Sir William Temple	58	72, ss. 8	
Adam Gottlob Öhlenschläger	60	70, 71	
Man's Head	63	55	
Cape Diamond, Quebec	64	74, ss. 10	
Castle St. Lewis	65	75	
Quebec from the Old Mill	66	77, ss. 7	MTL, NYPL
École Élémentaire	71	78, ss. 13	ANQ, ASQ
New Roman Catholic Church, Montreal	74		ASQ, BVMG, McC, McG.RBD.LR, MTL, NA, ROM

Maps	Cat. No.	Scrapbook No.	Other Collections Examined
Part of the Province of Upper Canada	9		ASQ
Plan of St. Gabriel	12		BVMG, NA
Section of Country Lying between the Old Seigniorial Settlements on the River St. Lawrence and Southern Boundary of the Province	52	42	BVMG, NA, ROM
Plan de la Rivière du Saguenay	53		BVMG, NA, ROM
Sketch of the Great Valley of the River St. John	54		BVMG, NA, NGC, NYPL, ROM
Plan of the New Settlements on the River Etchemin	68		NA

Book Illustrations and Sets of Prints	Cat. No.	Scrapbook No.	Other Collections Examined
Quebec and Its Environs			
	55a	48, ss. 4	MTL, NA, NGC, ROM
	55b	49, ss. 5	MTL, NA, NGC, ROM
	55c	50, ss. 12	MTL, NA, NGC, ROM
	55d	51, ss. 11	MTL, NA, NGC, ROM
	55e	57, 58	MTL, NA, NGC, ROM
	55f	56, ss. 9	MTL, NA, NGC, ROM
London and Its Vicinity			
	56a	61	NGC
	56b	63, ss. 14	NGC
	56c	64	NGC
	56d	66	NGC
	56e	65	NGC
	56f	67	NGC
Rocks and Fossils of Lower Canada			
	67a	27, ss. 2	MTL, NA, NGC
	67b	28, ss. 3	MTL, NA, NGC
	67c		MTL, NA, NGC
	67d		MTL, NA, NGC
Picture of Quebec			
	69a	80	MTL, NLC, ROM
	69b	81	MTL, NLC, ROM
	69c	82	MTL, NLC, ROM
	69d	83	MTL, NLC, ROM
	69f	85	MTL, NLC, ROM
	69g	88	MTL, NLC, ROM
	69h	89	MTL, NLC, ROM
	69i	90	MTL, NLC, ROM
	69j	91	MTL, NLC, ROM
	69k	92	MTL, NLC, ROM
The Huron Chief	73	94, ss. 15	NLC, NYPL
Plan for Moving Boats over Rapids	76		BVMG, NA

Commercial Prints	Cat. No.	Scrapbook No.	Other Collections Examined
Facsimile Legal Document	2	18	
David William Smith Bookplate	10		
Rev. L. C. Jenkins Bookplate	11	7	
Chasseur's Museum Entry Ticket	13		ASQ
J. Hoffman Bookplate	14		BVMG
Notes of Exchange	17	6, ss. 1	
Lindsay Trade Card	20	11	
Jackson Trade Card	21	12	
Leggo Bookplate	22	13	
J. Smillie, Sr., Trade Card	23	14	
Lenfestey Trade Card	25	19	
Dorion Trade Card	26	20	
Dalkin Trade Card	29	21	
Masonic Address	30	8	
Dalhousie Bookplate	41	93	NA, NGC, NSM
Maule Bookplate	42	54, ss. 6	
Quebec Fire-Assurance Company	43	43	
Note of Exchange	44	44	
Quebec Fire Assurance Company	59	69	McC
Thomas Drysdale Trade Card	62	68	

Drawings and Watercolours	Cat. No.	Scrapbook No.
Two Heads, after Raphael	1	2
Gaston de Foix	7	
The Holy Family	8	
Upper Town Market and Church	27	86
Upper Town Market and Church	28	87
Studies of Napoleonic Figure	31	facing 27
Bust of Charles J. Fox	33	36
Edmund Kean as Richard III	34	32
Hare and Foxes	35	34
Dog Gnawing Bone	36	30
Dog	37	31
Skull of Colonel Despard	38	40
Langhorne's Poems	39	33
An Old Canadian	40	35
Uncle's House, Quebec	45	37
Looking from Mountain Street towards Montmorenci Falls	46	38
Looking from Mountain Street towards Cape Diamond	47	39
Quebec Street Scene	48	46
Falls of Montmorenci in Winter	49	47
Habitant in Winter Landscape	50	53
Picturesque Views of Canada	51	29
Letterhead with Angel	57	62
William Smillie	61	between 71 and 72
Quebec Driving Club	69e	84
École Élémentaire	70	78
Indian Chiefs at Jeune Lorette	72	59
Catholic Church, Montreal	75	52

Selected Index

Individuals, Societies, Businesses, and Other Institutions